DATE DUE

~~MY 2 '08~~		
DE 1 8 '09		

DEMCO 38-296

MEDIEVAL FAMILY ROLES

GARLAND MEDIEVAL CASEBOOKS
VOLUME 15
GARLAND REFERENCE LIBRARY OF THE HUMANITIES
VOLUME 1727

GARLAND MEDIEVAL CASEBOOKS

JOYCE E. SALISBURY AND CHRISTOPHER KLEINHENZ
Series Editors

MEDIEVAL FAMILY ROLES
A BOOK OF ESSAYS

EDITED BY
CATHY JORGENSEN ITNYRE

GARLAND PUBLISHING, INC.
NEW YORK AND LONDON
1996

Library of Congress Cataloging-in-Publication Data

Medieval family roles : a book of essays / edited by Cathy Jorgensen Itnyre.
       p.   cm. — (Garland reference library of the humanities ; vol.
1727. Garland medieval casebooks ; vol. 15)
   Includes index.
   ISBN 0-8153-1329-2
   1. Family—History. 2. Marriage—History. 3. Social history—Medieval, 500–1500. 4. Family in Literature.   I. Itnyre, Cathy Jorgensen,
1952– . II. Series: Garland reference library of the humanities ; vol.
1727. III. Series: Garland reference library of the humanities. Garland medieval casebooks ; vol. 15.
HQ513.M43 1996   95-25381
                                                    CIP

Printed on acid-free, 250-year-life paper
Manufactured in the United States of America

To my family
Bob, Tim, and Erin

Contents

ACKNOWLEDGMENTS

I greatly appreciate the generosity of the scholars who contributed essays to this volume. It was a pleasure to work with all of them, and their cooperation was a great inspiration.

I would also like to thank the series editor, Dr. Joyce E. Salisbury, for her friendly support from start to finish.

Many students and staff members at Copper Mountain College assisted me, and my appreciation goes to them all. I would like to thank Carolyn Hopkins and Nell Engesser of the Greenleaf Library at CMC for their help in locating and obtaining materials; staff members Vicki Chambless, Karen Coghill, Cheri Dixon, Carolyn Emanuel, Daphne Gunnerson, Janie Hannah, Wanda Scott, Cindy Stephenson, and Carolyn Warner for their technical assistance; and my students Leslie Anthony, Jim Hauronic, Brigid Kelly, and Patricia Tabeling, who proofread and helped in various ways. Finally, I would like to acknowledge especially the assistance of my student Sandra Griesmeyer, whose aid was constant, enthusiastic, and invaluable.

INTRODUCTION

For decades now, historians have been busy studying the history of the family. Their interest and concern are, of course, natural—few would doubt that this institution is, and has been, of critical importance. With speculation about the "breakdown" of the family so rampant today, many look to the past to see how the family has weathered crises before. Peter Laslett's book *The World We Have Lost*, such a major spur to studies in the field, coincided with a period of dynamic change in modern industrial society: high divorce rates, increased geographic mobility and the attendant weakening of family presence, a growing illegitimacy rate. As these forces gather steam, many are wondering, "What *have* we lost?" While historians do not serve as counselors or prophets for modern society, the observations we make in our own areas are inherently interesting to all who consider the history of the family to be a topic worthy of attention.

The authors who contributed essays to this collection all have something important to say about how family members carried out their roles in diverse temporal and geographic settings. Diversity was not necessarily a quality perceived by the people who lived in the Middle Ages, but when we modern historians attempt to assess the many different "looks" that the family embodied, it is useful to have breadth of view in both the geographic and temporal sense. Some of the authors here are concerned with early or later medieval England; some examine Italian family issues; German families are investigated by others; several authors turn their attention to other areas of the medieval world. A collection that presents the latest research on the family must be concerned with the broad picture, for as Joseph Campbell wrote about the hero with many faces, the universality of the institution invites us to see it as the *family* with many faces.

As a microcosm of human activity that has a public as well as private aspect, the family reflects interior attitudes that shape exterior conditions.

Aristotle not surprisingly considered it the essential place for beginning to look at the state. The many positions that people take on in later life are first delineated in the context of family: rulers and ruled, appropriate behavior for young and old, producer and consumer. All of these attitudes are learned in the family first. The basic orientation toward life that the family provides is one of both accommodation to and acceptance of restraints, and this is engendered in the earliest days of one's advent into a family.

From the family's inception through marriage, to its replenishment through reproductive activity, to the accommodations its members must make in their dealings with each other, the family's functions provide valuable clues to our medieval past as well as thoughtful reflection on our present. The institution is resilient enough to provide for its members a shelter strong enough to sustain life through adverse times. I have divided the essays into three broad areas that highlight the family's temporal sequence. Despite the various areas of specialty the authors represent, it is certainly the case that common themes emerge. The institution of the family engendered support for family members within and without the immediate household; it cast a broad light on many areas of life that are today considered public responsibilities. Nurturing ties between family members and the wider community were often activated by events within the family: marriage, birth, and death. Relations between particular family members exhibited, Janus-like, a two-sided presentation of dysfunction and nurturing support.

MARRIAGE

Marriage establishes a relationship; it provides the conditions within which a family can be conceived and reared. The writers who examine marriage in this volume are interested in the ways in which it serves to create new ties within and without the household. Carolyn Edwards bases her study on the *Lives* of Ottonian royal abbesses, and finds that the acknowledgment of their sanctity influenced the foundation and provisioning of religious houses. She finds that, although royal abbesses like Mathilde and Hathumoda exercised power in circumscribed areas, it was primarily their nurturing function that was perpetuated after their deaths by the encouragement of their cults. Aline G. Hornaday inquires into the role of the family as an agent of social control. Her careful study demonstrates that by the Carolingian period, extrafamilial religious influences replaced the role formerly played by the kin-group. The remaining two essays in this section are concerned with the more private aspects of marriage. Specifically, these authors turn their attention to evidence for the development of affective feelings within the marriage. Albrecht Classen's thorough look at the growth of personal marital bonds as expressed in medieval German literature helps to establish how the institution of marriage was viewed by people of that time and place. He sees the emergence of a more modern aspect to the husband-wife relationship than other historians have allowed for thus far. Kimberly Keller finds, in her close reading of *Piers Plowman*, the expression of new attitudes about the marital union, ones that reflected the Church's sacramental notion of marriage and ultimately elevated the wife's position in the relationship.

CHILDREN

Children's role in medieval families has been of intense interest to scholars. This silent group has had its champions in historians who coax from sources that are necessarily concerned with other matters tantalizing evidence of the activities and concerns that constituted the world of children. The articles in this section focus on the role of children, but they do so from different perspectives. Fiona Harris Stoertz and Louis Haas, though concerned with different eras and locales, both affirm the efforts that medieval people expended in ensuring safe deliveries for pregnant women. Given the technological limitations of the premodern world, this was no easy task, and the full quiver of parental strategies was invoked: charms, prayers, paid medical help, and so forth. One's status as a parent was indeed precarious, since plague, illness, and accidents threatened to erase the fruit of one's reproductive activity. Dr. Haas uses the *ricordanze* of Florentine men to examine the extent to which women controlled the situations surrounding their maternal functions. He also notes an impressive coterie of women who were galvanized to act on a laboring woman's behalf—a telling example of how expectant women elicited the support of others outside the immediate confines of the birth room. Fiona Harris Stoertz's careful look at English childbirth customs reveals an extrafamilial concern not only for the safe delivery of children but also for the comfort level of laboring women.

Two essays explore the impact of death on children's lives: one from the point of view of adults whose children died in suspicious circumstances, and one on how children were affected when their parents died. Philip Gavitt applies modern medical research into Sudden Infant Death Syndrome (SIDS) to the late medieval Florentine population. He arrives at the conclusion that supposed "smotherings" may actually have been cases of SIDS, which still extracts its heartbreaking toll today. Timothy S. Miller, in his work on Byzantine orphanages, considers children as the objects of state strategies designed to cope with the survivors of parental death. If no close relatives were present to assume responsibility, such children were sometimes reared in the

Orphanotropheion, a state-supported institution that replaced parental care and supervision. Thus, according to Dr. Miller, orphans became the objects of charity, and this allowed the theocratic Byzantine state to bestow its care on them. In addition, by resorting to institutionalization only after exhausting all other avenues, the Byzantine policy foreshadowed more modern solutions to the care of orphans.

FAMILY TIES

Other relationships within the family are examined in the final section. The authors here concentrate on particular ties that characterize the family in various areas, and assess what some of the features of these relationships involved. Here we see dysfunctional aspects of family life, as well as general lessons that might be derived from them from the point of view of medieval authors. Elizabeth Archibald presents a fascinating discussion of the prevalence of incest in medieval literary texts. She argues that the inclusion of incest as a theme in hagiography and exemplary literature suggests that it served a moral tutelary purpose for medieval audiences. In my essay, I show some of the stresses that drew the attention of saga authors who remarked upon the father–son relationship, as well as some of the positive aspects of this important bond. María Luzdivina Cuesta investigates how medieval Castilian writers presented family relationships. Noting that the writers were interested in portraying the economic and social consequences of familial relations, Dr. Cuesta demonstrates that family roles in medieval Castile mirrored societal concerns. Joel T. Rosenthal's lively look at three-generation links in later medieval England is the final essay. His informative review of the post-Laslett literature, combined with his perceptive use of source material, yields a fresh look at the implications of multigenerational families in late medieval England. Professor Rosenthal's analysis of Laslett—whose seminal work helped to launch the great journey into detailed studies of family history—seems a logical place to conclude this volume of recent investigation in this important field.

I. Marriage

Dynastic Sanctity in Two Early Medieval Women's *Lives*

Carolyn Edwards

Despite the renown Charlemagne and his court have won, we do not usually hear of St. Charlemagne, or even of St. Alcuin or St. Gisela. Otto the Great, however, is surrounded by a throng of royal saints. His great-aunt Hathumoda; his mother, Mathilde; his brother Brun; and his second wife, Adelheid—are all saints. His great-grandmother Oda and his first wife, Edith, were also venerated for a brief time. Early researchers tried to explain this profusion of saints through discussions of inherited sanctity and the charisma of German and Anglo-Saxon rulers. Few scholars, though, have taken advantage of the opportunities for studying the family in the Ottonian *vitae*. The *Lives* of Hathumoda and Mathilde can be particularly valuable for studying early medieval women, early medieval ideals of holiness, and Hathumoda and Mathilde's connections to the history of their family.[1]

Saint Hathumoda and Saint Mathilde controlled the two most famous convents in Saxony: Gandersheim and Quedlinburg. These houses were founded and controlled by the Liudolfing family, who rose out of the obscurity of the Saxon nobility to become the Ottonian emperors of Germany. Gandersheim was founded in 845 by the Saxon duke Liudolf and his wife Oda; Liudolf and Oda travelled to Rome, where they received papal sanction for the house and relics and received permission for their twelve-year-old daughter, Hathumoda, to become abbess. After the Carolingian line died out in the East, Liudolf's grandson, Henry the Fowler, was crowned king in 919 (see figure 1 for a family tree). Upon his death in 936, Queen Mathilde founded a convent in Quedlinburg, on the eastern border of Saxony, as his memorial. Both convents prospered and maintained close ties to the family, choosing Liudolfing daughters as abbesses.

FIGURE 1. LINEAGE OF HATHUMODA AND MATHILDE

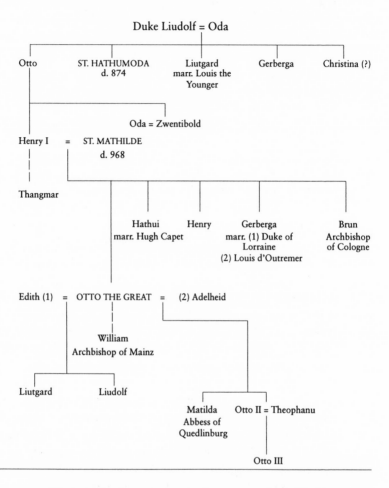

Hagiography, increasingly mined as a source for family history, can be of great value in the case of the Ottonians, since conceptions of holiness can be traced through several generations. A close reading of the *Vitae* of Hathumoda and Mathilde demonstrates that, between the late ninth and the late tenth centuries, saintliness became less associated with the monastery and became inextricably linked to the dynasty.[2] It is important to note, however, that merely being a member of this family did not make the women saints; the convents themselves cultivated Mathilde and Hathumoda as saints to secure the family's patronage. At the same time, as the saint became more closely tied to the family, tensions arose over her saintly behavior, which was increasingly defined and controlled by the dynasty.

Karl Leyser devotes almost a fourth of his ground-breaking study, *Rule and Conflict*, to Saxon noblewomen, focusing largely on their economic motives for founding convents. Since women were able to inherit lands and very often outlived their husbands and brothers, they could accrue significant amounts of land and resources that the endowment of a convent could secure from the claims of other heirs.[3] Although Leyser refers to the many Ottonian saints, especially to St. Mathilde, he does not explain the complex connections between the family, the convents, and the women's sanctity.[4]

The *Lives* of Hathumoda and Mathilde, while sharing many traits common to stories of female saints and highlighting the importance of the family, were written in very different family contexts. Hathumoda's *Vita* was written, so to speak, before the Ottonians were the Ottonians—before they held royal power and developed a family history. She is a noble, monastic saint who gave up her worldly status and comforts to be a bride of Christ and who successfully led a new foundation as the first abbess. Hathumoda's monastic discipline is stressed, as is her leadership and general virtue. Mathilde's *Vita*, however, was written after a generation of Ottonian imperial power. As the mother of the new dynasty, she was revered for her piety, probity, generosity, and care for the dead. However, there is more at stake than just Mathilde's sanctity. The *Vita* is not focused on her alone; it is just as concerned with the Ottonian dynasty as with her holy deeds, and possibly even more with establishing clear claims for her convent at Nordhausen.[5]

St. Hathumoda

Hathumoda, Otto the Great's great-aunt, was the first abbess of the Liudolfing foundation at Gandersheim. The *Vita Hathumodae*, as well as a verse *Dialogus*, was composed shortly after her death in 874.[6] The author, Agius of Corvey, was well known to Hathumoda and the sisters of Gandersheim, perhaps having served there as a confessor.[7] Following the hagiographic convention, Agius addressed his work to the sisters, explaining that he wrote to console them, for although they could no longer see Hathumoda corporally, through this account of her deeds they might yet hold her before their eyes.[8] In his conclusion, Agius followed up on this image, telling the sisters that, although they were no longer in daily conversation with her, they might still read of her life in this little work and use it as a rule and as a mirror. Just as they followed her corporal steps, so they should follow her spiritual strides.[9] He concluded by begging the sisters not to grieve, for Hathumoda is one of the elect, one of the 144,000 who stand unspotted before the throne of God.[10]

Hathumoda fits many topoi of female saints. She was noble, the "most pleasing flower from the good seed of the good tree, who later grew up to be its sweetest fruit."[11] As a child she scorned childish play; empty vain things irritated her (chap. 2). Instead, she preferred the Church. She had no desire for precious things, and if she were dressed according to her station, she cried out in a holy tantrum. Educated at the Saxon convent at Herford, Hathumoda became the model abbess of the new foundation of Gandersheim when she was only twelve. Eager to learn, humble and generous, full of charity—she ruled her abbey as a mother and constantly cared for the sick. The Lord was always in her mouth in psalmody and prayer, and Christ was always in her heart (chap. 22). Hathumoda fell ill at age 34 after nursing the nuns through an epidemic in 874, and on her deathbed she experienced many visions, including those of her own grave, the time of her death, and St. Martin, to whom she was especially devoted (chaps. 11–13). Upon her death, there was great if not excessive grief, and her grave was immediately revered.

Hathumoda's lifestyle is described more in terms of abstinence and discipline than of extreme asceticism. For example, in glossing the Benedictine rule, the *Vita* stressed that, although she was of the highest nobility, she, along with all the other sisters, did indeed live a common life under strict observance of the Rule (chaps. 5–6). She maintained strict enclosure, kept the canonical hours of prayer, had no servants, and did not even eat meat when it was allowed to the sisters (chap. 6). Agius constantly stressed how much she had given up: "For she scorned, despised, and gave up so much for divine love; certainly whatever she gave up for God, to that degree she will have more merit with God, and will receive the greater reward."[12] Although she could have had whatever she wanted because of her birth and position as abbess, at the time of her death there was nothing left to be given away, for she had only a pall for her burial.[13]

Agius reported that Hathumoda's family gathered around her deathbed. Ludwig Zoepf underscored the centrality of family in tenth-century sanctity and pointed out the family's highly visible and unquestioned role in all the Ottonian *Vitae*, although earlier hagiographers emphasized saints' withdrawal from the world as well as from the family.[14] Yet, while family plays an important role for Hathumoda, her relatives only surface to found the convent and to stand beside her deathbed. The emphasis of the *Life* is on her role as abbess and on her model conduct as a nun. Since she was cloistered all of her life, the monastery was Hathumoda's real family.

In addition, even the identifications of people as Hathumoda's relatives are not without their problems. For example, Agius, Hathumoda's hagiographer, was previously designated as her blood brother, merely because he referred to her as "soror." More recent research, such as that of Winfred Glocker, now refutes this relationship.[15] With this revision in mind, the status of Gerberga and Christina, the two abbesses who succeeded Hathumoda, could equally be called into question, prompting new questions about the family's composition and its relationship to family sanctity. The usage of the generic term *soror* and the more specific term for biological sister, *germana*, is not clear. Gerberga and Christina have both been assumed to have been Hathumoda's blood sisters although they were not designated as germana, while Hathumoda's sister Queen Liutgard explicitly was. Also, while Gerberga and Liutgard were family names, Christina was not. Although offering three daughters to a foundation would presumably have brought honor to a family, their relationship was not spelled out.

This lack of precision in the *Vita* seems problematic, considering the close attention family relations were given in all the sources surrounding the family and the *Hausklöster*. The accounts of Gandersheim's foundation, in the *Vita Hathumodae* and in the *Primordia Gandeshemenensis*, clearly set out Liudolf and Oda's pilgrimage to Rome and the establishment of Hathumoda's abbacy, with no mention of other daughters.[16] The brief history provided in the charter given to Gandersheim by Otto I in 956 likewise mentioned only one daughter in terms of the foundation.[17] Neither Gerberga nor Christina is addressed explicitly in the prologue of the *Vita*. Indeed, no discussion of family members at the convent occurs whatsoever until Hathumoda's deathbed (chap. 15). Here we find "germanae" (plural) at her deathbed who refused to be separated from her. However, when Christina is named, she is merely "soror eius." Gerberga likewise is "soror eius," although it is to Gerberga alone that Hathumoda was able to tell her vision of the afterlife.[18] Queen Liutgard, however, mourned specifically for her germana.[19]

Although the foundation account in the *Primordia* similarly discussed only one daughter, Hathumoda, the work also mentioned Liudolf and Oda's other children, beginning with Liutgard (l. 305), then Hathumoda (l. 315), Gerberga (l. 318), Brun (l. 362), and Otto (l. 367). Christina, however, was not introduced until line 485 upon Gerberga's death, when she became abbess. Here Hrotsvitha says that Christina was as great in probity as in lineage.[20] Why would it be necessary for her lineage to be described if she were of the Liudolfing dynasty? At the time of Oda's death in the monastery, Christina was designated not as her daughter, but as her "alumna" (l. 581). However, upon Christina's own death, she joined her "germanis" in heaven.[21] Gerberga and Christina were named specifically as her biological sisters only in the *Vita Bernwardi*, written in the eleventh century.

It seems peculiar that if both Gerberga and Christina were indeed Hathumoda's biological sisters, this was not stated explicitly and without apology, as were other family connections. Was their familial relationship assumed, and did the authors find it far more important to stress that the women were nuns in the convent than to state that they were Hathumoda's sisters? Perhaps the authors of the *Vita* and the *Primordia* and the charter were privileging the monastic over the dynastic family.

Hathumoda was made abbess of Gandersheim thanks to her family connections. As abbess, however, she could exercise relative autonomy within the monastery and serve as a model of saintly behavior. Her social status and relationship to her family only became apparent at her deathbed, with her *Vita* assigning no great importance to the Liudolfing "dynasty." Indeed Agius' careless and ambiguous use of language to designate Hathumoda's family members underscores the insignificance of her family in comparison to her saintly way of life. St. Mathilde's family, by contrast, is at the forefront of her *Vita*. Although she was able to maintain her independence outside the cloister, Mathilde was not able to exercise her sanctity, in the patronage of convents and generosity to the poor, without great struggles.

St. Mathilde

By the end of the tenth century, the relationship between the family and holiness had changed. Mathilde's saintly activities and even the structure of her *Vita* are directed toward, and defined by, the dynasty. Agius of Corvey provided no formal prologue to Hathumoda's *Life* and addressed the sisters directly in relatively straightforward Latin. In contrast, the unnamed monk from Nordhausen who wrote the *Vita Mathildis Reginae Antiquior* addressed his work to Otto II in an artful prologue that echoes Sulpicius Serverus.[22] The hagiographer juggled several thorny issues, combining an account of Mathilde's life with a history of the dynasty, as well as an encomium for Nordhausen. Oddly, the *Vita* opens with an account of Henry I's family rather than her own, and devotes a great deal of attention to the history of the dynasty. Upon Henry I's election, the author launches into an exhortation to Saxony to give support to this dynasty, lest the region again fall into the state of servitude.[23] It reports Otto the Great's imperial coronation and Mathilde's prophecy of Otto II's future greatness. Continuing beyond her death, the *Vita* concludes with Otto I's death and Otto II's marriage and coronation.

After the account of Henry's lineage, the hagiographer briefly harkened back to her ancestor, the Saxon Widukind, and then recast Mathilde and Henry's meeting (chap. 2). Having heard reports of her great beauty and virtue, Henry went with a troop to the monastery at Herford, where she was being educated. Overcome by her great beauty, he immediately sought her hand in marriage. This fairy-tale account, lifted directly from Terence's *Andria*, effectively concealed Henry's first marriage and son Thangmar, and so served to legitimize a narrower field of heirs.[24] The hagiographer painted a careful, limited family portrait, omitting other family members as well. Although Mathilde bore Henry at least five children, only four are mentioned in this first *Vita*, and only the sons are included in the second *Life*, perhaps to emphasize Mathilde's chastity even in marriage or to narrow the definition of the family and possible heirs.[25] Mathilde's *Life* mentions only two of her grandchildren, Matilda[26] and Otto II. The hagiographer thereby omitted Otto I's children of his first marriage—the rebellious Liudolf and Liutgard (who married the Duke of Lorraine and was the progenitor of the Salian dynasty)—who had been excluded from the succession, as well as his illegitimate son, William, Archbishop of Mainz.

Despite her marriage, Mathilde felt herself closer to Christ than to her husband and preferred times spent in Church to her husband's bed. Like other saintly queens, she encouraged Henry's generosity and intervened for prisoners. After Henry's death Mathilde led a life of even greater piety and humility. She added to her previous virtues chaste widowhood, abstinence, and most of all, generosity to the Church and probity (chap. 8). She is praised for founding convents at Quedlinburg and Nordhausen, for feeding the poor twice daily, and for personally ministering to poor women. Further, she lived a life of abstinence in food and comforts (chap. 11). She read or was read to constantly, and citing St. Paul, she declared that he who does not want to work shall not eat. Her hagiographer stressed that through her deeds she nearly acquired the "palm of virginity."[27]

As the author admitted, though, Mathilde shone out more in inward wonders than in outward miracles. Those miracles that she did perform were rather unusual and demonstrate a folkloric undercurrent in the *Vita*. First, standing on a hill in Quedlinburg and overseeing food distribution to a crowd of poor people, Mathilde saw that the people in the valley were not being given bread. As if angered at the minister, she seized a piece of bread and, making the sign of the cross and invoking the name of the Lord, she threw it. It tumbled over rocks and hedges until it fell unharmed into the lap of a poor man.[28] In another, equally novel miracle, a doe tamed in the monastery swallowed a small flask of sacramental wine. During mass, the deer entered the church enraged and could not be shooed away. However, Mathilde stretched out her hands and asked the deer to give back what it had taken. The deer miraculously quieted and vomited the little flask. This occurrence is all the more amazing since deer are biologically incapable of vomiting.[29]

The author of the *Vita* devoted the last three crucial chapters to Mathilde's deathbed and her beloved foundation at Nordhausen. After receiving assurances for the monastery from Otto I following the great Pentecost celebration of 965 in Cologne, she appointed her dear servant Ricburga as abbess. She lamented that familial expectations demanded that she be buried in Quedlinburg next to Henry, when she would have preferred to be buried in Nordhausen. On her deathbed she performed her final miracle. After dividing all her goods among the clergy, the poor, and her monastic foundations, she received the last rites from her step-grandson, William of Mainz. When she gave him her pall, foreseeing that his death would fall suddenly, even before her own, her daughter Gerberga arrived with a finer double pall for the double grave. On her deathbed, Mathilde entrusted the destitute convent Nordhausen to her son Otto (then in Italy). Finally, in perhaps the best-known scene of the *Life*, Mathilde presented her thirteen-year-old granddaughter and namesake, Abbess Matilda of Quedlinburg, with a *computarium,* or necrology, entrusting her with the care of the dead for the dynasty.[30] Consoling the nuns, Mathilde died and was buried beside her husband.

THE CONVENTS—CARE OF THE DEAD, AND OF THE LIVING

The Ottonians were deeply concerned with the care of the dead, as witnessed by Mathilde's *Life* and other contemporary sources. Gerd Althoff has demonstrated the role that Gandersheim and especially Quedlinburg played as cult centers for the care of the dead, focusing his attention on the writing of histories and necrologies.[31] He states that noble families conceived of the houses they founded as centers of memory for their members, relatives, and friends. Ruled by Ottonian daughters to assure the continuity of the family's influence, Gandersheim and Quedlinburg were richly endowed so that freed from material worries, the nuns might concentrate their attention on the memory of the family's deceased members.[32] Certainly prayers from relatives would be more zealous than those from strangers.

Further, the Ottonians left careful instructions about their own burials. Quedlinburg is often described as the new royal mausoleum for the Ottonians, replacing the merely noble foundation at Gandersheim. Indeed, except for the abbesses of Gandersheim, the only family member who was buried at Gandersheim after 936 was Henry the Wrangler, who fell ill while visiting his sister, Abbess Gerberga, in 995. Yet, while Henry I's body was carried from Memleben to his burial in Quedlinburg and Mathilde's *Life* stressed that, except for familial expectations, she would have preferred to have been buried in Nordhausen, these two and the abbesses Matilda and Adelheid were the only members of the dynasty buried at Quedlinburg. Otto and his first wife, Edith, are buried at Magdeburg, in the cathedral they founded. Otto's second wife, Adelheid, is buried at her foundation of Selz in Alsace. St. Brun's body was carried, according to his instructions, from Reims to his foundation at St. Pantaleon in Cologne. Otto II is buried at St. Peter's in Rome. Otto III had his body carried from Paterno, north of Rome, to Aachen to be laid at the side of Charlemagne. Henry II and his equally saintly wife, Kunigunde, were both buried in their foundation, the cathedral of Bamberg.

St. Adelheid, Mathilde's daughter-in-law, was also zealous in her care for the dead and was a great patron of Cluny.[33] Both the *Vitae* of Mathilde and Adelheid devote considerable time to describing the monasteries they founded and their exertions for the memory of the family. On the other hand, while the family is very visible in the *Life* of Otto's brother, St. Brun, his achievements are framed in terms of his contributions to the Reich and the church as Archbishop of Cologne, his close connection to Otto I, and his great talents. His *Vita*, in stark contrast to those of the Ottonian women, mentions neither Quedlinburg nor Gandersheim, nor the efficacy of his own prayers and care for the family.[34]

Indeed, the care of the dead was the particular responsibility of the women of the family. Liutprand of Cremona said he had never seen a woman as pious about the dead as St. Mathilde.[35] Thietmar of Merseburg described Mathilde as a model for the behavior of a noble widow, saying:

> Now I will briefly portray to all believers the holy picture of the venerable Mathilde who, after the death of her lord accomplished great deeds. . . . Mathilde followed this example after her husband was struck into the chains of temporal death, in which she fed not only the poor, but even the birds. Also, thirty days after his death, with the consent of her son, she founded a convent in the city Quedlinburg, endowing it with all that it needed for provisions and clothing, and provided a written confirmation.[36]

Feeding the poor was directly linked to the care for the dead. Alms were given in memorial, especially on the anniversaries of deaths. Donations to monasteries were also often given shortly after the death of a family member or on the anniversary of the death.[37] Mathilde had ensured the continuance of the dynasty's memory by entrusting the computarium to her granddaughter on her deathbed. Establishing convents institutionalized prayer and alms and was another way of caring for the dead. Many of the Ottonian women—including the queens Mathilde, Adelheid, and Edith; Otto's married sister, Gerberga; as well as abbesses Gerberga, Matilda, and Sophia—founded convents, as did many other Saxon noblewomen.[38] Since these grants remained within the family, rather than entering a possible rival's hands though marriage, the king or emperor could truly afford to be generous.

But as the *Life* of Mathilde and the charters for Gandersheim and Quedlinburg reveal, the houses were not just for the care of the dead but also for the care of the living. Quedlinburg was often frequented by the Ottonians, and starting with Henry I, it was a center for the administration of the Saxon lands and became a family cult center for Easter.[39] The houses cared for the family's widows and daughters, for which the house received many donations and gifts. Specifically, grants were made for the upkeep of Hathumoda and the other daughters entrusted to the houses; for the upkeep of Liudolf's widow Oda; for thanks for the safe delivery of royal children; as well as in memoriam (for example, on the death day of Queen Edith).

The houses provided much more than financial and physical security. They also offered the Ottonian women opportunities for education and leadership on behalf of the family, instead of marriage. Peter Dronke comments that

> at least in Hrotsvitha's lifetime, that is, Gandersheim was a small, proudly independent principality ruled by women. Such independence will also have suited the Ottonian dynasty politically, since it gave the unmarried women of royal blood a certain power and intellectual scope, and lessened the danger of their marrying princes outside the family, who might loom as rivals for the throne.[40]

Constance Bouchard describes how the increasing number of canonically prohibited degrees of marriage in the tenth and eleventh centuries influenced marriage strategies. Since the royal families of France, Germany, Burgundy, and England were too closely related for the future marriage alliances, royal women often married "beneath them." For example, in this period the king of France's daughters generally married counts' sons.[41] The Ottonians tried to follow the proscriptions against marrying within the seven canonical degrees (as evidenced by their marriage negotiations for the Byzantine princess Theophanu and the negotiations on Otto II's behalf). However, rather than marrying their daughters to less-than-royal suitors, the Ottonians placed them in royal convents. The family could restrict the further intertwining of families, and could thus allow better marriage options for the family's sons and grandsons. Indeed, the only Ottonian daughter in five generations who married beneath the rank of king or duke was Matilda, Otto II's sister (978–1025), who married the Count Palatine Ezzo. This was apparently so extraordinary that a story sprang up to explain it in which Ezzo had beaten Otto at chess and asked for Matilda's hand as his reward.[42]

Struggling to maintain control within Germany at large, the Ottonians had enough problems with the other leading families without giving them the legitimization and dowry of a royal princess. This was especially true, since inheritance through women was not in itself an impediment, even for the crown. (Conrad II, for example, gained the throne through his great-grandmother Liutgard, Otto's eldest daughter.) Thus, the dynasty kept the daughters' dowries, which were invested in the family monasteries, as well as their talents and piety for the maintenance of the family honor and memory. Likewise, Ottonian widows did not remarry. Otto I married the young widow, Adelheid, to gain his claim for Italy, but Oda, Mathilde, Adelheid, and Theophanu all survived their husbands by a number of years, never remarrying—another example of keeping family properties intact and reserving these women's industry and piety for the cult of the family's dead.

St. Mathilde, the Dynasty, and Conflict

Karl Leyser has argued that, through the foundation of convents, Saxon women were best able to maintain control over their lands. Certainly the founding of monasteries, often as memorials, was a praiseworthy, saintly activity singularly suited to the women of the Ottonian royal family. However, as glimpses of Adelheid and Mathilde's experiences show, this mutually beneficial and laudable activity was not exercised without a struggle. Even in the founding of convents, the Ottonian women did not have secure control over their lands.

In discussing Adelheid's administration and control of her dowry, the historian Mathilde Uhlirz describes the losing battle Adelheid waged to control the lands of her German dowry, while she successfully maintained control over the Italian and Burgundian lands she received from her first husband, Lothar.[43]Although according to the language of the grants she held the German lands "in proprium," "potestatem donandi, vendendi, commutandi," and "iure herditario," Uhlirz argues that Adelheid was in no way able to administer these lands freely, as she did her lands in Italy.[44] Nearly the same words were used to describe the grants, but the rights she could exercise over them were very different. Such a discussion demonstrates that "ownership" depends very much on context and is deeply implicated in dynastic concerns and strategies regarding familial lands.[45] Adelheid's struggles over control of her dowry shed important light on Mathilde's administration of the lands she received as dowry—a problem that has received little attention in the historiography.[46]

Mathilde's hagiographer, in presenting her sanctity and the central position of Nordhausen, refers explicitly to the charters given to her foundations. An analysis of the *Vita Mathildis* along with these charters reveals that Mathilde's relationship with her son Otto I was full of tension. Although she was exercising her sanctity within and for the family, her independent control of lands and generosity to the poor met with great resistance.

Upon her marriage, Mathilde was given five cities: Quedlinburg, Nordhausen, Pöhlde, Duderstadt, and Grona. In 929 Henry confirmed his grant with Otto's consent, with the proviso that Mathilde should keep the lands only as long as she remained a widow.[47] Mathilde founded religious communities in four of the five cities, but even so, her control over the lands was not secure. The hagiographer dramatizes her difficulties by cleverly juxtaposing descriptions of Mathilde's virtuous widowhood with accounts of Otto's uncharitable greed. Although Mathilde was a widow of such great probity that few of either sex could imitate her, the devil incited Otto to demand back her dowry. Otto did not succeed in pressuring her to take the veil but he did waylay her servants carrying money to her monasteries (chap. 8). Perhaps Mathilde's great generosity to the poor was too taxing on the familial resources, especially during a time of great rebellions. Finally, through the mediation of Otto's first wife, Edith, who interpreted Otto's loss of several battles as signs of divine disfavor, the two were reconciled. With Otto prostrate at her feet, Mathilde gave up control of her dowry (chaps. 8–9). The charters confirm this rift: until Edith's death in 946, Mathilde only appears as an actor in one charter.[48] After their reconciliation Mathilde appears more frequently in the charters—"at the request of," or "by the intervention of our beloved lady and mother Mathilde." Nevertheless her patronage was still very limited.

The *Vita*, which seems unconcerned with giving more than a cursory mention to the nobility of her lineage, also does not report her patronage to the monastic houses on the lands she received from her own family. The *Life* makes no mention of the grants Henry made at her request to Herford, where she was educated, or to her foundation at Enger. Indeed, Enger was supposedly established long ago by her illustrious ancestor, the Saxon Widukind. The *Vita* mentions only her lands in the west tangentially, when she retired to them briefly during her conflict with Otto. Perhaps the author chose to ignore this material to keep the Ottonian dynasty in the forefront, and to keep these lands out of future inheritance struggles.

The charters amplify material in the *Vita* concerning Mathilde's pet foundation at Nordhausen. Mathilde's hagiographer assigns a particular efficacy to her prayers for Otto and claims that Otto credited her with his conquests in Italy (chaps. 13 and 14). In response, in 965, Otto promised her unending support for the convent at Nordhausen, which she had founded in thanks for her two safe deliveries there.[49] Mathilde's last petition was to beg again for support for Nordhausen.[50] After her death, Otto, distraught with grief, granted her dying wish, firmly establishing the house; and thus the *Vita*'s story ends happily.[51] However, while the *Vita* clearly states that Otto confirmed these grants for Nordhausen with his own hand, there is only one charter for Nordhausen granted by Otto after Mathilde's death, and it was given two full years later. Either the earlier and more complete grants have been lost, or more likely, the author invented donations that had never been made, in order to shore up the position of the house.

Nor did the struggles over Nordhausen end with Mathilde's death. Although the women of the Saxon aristocracy often founded convents on their lands, the lands given in dowry by the Ottonian kings to their wives remained the same for almost 200 years. This could create problems when a previous queen had removed the land from the familial pool by founding a convent there. For example, four years after Mathilde's death, Otto II married the Byzantine princess Theophanu and granted her in dowry the city of Nordhausen, along with many other cities. This gave Theophanu the revenue and control over the city, which had been in the hands of the convent, and thus the convent at Nordhausen was in jeopardy. In response, that same year, Mathilde's first *Vita* was written, which praised the dynasty generally and presented Nordhausen's credentials, as it were, to Otto II. Apparently the *Vita* was convincing, for in 974 Otto II confirmed Nordhausen's endowment.[52]

The limited nature of Mathilde's patronage is revealed by the fact that Nordhausen was threatened after her death. Moreover, there are no extant charters providing lands or protection to her foundations at Pöhlde and Grona. Twenty-one grants were made at Mathilde's request. None extended beyond Saxony. Of these twenty-one, five are for Quedlinburg and sixteen are for either Herford, Enger, or Gandersheim. These twenty-one charters do not compare favorably with the 404 charters issued by Henry I and Otto I up to her death in 968. In the few grants where she is an actor, she seems to be exercising some control over Otto's rights of her dower lands. Perhaps the only way to maintain any control of her lands was to give them up!

Thus, although generosity to convents was an eminently suitable and laudable—if not expected—activity for an early medieval royal saint, Mathilde's agency was limited. She was forced to relinquish her dowry, although she maintained some control over Otto's donations to the houses she founded in these locations. Further, the scope of her patronage was small, confined to Saxony, and completely dependent upon her son and grandson's goodwill. As saintly a woman as Mathilde had great difficulty exercising even that power which was allotted to her.

CONCLUSIONS

The *Vitae* of Hathumoda and Mathilde reveal the linkage between the dynasty and its foundations and the great importance of family (for better or worse) for the Ottonian women. Most scholarship has either slighted the central role these women played for the monasteries or has exaggerated their power, ignoring the problems they had in exercising their patronage. Gandersheim and Quedlinburg, along with a number of less visible convents, received rich endowments and lavish expenditures of time and human resources. The houses provided great benefits for the Liudolfing-Ottonians, as visible manifestations of their wealth and piety, as cultic centers, as residences, and as producers of history and care for the dead as well as the living. No one of these functions alone can enable one to decipher the range of motivations for this patronage. Women, though, are the common denominator for most of the generosity.

The motivations for the patronage of Gandersheim and Quedlinburg cannot be easily summarized because of their range but also because they were not static. The contrasts between the *Vitae* of Hathumoda and Mathilde reveal a shift in the ideals of sanctity. Hathumoda was a typical noble, monastic saint. She was free to exercise her sanctity in a cloistered but relatively autonomous life, in which the convent at Gandersheim, not the Liudolfings, served as her family. However, during the tenth century, what was acceptable for and expected of a saint was redefined. Patrick Corbet describes a change in the hagiography which accommodated lay saints, shifting from the earlier ascetic, monastic ideals to a more positive view of marriage and queenship.[53] While Mathilde could lead a holy life, even though she was married and not cloistered, and employ a limited degree of patronage, she had to struggle with her son to exercise her sanctity. Although she spent her resources and energy cultivating the memory of the dynasty, her independent control of familial resources, even for the family, was suspect.

Mathilde's conflicts with her son have forced a more critical appraisal of her sanctity. Her foundation at Nordhausen fostered her cult as it sought continued Ottonian patronage. The family provided for and required its daughters and widows to lead a holy life and care for the cult of the family; this afforded the women opportunities for education, leadership, etc. While family membership did not confer sanctity, it ensured a life-style and family connections that encouraged the production of a cult.

Some historians have looked back to a golden age in the early Middle Ages, when women served as abbesses and patrons of richly endowed convents or as regents. Powerful English, Merovingian, and Ottonian women are trotted out as examples. The lives of Hathumoda and Mathilde, however, demonstrate first that whatever autonomy or power these women might have held, they wielded it within the bounds and confines (whether monastic or dynastic) of the family and often not without a struggle. Secondly, they show significant change rather than continuity in noble women's status and even in the characteristics of sainthood in the early Middle Ages. In the course of one century, substantial shifts occurred in the relationship between these women's sanctity, the monasteries, and the family, as this family produced itself as a dynasty.

NOTES

1. The Ottonian saints have received more attention in recent years. See Karl Leyser, *Rule and Conflict in an Early Medieval Society: Ottonian Saxony* (Bloomington, Ind.: Indiana Univ. Press, 1979); Patrick Corbet, *Les saints ottoniens: saintete dynastique, saintete royale et saintete feminine autour de l'an mil* (Sigmaringen: J. Thorbecke, 1986); Gerd Althoff, "Gandersheim und Quedlinburg: Ottonische Frauenkloster als Herrschafts- und Überlieferungszentren," *Frühmittelalterliche Studien*, vol. 25, Berlin: W. de Gruyter, 1991), 123–44; and "Causa scribendi und Darstellungsabsicht: Die Lebensbeschreibungen der Konigin Mathilde und andere Beispiele," *Litterae medii aevi: Festschrift fur Johanne Autenrieth zu ihrem 65. Geburtstag* (Thorbecke, Sigmaringen, 1988), 117–33.

2. Leyser, Corbet, and Althoff use the *Lives* of Mathilde; Stephen Jaeger and Irene Schmale-Ott have discussed the life of Brun; but Hathumoda is generally mentioned only to fill in material on the origins of Gandersheim.

3. Leyser, *Rule and Conflict*, 63

4. Leyser, *Rule and Conflict*, 78, 88–89. Patrick Corbet's *Les saints ottoniens* seeks primarily to explain the accommodation and status of queens in the hagiography. Gerd Althoff has focused on spiritual connections between the dynasty and the houses and discusses their role as familial cult centers, through the charters, necrologies, and production of the *Vitae*. See especially, Gerd Althoff, "Beobachtungen zum liudolfingisch-ottonisch Gedenkwesen," *Adels- und Konigsfamilien*, ed. Karl Schmid and Joachim Wollasch (Munich: W. Fink, 1984).

5. Rather than focusing on the houses at Gandersheim and Quedlinburg, the *Vita* completely ignores the existence of Gandersheim and begrudges Quedlinburg even Mathilde's resting place.

6. *Vita Hathumodae* Monumenta Germaniae Historica (MGH) SS IV, ed. M. Pertz (Hannover: Hahn, 1828–), 165–75.

7. Previously he was assumed to be her biological brother, but this connection has been dismissed. See below. Also Winfred Glocker, *Verwandten der Ottonen und ihre Bedeutung in der Politik* (Köln: Bohlau, 1989), 258.

8. *MGH* SS IV, 1:166.

9. *MGH* SS IV, 28:175.

10. Revelation 14:3–4.

11. *MGH* SS IV, 2:167.

12. *MGH SS IV*, 1:167.

13. *MGH SS IV*, 28:175.

14. Ludwig Zoepf, *Das Heiligen-Leben im 10 Jahrhundert* (Leipzig and Berlin: B.G. Teubner, 1908), 164.

15. Winfred Glocker, *Die Verwandten der Ottonen und ihre Bedeutung in der Politik* (Köln: Bohlau, 1989), 260.

16. Hrotsvitha's *Primordia Gandeshemenensis* was written under Otto II (973–983). This incomplete verse account begins with Liudolf and Oda's pilgrimage to Rome, the foundation of Gandersheim, and Hathumoda's abbacy and ends incompletely with Christina's abbacy.

17. *MGH DOI* 180. "monasterium . . . cum filia velo consecrata."

18. *MGH SS IV*, 17:172.

19. *MGH SS IV*, 26:175.

20. *Primordia Gandeshemenensis*, l. 468.

21. *Primordia*, l. 585.

22. *Vita Mathildis Reginae Antiquior, MGH SS* X, 573–82. Gerd Althoff, "Causa scribendi und Darstellungsabsicht," 117–33. A second *Life*, directly based on the earlier version, was written by another unnamed monk at Nordhausen, but at the request of Henry II. *Vita Mathildis Reginae, MGH SS IV*, 282–302.

23. *MGH SS IV*, 4:576–77.

24. Zoepf, 47.

25. Their children were Otto I; Gerberga, first Duchess of Lorraine and then West Frankish Queen; Henry, Duke of Bavaria; and Brun, Archbishop of Cologne. Hathui, who married Hugh the Great, is not included in this list.

26. I will use the spelling Matilda to refer to the abbess of Quedlinburg, Queen (St.) Mathilde's granddaughter, to avoid confusion.

27. *MGH SS IV*, 11:579.

28. *MGH SS IV*, 12:579. No multiplication of food occurs, nor is there any evidence of great eucharistic devotion in the *Vita*. The only sacraments discussed at all in detail are those surrounding the care of the dead.

29. *MGH SS IV*, 12:579.

30. *MGH SS IV*, chap. 15.

31. Gerd Althoff, "Gandersheim und Quedlinburg," "Beobachtungen," *Adels- und Konigsfamilien*.

32. Althoff, "Beobachtungen," 652.

33. The *Epitaphium Adelheidae*, written by Odilo of Cluny, was written long after her death in 999 and does not fall within the tradition of Saxon hagiography. A book of miracles follows considerably later. *MGH SS* I, 637–45.

34. The *Life* of Brun was written between 967 and 969, shortly after his death in 965. The *Life*, requested by Brun's successor, Folkmar, archbishop of Cologne, was written ostensibly by Ruotger, a monk at Brun's foundation of St. Pantaleon in Cologne. *MGH SS rer. germ. n.s.*

35. Liutprand IV, 15. Thietmar I, 21. Althoff, "Beobachtungen," 650.

36. Thietmar of Merseburg, *Chronik* I, 21.

37. For example, for Edith: DOI 74, 75; for Otto I: DOII 29–32; for Adelheid: DOIII 344. Althoff, "Beobachtungen," 654.

38. Thirty-six communities for noblewomen were founded between 919 and 1024 in Germany. For example, Fischbeck, Kemnade, and Hilwartshausen were all founded by noble Saxon women from their inheritances. Timothy Reuter comments that houses of canonesses were more available to the aristocratic families (including the Liudolfingers) than Benedictine monasteries, which were necessarily larger and much more expensive. Reuter, *Germany in the Early Middle Ages c. 800–1056* (London: Longman, 1990), 241. See also Leyser.

39. Henry I stayed in Quedlinburg four times, Wallhausen and Pohlde three times. Otto, however, stayed only at Magdeburg (twenty-two times) more times than

at Quedlinburg (seventeen). Carl Richard Brühl, *Fodrum, Gistum, servitium Regis*, (Köln: Bohlau, 1968), 119. Otto spent a total of eight Easters at Quedlinburg, including in 941, when his younger brother, Henry, attempted a coup.

40. Peter Dronke, *Women Writers of the Middle Ages: A Critical Study of Twenty-Six Texts from Perpetua (+203) to Marguerite Porete (+1310)* (Cambridge and New York: Cambridge Univ. Press, 1984), 55.

41. Constance Bouchard, "Consanguinity and Noble Marriages in the Tenth and Eleventh Centuries," *Speculum* 56 (Apr. 1981): 268–87.

42. Gerd Althoff, *Verwandte, Freunde und Getreue* (Darmstadt: Wissenschaftliche Buchgesellschaft, 1990), 52–53. Fundatio monasterii Brunwilarensis, *Archiv der Gesellschaft fur altere deutsche Geschichtskunde* 12, ed. H. Pabst (Frankfurt A.M.: 1872) 147–92; chap. 6, 158ff.

43. Mathilde Uhlirz, "Die rechtliche Stellung der Kaiserinwitwe Adelheid im Deutschen und im Italienischen Reich," *Zeitschrift der Savigny Stiftung für Rechtsgeschichte* vol. 74 (Weimar: H. Bohlau, 1880), Germ. Abt., pt. 2, especially 92–97.

44. Uhlirz, 93.

45. Barbara Rosenwein's *To Be the Neighbor of Saint Peter* (Ithaca, N.Y.: Cornell Univ. Press, 1989) also argues for the complexity of land transfers and land tenure, describing a fluidity of ownership as well as a multitude of motivations for the donations to Cluny in the tenth and eleventh centuries.

46. See Gerd Althoff's forthcoming work, which traces these conflicts over dowries through Henry II's queen, Kunigunde.

47. DHI 20. "si nobis superstes extiterit et in sanctae viduitatis pudicitia permanserit, praedicta loca ei concendendo tradimus ut libera atque secura potestate cum omni quaesitu eidem."

48. DOI 18, for Quedlinburg in 937.

49. *MGH* SS IV, 14:580.

50. *MGH* SS IV, 15:580.

51. *MGH* SS IV, 15–16:581.

52. DOII 21. Althoff, "Causa scribendi," 126. Althoff further argues that the *Primordia* was written as an attempt to restore Gandersheim to its former central position. The constant didactic theme is that the Ottonians' great success is the result of the grace due to their patronage of Gandersheim. Both the *Primordia* and Mathilde's first *Life* were composed after the houses had lost their particular *Konigsnähe*. Neither work is a dynastic history; rather, they remind the ruler of the needs of the house, either with an undertone of criticism or with an admonitory tone.

53. Patrick Corbet, *Les saints ottoniens*.

EARLY MEDIEVAL KINSHIP STRUCTURES AS SOCIAL AND POLITICAL CONTROLS[1]

Aline G. Hornaday

"The reader [of Gregory of Tours] may often wonder whether it is worth while to speak of justice at all in connexion with the Merovingian kingdoms, so flagrant was the lawlessness, so cheaply might the worst criminal who had the means compound for his offense."[2] When he wrote these lines, did Gregory's translator, the historian O.M. Dalton, present an accurate picture of early medieval society? Or did he overlook social controls that helped early medieval rulers and people to survive in turbulent societies whose rudimentary administrative systems were more honored in the breach than the observance? Kinship structures may well have functioned as such controls even if Dalton and other historians like him believed that "whole cities, groups of citizens, and individuals [took] the law into their own hands." For at all levels of community the invisible glue of kinship cemented factions and bound families together for mutual help, even though that help could oppose kindreds in deadly conflict. And these kinship structures could be exploited by rulers and administrators from outside the family, to serve the ends of rough justice.

As historians have tried to discover medieval people's own reactions to their kinship patterns, they have clarified hitherto obscure or unconsidered aspects of kinship through genealogical studies, prosopographical dictionaries, and analyses of the self-perceptions of aristocratic kindreds.[3] Some historians have traced the use of genealogies as propaganda to support dynastic legitimacy by stressing exalted lineage.[4] A few have examined dynastic reproductive strategies.[5] Theories of patriarchal and matriarchal social structures, too, can be seen as specialized applications of kinship theory. Bachofen's 1861 recognition of prehistoric matriarchy, which he deplored, eventually evoked a polemical counterliterature, since the existence and nature of prehistoric matriarchy, and its possible survival into historic times, have been major concerns for feminist historians.[6]

In all this varied literature, the notion that kinship structures that determined inner relationships within a family or kin group could also function as outside social controls exercised through the institution of feuding remained largely the province of legal historians and anthropologists. Yet the relevance of this point to early medieval social conditions in northern Europe is attested by the numerous citations anthropologists make to the histories of Gregory of Tours when they discuss feuding as a social model.[7] And some perceptive historians of medieval northern Europe have taken the point, for Dalton's view of Merovingian lawlessness did not win unanimous agreement nor was Frankish feuding totally ignored.

As early as 1959, J.M. Wallace Hadrill proposed that a positive side of feuds in Merovingian Francia was that they provided "a way for the settlement of differences, whether through violence or negotiation or both."[8] More recently, other historians have drawn attention to social controls inherent in medieval northern European kinship structures allied to feuding. In 1982 Jesse Byock saw feud as a "cohesive and stabilizing force in Old Icelandic society." Byock thought that tenth-century Icelanders created their court apparatus "to endorse resolutions arrived at by private parties," in which middlemen acted to "initiate, maintain and resolve disputes."[9] In 1987 Richard A. Gerberding noted the Pippinids' political manipulation of Frankish kinship structures as they rose to power.[10] In 1987 and 1989 respectively, Katherine Fischer Drew and Emanuel J. Mickel observed that kinship groups operated as supplemental agencies for Germanic courts in Rome's successor states.[11] David Abulafia has put the point succinctly concerning a Venetian context: "[W]hat is striking about the vendetta is precisely that it operates within constraints; it is a controlled system of justice apportioning responsibility for its execution to the kin network of the contesting parties."[12]

Such comments support the notion that in poorly organized prebureaucratic states without police forces, rulers deliberately used the legal obligations imposed on kindreds as rudimentary controls on antisocial behavior, acting as middlemen to reach quasi-administrative solutions for justice problems. But understanding early medieval kinship structures and the law codes governing them is a prerequisite to interpreting how rulers manipulated early medieval kinship in real life. For though formal law does not always coincide with actual social practice, it expresses cultural ideals or their antecedents in preexisting social norms. Among Celts, Germans, and Scandinavians alike, early medieval law codes recognized groups of kin who were bound together in structurally cohesive units. Their members were charged with well-defined individual duties and enjoyed specific privileges in the areas of wergeld and inheritances, and precise responsibilities were assigned to the whole group to enforce these commands through the medium of feuding.

In a recent work Nerys Patterson analyzed how, within the complex Irish organization of kinship, individuals belonging to the kin group, or *fine*, exercised authority over other members of it in specific, well-recognized situations. In early medieval Ireland, a system of restraints upon individual action "was implemented through the general rule that people could not alienate more than their honor price in general social transactions [motivating them] to act as watchmen upon each other [and benefiting] the lords . . . because it was in their interest that feuds be settled."[13] Patterson here describes a typical early medieval situation in which feud and feud settlement were open to manipulation, even though the patrilineal agnatic organization of the Irish *fine* differed from the bilateral structure of kinship organization found in Germanic regions of northern Europe in the same era.

Historians who do not have a command of the Irish language can best examine the notion of official manipulation of feuds in the interests of chiefly or royal profit and social justice in Germanic law codes and chronicles, whose texts have long since been established by the devoted scholars of the *Monumenta Germaniae Historica*. I shall therefore discuss Germanic kinship primarily; and to keep this essay within reasonable bounds, I shall take Frankish law as an exemplar for Germanic ideas about family, feuding, and social controls, since Frankish law codes reflect general Germanic social patterns. I shall also examine some Roman ideas about family structure, for officials using Latin to record Germanic laws and write legal documents perforce used the vocabulary of Roman family models. In like manner, existing recensions of early Germanic family law also contain elements borrowed from West Roman vulgar law and from the treatment of inheritance in the Theodosian Code.[14] But Germanic invaders did not always use the material they were adopting in ways a Roman would have recognized. Nor did Frankish referendaries, notaries, chroniclers, and hagiographers always know how to apply specific Latin relationship terms.[15]

The Latin kinship vocabulary revealed a bilateral core kindred through etymologically distinct words for each member of a family related in the Roman fourth degree of relationship.[16] The vocabulary of the Roman *Digest* segregated remoter relations by employing words for them compounded from prepositions added to the basic terms.[17] The Roman core family, plus this remoter kin group extending to descendants in the sixth generation, corresponded fairly well with the legal configuration of Frankish kinship structures. Thus Murray states that in compensation and oath helping "a range of second or third cousins is not an extreme estimate," while in *reipi* payments and inheritance, the bilateral kindred extended "to the sixth degree."[18]

Did any developmental links connect Roman and Frankish concepts of family relationships as expressed in law codes? Or did the latter evolve independently? The earliest recension of the Salic law cannot answer the question, since it probably dates from c. 511, after the Franks conquered Roman Gaul.[19] The patrician referendary Asclepiodatus authenticated its third recension in 596. His involvement in the process, together with similar evidence from other barbarian codes, led Patrick Wormald to argue strongly for Roman participation in codifying barbarian laws in general and Frankish law in particular.[20] Always supposing that officials concerned in the recensions of barbarian laws were not Franks with Roman names, if Wormald is right, "contamination" of Frankish family models by Roman law cannot be ruled out.

A late Roman family document from pre-conquest Gaul, the *Parentalia* of Ausonius, might be thought useful in settling this question. But it cannot help either. Ausonius composed this set of elegies about 382 to memorialize the bilateral kindreds and in-laws of himself and his late wife.[21] Since religious obligation compelled Ausonius to include even remote relatives whose deaths were recent, the extended family model he presented conformed to that of the *Digest* and does not conflict with the Frankish kin group.[22] But this preconquest work shows that the precise ancient Latin terminology for the Roman core family had already begun to disintegrate. For example, Ausonius employed the term *consobrina* to designate a paternal cousin who should properly have been called an *amitina*, and replaced the *Digest* terms *levir* and *glos* for brother- and sister-in-law with *adfinis*. Frankish notaries carried forward similar misunderstandings. Centuries later, in 739, the patrician Abbo's will likewise used *consobrina* for the daughter of an *amita*, and confused its usage of *amita* (paternal aunt) and *avunculus* (paternal uncle) by employing the words for maternal relatives.[23] To sum up, traces of an early clan system are embedded in Roman family vocabulary and ritual custom, but Roman written law retains neither legal definitions of ancient kinship structures nor codified feuding practices.

When the Franks conquered Roman Gaul, they brought with them new, different codes. These embodied a legal system in which kinship structures were intimately linked with the practice of feuding. The victorious Franks confronted a Romanized Celtic population whose own tribal system had been partially obliterated by installation of Roman law, under which this existing population continued to be governed under the Frankish system of "national laws."[24] The interconnections of these three social structures, or remnants of structures, and any developmental links they may have shared, are largely ir-recoverable at this distance of time and in view of the ambiguity of surviving records. In any case, if Roman family terminology was already degenerating into confusion before the Frankish conquest, comparison of the two family models could not detect possible Roman influence on Frankish law.

Whatever the course of their development, one important difference distinguished Frankish from Roman kinship structure. Frankish law defined the composition of a kin group, referred to by the Latin word *parentela* (a translation of the Frankish *chrenecruda*), as a legally specific bilateral kin-dred extending as far as third cousins, whereas Roman law as opposed to custom knew nothing of such kindreds.[25] The Salic law bound members of this parentela together by legal rights and obligations.[26] According to the Frankish system, wives did not belong to their husbands' *parentelae* unless the spouses were blood kin; therefore, unrelated spouses had no responsi-bilities for each other's kin and shared none of the benefits of each other's kindred. All members of the parentela shared receipts from compositions but also shared in paying compositions for individual members as required. Its members also shared some types of inheritances. All members were required to help each other to bring attackers to justice and to act for each other as oath helpers in court cases. As Patterson noted in her discussion of the Irish *fine*, the regulatory requirements laid on kin group members in such systems produced tremendous family pressure on individual action. And rather than avoiding conflicts of interest perceived as corrupt in modern times, the parentela system institutionalized mutual help by interested parties.

Salic law number 60 provided an escape from the parentela, but hav-ing escaped from its restrictions, a person without a parentela then stood alone and vulnerable.[27] For this reason, Murray interprets law number 60 as being designed to permit renunciation of obligations not to the parentela as a whole but to specific individuals within it.[28] But since Frankish law pro-vided procedures called *affatomie* to bring a new heir by adoption into a diminished parentela, may not release from the original parentela have rather been a prerequisite for adoption designed to avoid a confusing situation of doubled parentelae? This interpretation would explain the original creation of a "de-*parentel*ization" procedure. However, once in place the procedure might also offer escape from onerous legal and financial liability for espe-cially troublesome relatives.[29]

Through its formal definition of a bilateral parentela, Frankish fam-ily law institutionalized a fluid social structure by means of "horizontal" kin groups whose composition changed with each generation. These structures coexisted uneasily with a "vertical" lineage-based inheritance system that privileged males over females, and with a subsidiary set of close godparenting connections. Within overlapping bilateral kin groups, husbands and wives, parents and children, had rights and duties that did not completely coincide. And if a widowed parent remarried, one household could contain several parentelae. Within a family household, notorious emotional difficulties of step-relationships must have been magnified by differences in the familial, legal, and religious rights and obligations that each family member observed. And on the plane of political action, the shifting composition of parentelae accounts for much of the confusing appearance of Merovingian factions in contemporary chronicles and other historical writing.

Like modern newspaper reporters, chroniclers delighted in recounting the dramatic and violent conflicts that this social structure produced in plenty, as well as the constant shifts in loyalties that it entailed. But the parentela system also contained positive values. For example, private interventions to settle conflicts resulted from the economic interest of the whole parentela in preventing violence by its members, since the victims of their aggressions might claim compensation to which that parentela had to contribute—if, indeed, its members did not save money by feuding instead of paying up, which entailed other, more severe consequences.[30] The kin group also had an interest in preventing violence directed against the persons or property of its members, an interest served by the legal obligation of parentela members to aid each other in bringing attackers to justice.

In turn, these private interests benefited public law enforcement. For early medieval rulers and administrators had no practical means to assure prosecution for offenses except manipulating the web of kinship obligations. Frankish law courts and their officers had no centralized, standing paramilitary body like modern police forces at their disposal, and they had few prisons. Most murderers and thieves could only be caught and punished by using existing legal structures to enlist the victim's family to hunt them down.[31] Under existing law and in these general conditions, officials were theoretically *forced* to manipulate and arbitrate feuds in the interests of justice.

What is the evidence that rulers did, in fact, deliberately proceed in this fashion? While we know almost nothing about Merovingian administrative techniques—and indeed, procedures like those of modern states could not have existed at all in early medieval times—direct personal intervention in feuds by monarchs can be amply documented. Gregory of Tours, the authors collectively known as Fredegar, and other chroniclers and hagiographers, reported many instances in which kings and queens took a lively interest in feuds, acted as arbitrators of aristocratic feuds, or directed feuding into special procedures. Indeed, Gregory recorded that some

Merovingian rulers encouraged feuds and then settled them, in a rudimentary adaption toward controlling incorrigibly violent individuals. Having gathered such examples into a table (see table 1), we might rest our case. But one question still remains. Do such reports mean that monarchs took special interest in aristocratic feuds in general, and that court officials also manipulated them on a lower level of society, or just that feuds fascinated chroniclers so much that they carefully recorded all known instances that were, by definition, therefore exceptional? An analysis of some of these records may help answer this question.[32]

TABLE 1. SOME MEROVINGIAN FEUDS

Date	Instigator(s)	Victim(s)	Action/Result	Arbitrator(s)
c.509/510	Clovis I	Own kindred	Murder, gained undisputed rule.	
522/4	Clotild, Clovis I's widow	Burgundian kings	Defeat, execution; vengeance.	
c.531	Frankish Queen Amalaberga	Thuringian kings	Frankish conquest, capture of Radegund.	
c.545	Agyric, bishop of Verdun (?); partisan of Guntram Boso	Syrivald	Murder; vengeance on Syrivald by Agyric's son.	King Theuderic (?)
c.550	Frankish kings Childebert I, Chlothar I, and Theudebert I	Theudahat, king of Italy	Vengeance for their cousin Amalasuntha.	
c.550	Secundinus	Asteriolus	Murder; vengeance on both sides.	King Theudebert I, Queen Wisegard
? to c.585	Jovinus, supported by Vigilius	Albinus, supported by Dynamius	Attacks short of murder. Albinus ousts Jovinus from office, is fined for mulcting Vigilius.	King Sigebert I, King Childebert II
574	Deacon Lampadius	Deacon Peter and Silvester	Murder of Peter by Silvester's son.	Court of assembled bishops
578	Duke Dragolen Industrius	Dacolen, son of Dagaric	Dacolen executed; property forfeited to king; Dragolen attacks his *foedus* Guntram Boso, who kills him.	King Chilperic I
c.578	Frontonius	Marchar, count and then bishop of Angouleme	Poisoned; avenged by nephew Nantinus.	No arbitrator named
c.579	Husband	Wife	Accused of adultery; wife hangs herself.	King Chilperic I
c.584	Vedast Avo	Ambrosius and Lupus, husband and brother-in-law of instigator's mistress (also his cousin)	Instigator marries cousin; later, a follower of Saxon Chilperic kills instigator in unrelated quarrel, then compensates his sons.	King Chilperic arbitrates original offense
c.585	Austregisel	Priest of Manthelan	Feud between Austregisel and priest's friend, Sichar.	Citizen's tribunal, Gregory of Tours
585	Bobolenus	Domnola	Bobolenus kills Domnola; king orders Antestius to execute Bobolenus, thus avoiding feud.	King Guntram

Table 1. (CONTINUED)

Date	Instigator(s)	Victim(s)	Action/Result	Arbitrator(s)
c.587	Ingitrude	Bethegund	Property dispute.	King Guntram, King Childebert II
591	A Frank of Tournai	Brother-in-law of instigator	Instigator's brother-in-law neglects his wife; after murder, feud continues until arbitrator executes three remaining parties.	Queen Fredegund
627	Aighyna, a Saxon nobleman	Ermenarius, controller to Charibert, son of Chlotar II	Aighyna kills Ermenarius; Chlotar II sends him away; settles possible feud.	King Chlotar II
642	Ermenfred	Chainulf	Attacked by Chainulf's family, Ermenfred flees to sanctuary.	Queen Nantechild
642	Flaochad	Willebad	King orders pitched battle at Autun; Flaochad kills Willebad.	King Clovis II
643	Grimoald, son of Pippin of Landen, *maior palatii* of Austrasia	Otto, tutor to King Sigebert III of Austrasia, perhaps connected with Radult, duke of Thuringia	Murder by Grimoald protégé; Lentharius, duke of Alamannia, eliminates Otto's threat to Pippinids.	No arbitrator named
661/2	Wulfoald	Grimoald	Execution of Grimoald.	King Clovis II, Queens Balthild of Neustria and Chimnechild of Austrasia
688	Duke Gundoin, relative (?) of Wulfoald	Ansegisel, Pippinid heir	Murder, possibly related to ongoing feud instigated by Wulfoald.	King Theuderic III (?)
703	Dodo, *domesticus*, Charles Martel's maternal uncle	Lambert, bishop of Maastricht, Wulfoald's protégé	Murder by enemies in Liège-Maastricht region, possibly related to ongoing feud instigated by Wulfoald.	No arbitrator named

Condensed from Gregory of Tours, Fredegar, *Liber Historiae Francorum*, and PLRE. The great feud between Brunhild and Fredegund was too complex and long-lasting for a condensed chart.

Five reported feuds could not be arbitrated by Merovingian kings, or indeed anybody else, since they set the Merovingians themselves against one another and against other royal and princely houses.[33] This impossibility of arbitration permitted royal feuds to spread and endure from generation to generation, unchecked by any controls. Their ramifications and the resultant wars give one the impression that feuding represented the Merovingian concept of foreign policy. It was Merovingian royal feuds that gave rise to the often repeated historical judgment that under the rule of this dynasty, Frankish society disintegrated. In a way, unchecked royal feuds act as a control for the evidence of feud manipulation. They glaringly illuminate the instability of a society when the parties to feuds are beyond the reach of settlement procedures, and suggest that had aristocratic feuds not been manipulated and settled, they could quickly have embroiled whole kingdoms.

But royals did not only feud with other royals; since commoners shared in their parentelae, even kings carried out private interventions within their own families. Gregory of Tours recounted how King Guntram of Burgundy tried to quiet some female relations on his maternal, nonroyal side. Their dissensions had become embarrassing, since his cousins lived in the convent of Ste.-Marie in the atrium of St. Martin's church in Tours, an uncomfortably public location for private quarrels.[34] In this instance, Gregory tacitly presented Guntram in the character of a senior member of his own parentela rather than that of an administrator enforcing order or a middleman between kindreds. However, in this case Guntram may have been trying to mediate a feud between overlapping parentelae from within one of them, for the quarrel's apparent instigator, Ingitrude, supported the pretender Gundovald's rebellion against Guntram. Gundovald publicly gave Ingitrude as his reference. He offered as a second reference Radegund, the Thuringian princess and former Merovingian queen, who had good reason to feud with her Merovingian husband, Chlotar I, and his kin. This case presents an instance in which royal membership in a partly nonroyal parentela created an unstable situation in which an aggrieved party could try to bring down a royal adjudicator of an internal feud by absorbing her aggression into a nonarbitrable royal feud, in an interesting foreshadowing of how powerful kin groups like the Pippinids would come to exercise control over Frankish monarchs. Though Guntram defeated this ploy by successfully putting down Gundovald's rebellion, he ultimately failed to quell Ingitrude. His successor eventually had to settle her problems.

Gregory also reported ten apparent aristocratic feuds, nine of which he described being arbitrated by kings, queens, or bishops in cases involving priests. In one vicious blood feud at Tours, Gregory himself, as bishop of Tours, first tried to persuade two feuding parentelae to control their members, then put up the money for the guilty parties' compensation payment even though priests had been killed in the course of the quarrel.[35] In this case Gregory acted as a middleman outside the lay courts of Tours, which had unsuccessfully tried to settle the feud. In a later chronicle Fredegar recounted a feud between the Franks Flaochad and Willibad, in which royal arbitration confined their fighting within special procedures whose violation could jeopardize the cause of the responsible kin group.[36] Their enforced observance of well-defined rules in this feud is illuminated by a less socially lofty case in which a local *iudex loci* penalized one party to a feud for carrying it on in defiance of specific appropriate procedures.[37] In these three cases, we catch a glimpse of quasi-administrative techniques for mediating feuds.

J.M. Wallace Hadrill argued from the known course of five Frankish blood feuds that Merovingian kings did not wish to abolish feuding. He was clearly right. For in addition to its advantages in maintaining social order, royal arbitrators' activities as middlemen made feuds profitable to them. This profit is not a matter of surmise: Gregory of Tours, for example, reported how Severus planned to present rich gifts to a Merovingian king to influence his favorable decision in a feud begun by Dragolen.[38] Yet our knowledge of the actual steps kings and their queens took to realize their potential profits, manage the course of feuds, and announce their decisions rests largely on deduction and interpretation of such reports by chroniclers and hagiographers.

When the Merovingian dynasty was ousted by Pippin I and his parentela and followers in 751, the Carolingian house introduced administrative techniques that are more visible to modern historians than the shadowy procedures of the previous age. At the same time, documentary and literary evidence became more plentiful for the functioning of Frankish kinship structures and the procedures used in mediating feuds. But kinship structures were failing in the long run to enforce public order. Even as the workings of such structures emerged more clearly into history, lawgivers began to prohibit vengeance and feuding and to outlaw perjury and false accusations arising from the conflicts of interest encouraged by the parentela system.[39] A compensatory new emphasis developed on oaths of fidelity and relationships between lord and man. Such oaths and relationships formed one strand in the making of feudal military organization, which can been seen partly as a response to the ultimate inadequacy of kinship social controls to deal with violence.

Nonetheless, a spirit of aristocratic independence showed itself in the functioning of the old kinship structures that lingered on into the Carolingian age. Aristocratic kin groups began to restrain arbitrary rulers quite effectively. For example, in the most resounding royal scandal of the ninth century, the Bosonids successfully thwarted Lothar II of Lotharingia's efforts to divorce their barren kinswoman Theutberga in order to marry the Frankish noblewoman Waldrada, with whom he had fathered several children.[40] Rulers and subjects alike can be seen manipulating kinship patterns to attain political ends: Empress Judith maneuvered with the aid of her Welf kindred, and the Pippinids and Bosonids were helped by their parentelae to achieve royal status.[41]

Prime royal tools in counteracting such aristocratic maneuvers in the past had consisted of standard Frankish "kin control" methods: fostering, guesting, and promotion of palace schools, all of which could be thinly disguised forms of hostage taking to control unruly or hostile aristocrats through an implied threat to their sons.[42] The Countess Dhuoda's qualms for her son at court illustrate this point.[43] Hostage holding easily slipped into brutality toward the hapless hostages; it had always facilitated outright execution if monarchs foiled treason in advance by destroying their kin, as Clovis did at the outset of his reign.

When Carolingian rulers seized the throne and found their fellow great aristocratic kin groups of Francia attempting to restrain their autocratic power, did they institutionalize these means of resisting treason by making whole parentelae answerable with their lives for their individual members' treachery? Even though the *Song of Roland* depicted Charlemagne executing the traitor Ganelon's whole family, one must answer, "Probably not." In practice, forcible tonsuring generally replaced execution at the Carolingian court. Pippin I hustled the last Merovingian king into a cloister.[44] Later, Charlemagne cloistered his cousin, the duke of Bavaria, and the latter's immediate heirs when they rebelled against his rule.

As the Carolingian age drew to a close, the uneasy balance between royalty and aristocratic kindreds began to tip toward the power of aristocrats organized into recognizable factions. This evolution was aided by the Carolingian system of oaths of fidelity, which placed kings and their subjects in direct relationship and extended itself into the relations between lords and their men. Patrilineal inheritance had always coexisted with the bilateral parentela system; now it began to replace the latter as a familial organizing principle. Yet the bilateral parentela maintained its strong effects on family organization in a strange development in which it became transmogrified into a mirror image of its old self.

This transformation of the ancient parentela began as Christianity took firm hold among the Frankish elite, whose members began to pay real attention to canonical marriage regulations. But these regulations forbade marriage to a set of relations who coincided with those specified in the old Frankish kindreds, and thus redefined "inside out" in the tables of forbidden degrees of kinship. The canonical rules did more: they asserted that since husband and wife were one, so too were their parentelae one and the same, so that all members of these expanded kindreds fell within the purview of the Church canons.[45] These rules in fact present a negative image of the old Frankish parentelae, as the thirteenth-century jurist Beaumanoir later recognized in his *Coûtumes de Beauvais* when he commented that the rules of feud and the rules of kinship degrees for regulating marriage corresponded with each other.[46] No case more clearly illustrates the new attitudes than the previously mentioned relegation of Waldrada to the status of Lothar II of Lotharingia's concubine and the bastardization of her children. Lothar had to attempt to divest himself of his existing wife Theutberga before he could try to marry Waldrada—a far cry from the polygamous households of Merovingian kings. And Theutberga's Bosonid kin successfully prevented him from doing so. Their maneuvers to protect her materially aided Lothar's uncle Charles the Bald in his efforts to absorb the short-lived Lotharingian state into his West Francian realm, and they managed to achieve a marriage between Charles and a Bosonid daughter.

By the middle of the ninth century, the Church prohibited marriage within the seventh degree of relationship, counted back to a common ancestor instead of from a spouse up to a common ancestor and down again.[47] Yet stringent as it might seem, this negative reinterpretation of old forms of kinship organization, while turning them to a new purpose, offered a new way to manipulate marriage regulations profitably by shedding spouses to preserve or gain valuable property. By the high Middle Ages, it became fairly frequent to take advantage of canonical marriage regulations for these decidedly uncanonical ends. A case in point is presented by the French queen Eleanor of Aquitaine's maneuvers on behalf of her younger sister Petronilla, in which she employed canonical marriage regulations to encompass just such a purpose. In 1141, when Count Raoul of Vermandois wished to marry Petronilla, Eleanor quickly discovered that his existing marriage was invalid due to his forbidden degree of consanguinity with his wife. Raoul then exchanged his current wife's less desirable status and estates for Petronilla's, annulling their marriage in order to marry the queen's sister and have Petronilla's dower lands in Burgundy at his disposal.[48] His remarriage to Petronilla embroiled the French court and the newlyweds with Bernard of Clairvaux and the Pope, but it was canonically correct even if morally specious.

The old Frankish kinship system organized around parentalae had functioned as a rudimentary social control precisely because it encouraged feuding, which, in spite of its accompanying violence and apparent lawlessness, was a cohesive force in Germanic society in general. Feuding created opportunities for early medieval rulers to direct events and secure punishments. A feuding society contains violence, so far as it actually does do so, by punishing random assaults and frauds. Thus feuds permit people to make sense of their experience, however painful, for the violence of feuding is neither random nor senseless (whereas the random shootings of our own time, generally condemned as "senseless," leave their victims confused and bitter).

As Byock pointed out in the case of Iceland, management of such a system can make it into a substitute for a court system or even lead to the construction of a viable court system. The kinship-based obligations of early medieval feuding provided a substitute of sorts for effective administration of justice, and also offered considerable benefits to Merovingian monarchs exploiting their position as middlemen in aristocratic Frankish feuds. But although the Merovingian kings of Francia used feud management as an administrative tool to supplement their court systems, they never seemed to have taken the next step of uniformly turning prosecution for violent crime over to established courts.

Though kinship structures become more visible to us in the following Carolingian age, as kindreds exerted more truly political influence and record keeping improved, their power was waning and feuding was increasingly unacceptable to a Christian society. Now former notions of kinship lingered on chiefly in their negative mirror image, canonical marriage regulations. The ultimate failure of the bilateral kinship system to control violence led to its eventual replacement by proto-feudal relationships between lord and man, while lineage-based inheritance, which had always coexisted within it, became paramount over the bilateral kindred. As negative consanguinity replaced positive kinship, a changing *mentalité* signaled a shift in social controls from early medieval kinship obligations to religious sanctions that were no longer based on family responsibilities.

NOTES

1. Earlier versions of this article were read to the Work in Progress group of San Diego Independent Scholars and delivered at a panel discussion moderated by Professor Constance B. Bouchard at the joint meeting of the Medieval Academy and the Medieval Association of the Pacific in Tucson, Ariz., on April 1, 1993. I am grateful to my listeners on both occasions for helpful feedback and especially to Professor Bouchard for including this essay in her panel.

2. O.M. Dalton, ed., *The History of the Franks by Gregory of Tours* (Oxford: Clarendon Press, 1927), I:204.

3. A selection of kinship studies must at least include Léopold Génicot's fundamental *Les Généalogies* (Turnout: Brepols, 1975); Martin Heinzelmann, *Bischofsherrschaft in Gallien* (Munich, 1976), and "Prosopographie et recherche de continuité historique: l'exemple des V–VII siècles," in *Mélanges de l'Ecole francaise de Rome*, 100 (Rome, Artenis, 1988), 227–39; Patrick Geary, *Aristocracy in Provence* (Philadelphia: Univ. of Penn. Press, 1985); Eduard Hlawitschka, "Studien zur Genealogie und Geschichte der Merowinger und der frühen Karolinger," *Rheinische Vierteljahrsblätter* 43 (1979): 1–99; Régine Hennebique, "Structures familiales et politiques au neuvième siècle: un groupe familiale de l'aristocratie franque," *Revue historique* 538 (1981): 233–289; Constance B. Bouchard, "The Origins of the French Nobility: A Reassessment," *The American Historical Review* 86 (1981): 501–32, and "Family Structure and Family Consciousness among the Aristocracy in the Ninth to Eleventh Centuries," *Francia* 14 (1986): 639–58; Georges Duby, "Structures de parente at noblesse dans la France du Nord aux XIe et XIIe siècles," in *Hommes et structures du Moyen Age* (Paris: Mouton, 1973); and Gabrielle Spiegel, "History, Historicism, and the Social Logic of the Text in the Middle Ages," *Speculum* 65 (1990): 59–86. Citations in these works can be supplemented by bibliographies printed in such journals as *Medieval Prosopography* and *Genealogists' Magazine*.

4. See Bernard Guénée, "Les généalogies entre l'histoire et al politique: la fierté d'être Capétien, en France, au Moyen Age," *Annales* ESC 33 (1978): 450–77; Jean-Marie Moeglin, *Les ancêtres du prince: propagande politique et naissance d'une histoire nationale en Bavière au Moyen Age* (1180–1500) (Geneva: Librairie Droz, 1985) and Gabrielle M. Spiegel's review, *Speculum* 63 (1988): 195–99; and Aline G. Hornaday, "Les saints du 'Cycle de Maubeuge' et la conscience aristocratique dans le Hainaut médiéval," *Revue du Nord* 73 (1991): 583–96.

5. See Jenny M. Jochens, "The Politics of Reproduction: Medieval Norwegian Kingship," *The American Historical Review* 92 (1987): 327–49; and Jerome Kroll and Bernard S. Bachrach, "Medieval Dynastic Decisions: Evolutionary Biology and Historical Explanation," *The Journal of Interdisciplinary History* 21 (1990): 1–28.

6. Johann J. Bachofen, *Das Mutterrecht* (1st ed. 1861; rpt. in R. Manheim, trans., *Myth, Religion and Mother Right: Selected Writings*, Princeton, N.J.: Princeton Univ. Press, 1967). From recent matriarchal interpretations of prehistoric archeological material one might select the influential works of Marija A. Gimbutas, *The Goddesses and Gods of Old Europe, 6500–3500 B.C.* (London: Thames and Hudson, 1982), and *The Language of the Goddess: Unearthing the Hidden Symbols of Western Civilization* (San Francisco: Harper & Row, 1989), and Riane T. Eisler's manifesto, *The Chalice and the Blade: Our History, Our Future* (Cambridge, Mass.: Harper & Row, 1987), from a host of works on this subject. For claims of medieval survivals of matriarchy, see William O. Farnsworth, *Uncle and Nephew in the Old French chansons de geste: A Study in the Survival of Matriarchy* (1st ed. 1913; rpt. New York: Columbia Univ. Press, 1966). A short, not unsympathetic deflation of some exaggerated contentions of matriarchal control over prehistoric societies appears in Ronald Hutton, *The Pagan Religions of the Ancient British Isles* (Oxford: B. Blackwell, 1990), 37–42, 249–52, 338–39.

7. Some basic works on legal aspects of kinship and feud are H. Brunner's *Deutsche Rechtsgeschichte*, I (Leipzig: Duncker and Humblot, 1906); Bertha S. Phillpotts, *Kindred and Clan in the Middle Ages and After* (1st ed. 1913; rpt. Cambridge: Cambridge Univ. Press, 1974); Julius Goebel, Jr., *Felony and Misdemeanor* (New York: Commonwealth Fund, 1939); Hermann Conrad, *Deutsche Rechtsgeschichte*, I (Karlsruhe: C.F. Muller, 1954); K.A. Eckhardt's editions of *Lex Salica* (Hannoverae: Impensis Bibliopolii Hahnioni, 1969); and Alexander C. Murray, *Germanic Kinship Structure* (Toronto: Pontifical Institute of Medieval Studies, 1983). For anthropological views on kinship and feud, see E.E. Evans-Pritchard, *The Nuer* (Oxford, 1979); Jacob Black-Michaud, *Cohesive Force: Feud in the Mediterranean and the Middle East* (Oxford: B. Blackwell, 1975), with especially numerous citations to Gregory of Tours; Murray Gluckman, "Peace in the Feud," in *Custom and Conflict in Africa* (Oxford: Blackwell, 1986); and Keith Brown, *Bloodfeud in Scotland 1573–1625* (Edinburgh: J. Donald, 1986).

8. J.M. Wallace Hadrill, "The Bloodfeud of the Franks," *Bulletin of the John Rylands Library* 41 (1959), reprinted as chapter 6 in *The Long-Haired Kings* (London: Methuen, 1962), 121–47, 122.

9. Jesse L. Byock, *Feud in the Icelandic Saga* (Berkeley/Los Angeles: Univ. of Calif. Press, 1982), 205–6; and Byock, *Medieval Iceland* (Berkeley/Los Angeles: : Univ. of Calif. Press, 1988), 36. Byock's conclusions are supported by the anthropological studies cited above.

10. Richard A. Gerberding, *The Rise of the Carolingians and the* Liber Historiae Francorum (Oxford: Clarendon Press, 1987), especially chapter V, "The Age of Saint Audouin."

11. Katherine Fischer Drew, "The Origins of the Middle Ages," *Speculum* 62 (1987): 803–12, 805; and Emanuel J. Mickel, *Ganelon, Treason and the "Chanson de Roland"* (University Park, Pa./London: Penn. State Univ. Press, 1989), especially chapter 2, "Accusation and Defense."

12. David Abulafia, "Not Quite so Serenissma," *Times Literary Supplement*, 29 October 1993, p. 25.

13. Nerys Patterson, *Cattle-Lords and Clansmen Kinship and Rank in Early Ireland* (New York: Garland, 1991), especially chapters 9, "The Corporate *Fine*: Control of Economic Behavior," 238–70, and 11, "Kinship and the Proto-State," 316–350. In her work Patterson applies the methods of historical sociology to the society mirrored in the ancient Irish law-tracts.

14. See Murray, *op. cit., passim*, for the legal background of Germanic kinship patterns, and 177–81 for an exposition of the similarities of Germanic law codes to late Roman law.

15. See D.A. Bullough, "Early Medieval Social Grouping: The Terminology of Kinship," *Past and Present* 45 (1969): 5–18, for a typical confusion that arose when the meanings of the words *agnate* and *cognate* shifted as late Roman usage mingled with early medieval concepts. For bilateral kinship terminology in general, see Jack Goody, *The Development of the Family and Marriage in Europe* (Cambridge: Cambridge Univ. Press, 1983), 262–78 (appendix 3).

16. Murray, *op. cit.*, 175: Germanic and canonical degrees of relationship count each generation as a degree, so that siblings are related in the first degree, cousins in the second degree; the Roman system counts each step up or down to a common ancestor as a degree, so that siblings are related in the second degree, cousins in the fourth.

17. Keith R. Bradley, *Discovering the Roman Family* (Oxford/New York: Oxford Univ. Press, 1991), 141–43 (table on 141).

18. Murray, *op. cit.*, 218. Murray's shift in wording from "second or third cousins" to "sixth degree" is perhaps unfortunate; presumably he was counting degrees in the Germanic mode in which the sixth degree of relationship is equivalent to third cousins. *Reipi* payments are betrothal fines paid by a widow's prospective husband to the nearest individual heir from her dead husband's kin within the six degrees of kinship.

19. See Rosamond McKitterick, *The Carolingians and the Written Word* (Cambridge: Cambridge Univ. Press, 1989), 40–46, for the manuscript history of *Lex Salica*. Its earliest extant manuscript, which embodies the recension of c. 511, dates from c. 770.

20. See Patrick Wormald, "*Lex Scripta* and *Verbum Regis*: Legislation and Germanic Kingship, from Euric to Cnut," in P.H. Sawyer and I.N. Wood, eds., *Early Medieval Kingship* (Leeds, 1977), 105–38, 108–109, 118, 126–28.

21. Hugh G.E. White, tr., *Ausonius, Parentalia* (London/Cambridge, Mass.: W. Heinemann, 1919), Loeb Classical Library 96, I: 56–95.

22. Ibid., 59. Viewed as a kinship diagram of Ausonius's recently deceased eighteen blood relations and twelve in-laws, his elegies are so oddly disordered that they must rather have been arranged at least partly according to the chronological order of his kinsmen's deaths.

23. The latest edition of Abbo's will is in Patrick J. Geary, *Aristocracy in Provence: The Rhône Basin at the Dawn of the Carolingian Age* (Philadelphia: Univ. of Penn. Press, 1985), 38–79; for Abbo's cousin, see 64–65. Such muddles prevent Roman kinship words from being taken as guides to exact relationships in early medieval hagiography, chronicles, or legal instruments.

24. It is worth noting that Ausonius's elegy on his wife stressed her Aeduan Celtic inheritance and, chiefly, ancestors.

25. See J.F. Niermeyer, *Mediae Latinitatis Lexicon Minus* (Leiden: Brill, 1984), 763–64, *sub parentela*. The word is related to Ausonius's title *Parentalia*, the name of the Roman festival commemorating the dead.

26. Katherine Fischer Drew, trans., *The Laws of the Salian Franks* (Philadelphia: Univ. of Penn. Press, 1991), 39–45, concisely summarized legal benefits and duties of Germanic kinship as expressed in the Salic law.

27. K.A. Eckhardt, ed., *Pactus Legis Salicae, Lex Salica* 60, *Monumenta Germania Historica (MGH) Leges* I, 4, pt. 12 (Hanover, 1962–1969), and Drew, *Laws of the Salian Franks*, 40–41, 121–24.

28. Murray, *op. cit.*, 150–55.

29. Murray cites no instance of the procedure for removing oneself from a parentela having occurred in practice.

30. D. Whitelock, *The Beginnings of English Society* (Baltimore: Penguin Books, 1952), 43, cited by J.M. Wallace Hadrill, *Long-Haired Kings*, 122, pointed out that saving money by feuding produced much endemic violence in early medieval societies.

31. Mickel, *op. cit.*, 54, remarks that "relatives of the deceased [in a homicide are] only to pursue the killer himself . . . there is here the notion that a killer has been so judged by society and that the business of apprehending him becomes the affair of the people and, above all, the family concerned. The concept of the outlaw presumes that anyone may slay the man who has been placed outside the protection of the law. Naturally, the offended family could be counted upon to hunt him down." Citing R. de Salis, ed., *Leges Burgundionum, MGH* LS I, vol. 2, pt. 1 (Hanover, 1892), 43.

32. Note that J.M. Wallace Hadrill, *op. cit., passim*, discusses blood feuds only. Therefore, in discussing Frankish feuds, he reports fewer instances than those that actually occur in contemporary historical writing.

33. Merovingians feuded with each other as well as with Burgundian, Visigothic, and Gothic royalty; the dukes of Thuringia; and the great Lombard clan of Agilofings. See Gregory of Tours, *History,* III, chaps. 4, 6–8, 9–10, 16, 20, 28, and 31. The great feud between Queen Fredegund and the Visigothic Queen Brunhild that embroiled three generations of Merovingians and their followers appears so often in Gregory's pages that citing each of his references to it is not practicable.

34. Gregory of Tours, *History*, 9:33; chap. 10; chap. 12. See Murray, *op. cit.*, 197–200, on legal considerations involved in the property dispute that triggered this squabble. Since the quarrel did not appear to involve a blood feud, J.M. Wallace Hadrill did not discuss it.

35. *History*, 7:47, 9:19, reporting how the feud broke out again and the king and queen took sides until Gregory succeeded in finally settling it.

36. Fredegar, *Chronicorum libri IV cum continuationibus*, ed. B. Krusch, *MGH Script. rer. mer.* 2, 4:90.

37. Gregory of Tours, *Vitae Patrum*, 8:7 (printed in *MGH* SRM I, pt. 2, 247, "Life of Nicetus, Bishop of Lyons").

38. *History*, 5:18.

39. Drew, *Origins*, and Mickel, *op. cit.*, 53–56, summarize the increasingly numerous laws against feuding. Note also a capitulary from Pippin, king of Italy edited by Alfred Boretius in *Capitularia Regum Francorum, MGH* I, 208: "4. De illis hominibus vel sacerdotibus aut quibuslibet per regnum nostrum, qui propter premia aut parentellam de nostra iustitia inquirentibus aut emendantibus vicia veritatem obfuscare volunt missis vel fidelibus nostris ut se in periuria mittant."

40. Regino of Prum, *Reginonis chronicon, MGH* SS I, 537–612; Jean Devisse, *Hincmar Archevêque de Reims 845–882* (Geneva: Droz, 1975), 380–459; and Jan Dhondt, *Le haut Moyen Age (VIIIe-XIe siècles)* (Paris: Bordas, 1967).

41. For Empress Judith, see Elizabeth Ward, "Caesar's Wife: The Empress Judith," in Peter Godman and Roger Collins, eds., *Charlemagne's Heir: New Perspectives on the Reign of Louis the Pious (814–840)* (Oxford: Clarendon Press, 1990), 205–27; for the rise of the Pippinids to the united Frankish monarchy, see Gerberding, *op. cit.*; for the Bosonids' maneuvers to achieve the thrones of Burgundy and Provence, see René Poupardin, *Le Royaume de Provence sous les carolingiens* (Paris: E. Bouillon, 1901), and Constance B. Bouchard, "Family Structure and Family Consciousness," 646–47.

42. For royal fostering see John J. Contreni, trans., Pierre Riché, *Education and Culture in the Barbarian West* (Columbia, S.C.: Univ. of South Carolina Press, 1976), 236–46; for Queen Balthild's organization in the 680s of the care of her hus-

band Clovis II's young aristocratic entourage, see Janet Nelson, *Politics and Ritual in Early Medieval Europe* (London: Hambledon Press, 1986), 203, with footnote references for Charlemagne's palace school.

43. See Pierre Riché, ed., *Manuel de mon fils/Dhuoda* (Paris: Editions du Cerf, 1975).

44. Mickel, *op. cit.*, 128–29, 155, concludes that Ganelon's execution had no parallel in real life but that the poet was "passing his own judgment." F.R.P. Akehurst concurs in his review of Mickel's book, *Speculum* 67 (1992): 726–28. Mickel believes that the factual inaccuracy of the Ganelon story supports a late date for the poem's composition, 137.

45. See, for example, Alfred Boretius and Victor Krause, eds., *Capitularia Regum Francorum, MGH*, II, pt. 1, 232, cap. 2, forbidding marriage between persons related in both fourth and fifth degrees, and ibid., 336, cap. 9, forbidding *propincuas* to marry because a wife's parentela shall be to her husband as his own. Similarly, ibid., 183, cap. 30, explains that marriage within the fourth degree is forbidden because husband and wife are one flesh, so that the parentela of each is common to both. Of course, these examples are but a tiny fraction of relevant texts.

46. Phillpotts, *op. cit.*, 193, quoting Beaumanoir: "one could take revenge by right of feud as far as the seventh degree of kinship and this was not strange in the days of yore, for marriages could not be made within the seventh degree. But as the degree for marriage has been made closer, beyond the fourth degree, so also one ought not to attack in feud anyone who is further removed from the kindred than the fourth degree." (*Coûtumes de Beauvais*, art. 1678, chap. lix, from the year 1283.)

47. See Constance B. Bouchard, "Consanguinity and Noble Marriages in the Tenth and Eleventh Centuries, *Speculum* 56 (1981): 268–87, 269–71; and Richard Southern, trans., Jean-Louis Flandrin, *Families in Former Times: Kinship, Household and Sexuality* (Cambridge: Cambridge Univ. Press, 1979) 19–26.

48. There are newer lives of Eleanor, but Amy Kelly, *Eleanor of Aquitaine and the Four Kings* (Cambridge, Mass.: Harvard Univ. Press, 1950), remains a rare combination of scholarly accuracy and delightful writing. She recounts the vicissitudes of Petronilla's marriage problems on 22–23, 27.

Family Life in the High and Late Middle Ages

The Testimony of German Literary Sources[1]

Albrecht Classen

Héloise, in the first of her famous letters to her teacher and, later, husband Abélard—writes in the early 1130s: "If Augustus, Emperor of the whole world, thought fit to honour me with marriage and conferred all the earth on me to possess for ever, it would be dearer and more honourable to me to be called not his Empress but your whore."[2] This is a strong rejection of marriage in theological and also emotional terms, formulated by a leading representative of the medieval Church and in conformity with its religious ideology. At the same time, however, Héloise outlines principles of how one should decide on the proper marriage partner, and thus reveals her ambivalent attitude toward human love and happiness. If we can take her statement in any way as representative for her time, then it becomes evident how negative was the perception of marriage and family life that the Church in the High Middle Ages harbored for this institution. If we consider, however, literary documents produced by secular poets, we gain a much more complex understanding of how marriage was viewed.[3]

We can undoubtedly assume that the values attached to "family" changed over time, and that they differed depending on which historical testimony we consult. In this article I will examine the evidence as displayed in the history of medieval German literature, which does not discuss very often where this form of social cohabitation ranked and what role it assumed. Therefore we will be forced on many occasions to search in the margins and subtexts for statements about marriage and family life. I will argue that both these social functions were considered to be a given, mundane factor and, hence, did not require special attention on the part of the poets and artists. Nevertheless, many of their works contain significant information about marriage and the family because happily married couples and their children serve as the backdrop for the major events. Even if a romance or a lyric poem does not specifically deal with married life, many medieval German writers provide us with explicit information about how the family was viewed during that time. I believe that despite the scarcity of sources, a closer look at literary texts will reveal that the modern type of marital love and personal bonds between husband and wife emerged considerably earlier than has been heretofore claimed in historical and sociological studies.[4] Such an investigation will open an additional avenue for studies of the mental history, the *Alltagsgeschichte* (history of daily life), and the social history of suppressed groups in the past.[5]

Before we begin with our literary-historical exploration, a definition of the term *family* as understood in our study is in order. Normally, medieval documents reveal that the term *familia* was used to refer to, apart from the family nucleus, the wider circle of servants, maids, relatives, dependents, and many other people within the power range of the lord.[6] It was a house-based concept. In this sense, we deal with a public-social relationship among people and not with "family" in the modern sense of the word, a private unit of two to four or six people, which implies strong emotional, sexual, and intellectual bonds between husband, wife, children, and immediate relatives.[7] Only with the emergence of the class of burghers in the late medieval cities do we observe a reduction and specification of what the term *family* meant, since it began to assume more concretely the meaning that the modern use of the term carries.[8]

In other words, the formation of the family was obviously subject to considerable changes throughout the centuries, beginning with various types of polygamy among the German tribes, to early models of partnership of husband and wife with the coming of Christianity, to coexistence within marriage with the purpose of having progeny and preserving and building territorial power through marriage in the High Middle Ages, and finally to the evolution of the modern form of bourgeois family life since the eighteenth century.[9] My interest, however, is not with the legal, practical, and social realities of marriage and family life in the Middle Ages.[10] Instead I will focus on how German poets from the High and Late Middle Ages (ca. 1170–1500) dealt with conjugal love and emotional partnership between husband and wife.

Undoubtedly, the family as a political institution has been profoundly meaningful for man and woman since the High Middle Ages (ca. 1170–1220).[11] Yet the classical Arthurian romances do not provide much insight into medieval family life except for rather perfunctory remarks regarding the legal bonds between husband and wife or regarding strife and conflicts rupturing the harmonious relationship.[12] The actual interest rests in chivalric quests, battles, individual challenges, and in such aspects as "the individual versus society," "the individual versus the other," or "the individual versus God." The primary orientation of romance authors is toward developing an image of what is happening at court and outside, how society is functioning in political terms, and how a single knight rises out of the crowd to become the paragon of the chivalrous world, both as its defender and as its new leader.[13] Certainly, families do play a relevant role as far as political power relations are concerned, but this, again, would only be of relevance to the public appearance of the court and its members.[14] The emotional dimension, at least, does not receive adequate attention in the historical and literary sources.[15]

Wolfram von Eschenbach's *Parzival* (ca. 1205), in part built upon Chrétien de Troyes' *Perceval,* illustrates the dichotomy between the private and the public perhaps in the most dramatic fashion.[16] Parzival's father is married twice: once to the black queen Belacane, a Moslem, and once to the white queen Herzeloyde, a Christian. Neither woman is able to restrain the knight and keep him at home. Gahmuret, averse to being shackled to social and emotional obligations, first abandons Belacane and marries Herzeloyde, then leaves her behind as well and returns to the battlefield somewhere in the Orient, where he will eventually meet his death. In both cases, a child is the product of his temporary marital status. Parzival, like his brother Feirefiz, grows up without a father, and later faces grave difficulties in finding his way back into society after his mother has removed him from the court, which she considers to be a dangerous and evil place after Gahmuret's death; it was, at least, not the place to raise her child.[17] Later, once Parzival has encountered some Arthurian knights, he follows their path and returns to the world of his father. He marries only once and has, unbeknownst to him, two children, Loherangrîn and Kardeiz. But the first encounter between himself and his enlarged family does not occur until he has spent many years on his personal quests and adventures, such as rescuing the Grail and helping his uncle Anfortas, the previous Grail king, to receive redemption from his sin.

Parzival's reunion with his family takes place very late, five years after his marriage (799:3), and although it is described in deeply emotional terms (801), the poet scolds his protagonist for not having thought of his children and his wife earlier (742:27ff.). Characteristic of the lonely knight (*chevalier errant*), Parzival does not develop strong bonds with the two children, except for a fleeting show of love for his offspring. Wolfram introduces a number of other married couples (such as Orilus and Jeschute, and Gawan and Orgeluse) who are more or less representative of his ideals, but they operate only on a functional level. They never display any particular interest in family life in the modern sense of the word. Childbirth, for instance, is mentioned occasionally, but the majority of couples either seem to be infertile or are too young to settle down and have children.[18] Nevertheless, Wolfram presents in *Parzival* a world of chivalry in which conjugal relationships are an important (though not dominant) factor because the heroes' happiness depends not only on their knightly virtues but also on their personal relationships with their wives.[19] In Wolfram's *Titurel* fragments (ca. 1220), in which the author pursues some loose narrative ends of his Grail romance, the death of the protagonist's mother shatters the husband's confidence in the world, and both he and his brother retire from chivalry to lead the lives of hermits.[20]

Interestingly, Wolfram as narrator draws a poignant demarcation line between himself in biographical terms and his literary text: in a number of self-allusions, he opens a window on his personal life, indicating that he is married and has children. But real value judgments cannot be elicited from these scant remarks, since they could well be understood as parodistic or, at least, ironic comments that are not necessarily supported by realistic conditions and attitudes.[21]

In contrast to this Grail romance, with its strong religious orientation and little interest in secular and personal aspects, in some of his other works Wolfram presents strong married couples who love each other and share their emotional, political, and intellectual love in a profound manner.[22] For instance, Willehalm and Gyburg, in the crusade epic *Willehalm* (ca. 1211–1217), prove to be an ideal couple who fight and struggle together to survive an extremely dangerous situation. Both prove their loyalty and love for each other and demonstrate to the world that true happiness is possible only within a marriage of equal partners.

Hartmann von Aue does not offer many more insights into family life than does Wolfram.[23] In *Erec* (ca. 1182), he has husband and wife spend a wild period of sexual pleasures immediately after their marriage, but then the protagonist is called upon to defend his honor and embarks on a lengthy quest, accompanied by his wife, whom he has forced to come along to redeem her allegedly wrongful behavior. Joy does not return to the court and the Arthurian world until Erec and Enîte have achieved their goals and discovered their path back toward the realization of an ideal life-style within the world of chivalry through observance of obligations, honor, and morality.[24] Again, family life as such does not assume a significant role in this work, although the decisive turn of events in favor of Erec takes place at the moment when husband and wife learn that they need each other and depend on a communicative link as a basis for their political and personal role in life.[25]

Iwein—in Hartmann's second Arthurian eponymous romance (ca. 1185), translated and adapted from Chrétien de Troyes[26]—is even less focused on marital interactions, since the text concentrates exclusively on Iwein's efforts to win Laudine's trust, first after he has killed her husband and then, after a year's "vacation" from marriage, when he is banned from her lands for having forgotten his wife and his oath given to her after their wedding. Laudine has suffered deeply from her first husband's sudden death, but her grief seems to be more the result of political and military considerations that render her vulnerable as a widow ruler, rather than a reflection of deep, profound personal loss.[27] Nevertheless, the author explicitly emphasizes the high value attached to marriage, since Iwein's failure results both from his neglect of his wife in personal terms and the neglect of his duties in ethical and even political-military terms. Society reintegrates the hero only after he has proven to be a dedicated husband and a responsible member of chivalric society.

In Hartmann's famous novella "Der arme Heinrich" ("The Unfortunate Lord Henry," ca. 1200), the text concludes with the marital union between the peasant girl and Duke Heinrich (Poor Henry). In other words, marriage and family life do not really concern the author; he focuses on the path toward marriage and then breaks off. However, if we pay attention to marginal figures, such as the girl's father and mother, we notice that the family as a social institution could carry considerable value. The relationship between this peasant couple is not disturbed by strife and miscommunication. Instead, both work hard to maintain the family farm and to achieve a good standard of living. They have a number of children who appear to bring joy into their lives, among them the young girl who later offers herself as a sacrifice to heal Henry but is rejected at the last moment by the duke himself. The other children do not treat Henry badly, but they politely avoid him, whereas their sister tends to his needs and provides him with company.[28]

In the heroic epics such as the *Nibelungenlied* (ca. 1200) and *Kudrun* (ca. 1250–1270), marriage and family life are mentioned briefly, but they matter in significant ways. Kriemhild marries twice, and she bears a child to each husband. She lives with her first husband Siegfried in his home kingdom in the Netherlands (Xanten). When they return to Worms for a visit, her brothers allow the murder of Siegfried. Kriemhild now decides to stay with her family, although she suspects them of murder, and does not object to her father-in-law's decision to take her child back to Xanten.[29] During her second marriage to Etzel, the king of the Huns, she bears another child, but we are not really given any information about her emotional bonds to it. In a way, she "sacrifices" it to her bloody revenge against her first husband's murderers, for she uses the child's death to incite the Hunnish warriors to rise against her hostile Burgundian "guests."

One interesting point must be mentioned, however. Kriemhild, in contrast to most other Arthurian women married to knights, is allowed to spend a number of years with her husbands before tragedy strikes them. And Kriemhild and Siegfried are able to see their child grow up and bring joy to them, although the narrator neglects to pay any attention to this fact and mentions only that Kriemhild and Siegfried lived together in his own kingdom in the Netherlands (Xanten). Whatever the contemporary audience's interest in more personal aspects might have been, the historical outcome each time is a brutal act that wipes out any family bonds, erotic affection, and love for children. The genre of the heroic poem does not lend itself to the representation of the emotional aspects of people's lives.[30]

In the eponymous heroic epic *Kudrun*, the title character, along with her mother and grandmother, are depicted as married women who have children and spend time with their intact family. However, the combination of courtly with heroic elements in this narrative undercuts any tendencies toward idyllic description.[31] Kudrun is kidnapped before her marriage to Herwic and has to wait ten years for her fiancé and her brother to rescue her. Typically for a heroic epic, *Kudrun* concludes with a great battle and slaughter of enemies and portrays a triumph over the evil forces. There is one variation, however, from other heroic songs. In a remarkable turn of events, *Kudrun* ends with multiple marriages and the establishment of world peace through these new family bonds, woven by Kudrun herself. Nevertheless, the topic of "family" still does not receive adequate attention, and it is of no real concern to the narrator of this heroic poem, since he (she?) seems to take it for granted as the foundation of society.[32] The focus rests on the "bridal quest" motif, in which the poet glosses over the actual living conditions of husband and wife. But in a few fleeting moments, at least, the author captures intriguing interactions within one couple (Kudrun's grandparents), who seem to have achieved a well-established, functioning, communicative relationship.[33]

In courtly love poetry we would hardly expect to find any discussion of family life because this poetry deals mainly with extramarital or premarital relationships and focuses on men and women's purely erotic attraction for each other. For example, the genre of the *tagelied*, the "dawn song," indicates that the women, who lament their lovers' departure, are married and afraid of being discovered by their husbands. No mention is made of children and the actual conditions of conjugal living.

In the novella "Morîz von Craûn," written either around 1170 or around 1220, we gain a glimpse into the living quarters of a husband and wife who sleep in the same bed and are rudely awakened by the ghostly entry of Morîz von Craûn, who wants to obtain his award for his indefatigable efforts on behalf of his beloved lady. It is a novelistic tale closely related to the ideas and values of the *minnesang*, yet it stresses, more than the lyric texts, the lady's real-life situation, although children do not figure at all.[34]

Our quick overview of what possible literary sources can be used for such a social-historical study indicates that they reveal fairly little evidence. Yet there are hints and allusions, and they increase in pitch over the centuries. Marginal figures and subliminal themes reflect the basic conditions of the family, without which life at court would not be possible. In other words, the *argumentum e silentio* promises a number of valuable conclusions particularly regarding the earlier texts. We cannot say with absolute certainty that early and high medieval poets did not place any value on family life, but we know for sure that they did not consider it interesting enough for their audiences for them to spend much time on this topic. If they referred to family, they used the term sometimes in a tongue-in-cheek manner and sometimes as a backdrop to events. But in most cases—apart from the social, political, and legal importance attributed to marriage (probably a natural consequence for most human societies)—marriage and family do not carry emotional value. In most cases, the official function of marriage is to produce offspring, and the political theme of the queen supporting her husband is placed in the foreground. Family as an ideal in itself largely falls by the wayside.[35]

A much more complex model arises in Gottfried von Strassburg's *Tristan*, since the author has a whole sequence of married couples parade before our eyes, but no real family life as such can be observed from the examples.[36] Riwalîn and Blanscheflûr have hardly enough time to create offspring before their deaths. King Marke has decided not to marry at all and might (if we can trust one scholar) be considered to be homosexual; he later turns out to be bisexual.[37] King Gurmûn and his wife Isolde have one child, and at least here, in the far-removed western kingdom, we seem to be able to detect a functioning family, although formalities and political intrigues involving the daughter Isolde are of much higher relevance to the poet than the personal bonds among the family members.

However, Gottfried also presents a very positive image in Rual li Foitenant and his wife Floraete, who work and live together in complete harmony and love. They have a number of children, who later become Tristan's step-brothers, and they share their love for each other. Both Rual and Floraete are described as ideal characters, admirable parents, and highly reputable political representatives. As in Hartmann von Aue's "Der arme Heinrich," marginal figures reveal that already in the High Middle Ages, family and conjugal love could indeed be viewed as positive values.[38] This observation might contradict the general view taken by historians that most marriages far into the early modern age were concluded simply for economic and political reasons. Consequently, according to their view, conjugal love did not play any major role, although marriage, as such, had been acknowledged as one of the seven sacraments of the Church since the Council of Lyon in 1274.[39]

Admittedly, however, neither Rual and Floraete nor the parents of the peasant girl in Hartmann's novella openly display their love for each other. Instead, they are idealized as loyal subjects and servants and as friends and allies of their lords, to whom they dedicate all their efforts and resources. From this perspective, the family does not loom large on the poetic horizon, although both Hartmann and Gottfried have vested their marginal figures with strong ideals and values, which they share with their marriage partners.

Didactic poets such as Hugo von Trimberg summarized the standard view of marriage and family life and thus helped to ossify the traditional construction of courtly society. Hugo, in his lengthy moralistic and instructional poem *Renner* from around 1300, crystallizes the misogynist perception of women, casts them in a stereotypical role as wives, and thus programs a dialectic relationship between husband and wife. Couples are supposed to be loyal to each other, but love as a basic bond between them does not seem to play any significant role in Hugo's thinking.[40]

Similar features of married life arise in Wernher the Gartenaere's *Helmbrecht*, a moralistic novella from ca. 1225, in which husband and wife collaborate to spoil their son and thus pave his way toward his downfall. Their failure to instill social values in their children results in the collapse of the family *and* society! The father is entirely discredited by the poet for his laxity in enforcing parental authority; the mother is ridiculed by her children for her alleged adultery with a nobleman, which supposedly explains young Helmbrecht's pretended aristocratic character. His sister Gotelint, when she follows her brother into a life of crime and violence, proves to be a total fool because she has decried old Helmbrecht and has thus undermined basic family values. Parental love and family values are nonexistent, the social entity of the family seems to be destroyed, and as a consequence, the world represented by the protagonist and his parents appears to be on the brink of disaster.[41]

The relationship between the parents, as depicted in the *Helmbrecht* novella and in other documents from thirteenth-century German literature, is one of unemotional coexistence. Husband and wife appear to be in charge of separate areas on the farm, and they operate relatively independently of each other. Marriage as an erotic ideal does not figure in Wernher's universe either.[42] Both Hugo von Trimberg and Wernher the Gartenaere develop only didactic concepts and stay clear from emotional, personal aspects in their works. However, the Stricker, a popular novella author who flourished in the middle of the thirteenth century, provides many examples of conflicts in marriages. Through satirical criticism and irony, he suggests options for reaching harmonious forms of coexistence in married life.[43] But even he pursues mainly didactic purposes and does not idealize marriage and family as such. We observe, at least, a new interest in sexual deviation, adultery, divorce, and conflicts between husband and wife, all of which indicates the loosening of the patriarchal rule over the woman, who learns to maintain her personal status.

Undoubtedly, the various writers (among them the Stricker and Wernher the Gartenaere) are not really concerned with marriage as an institution but focus, instead, on the competition between the sexes in intellectual, financial, and social terms.[44] To observe any noteworthy transformations, we must move into the fourteenth and fifteenth centuries.[45]

THE LITERARY DOCUMENTATION OF FAMILY LIFE IN THE LATE MIDDLE AGES

Oswald von Wolkenstein (1376/77–1445) is well known to us through an astoundingly large number of historical documents.[46] His lyric poetry reveals more about the writer himself than does any other German poetry before that time. His "œuvre," which consists of 133 poems, covers a wide range of topics, among them courtly love, crusade, religious contrition, repentance, travel, military events, lovemaking in the tradition of the *pastourella*, marriage, and violent conflicts between the singer and members of other social classes.[47]

The most interesting aspect of Oswald proves to be his dedication to his wife, Margareta von Schwangau, about whom he sings in various songs. In "Ain tunckle farb" (Kl. 33), he laments his loneliness and the fact that his Gret is not with him. Many times, while lying in bed, he turns back and forth trying to sleep. But again and again, the memory of his beloved disturbs and tortures him, and he is not able to find rest:

> wie offt ich nach im greiffe,
> So ist neur, ach, mit ungemach feur in dem tach,
> Als ob mich brenn der reiffe.
>
> . . . .
>
> Also vertreib ich, liebe Gret,
> die nacht bis an den morgen.[48] (Kl. 33, ll. 18–26)

[Never mind how often I feel for my beloved (all to no avail—
Ach), there is only fire in the roof, as if the dew is burning me. . . .
Thus do I spend, dear Gret, the night until the morning.]

The mood changes, however, when we turn to another poem. In "Durch
Barbarei, Arabia" (Kl. 44), the poet reflects nostalgically on his glorious past
as an imperial diplomat in the service of Emperor Sigismund and describes
in a disgruntled manner the misery of his present life. Instead of travelling
around the world and experiencing the glorious excitement of international
politics, he is trapped in his mountainous castle in the South Tyrolean Alps.
Frustrated by his boring existence, he begins to beat his children: "vor angst
slach ich mein kinder/offt hin hinder" (Kl. 44, l. 50f.). He is immediately
interrupted by his wife, who comes rushing out of the house to protect them.
She, in turn, attacks her husband for his mistreatment of the children: "So
kompt ir mütter zü gebraust, / zwar die beginnt zu schelten; gäb si mir aines
mit der fawsst, / des müsst ich ser engelten" (ll. 52–55). [Their mother runs
to them, she begins to scold, and if she hits me with her fist, I would have
to pay for my beating [of the children] dearly.]

Obviously, the old tradition of misogyny plays a major role in this
stereotypical description, but at least it shows the poet in his daily existence;
he is interacting, though not in a pleasant way, with his family.[49] He has
children and blames himself for not having been a good father. Certainly
disgruntled about his personal life but willing enough to discuss it ironically
in his songs, Oswald is one of the first late medieval German poets to shed
some light on the intimate relationships between married couples. Previously,
this Tyrolean aristocrat had openly discussed the social pressure to get married and had revealed his feelings about being forced into family life:

> Ich han gelebt wol vierzig jar leicht minner zwai
> mit toben, wüten, tichten, singen mangerlai;
> es wēr wol zeit, das ich meins aigen kindes geschrai
> elichen hort in ainer wiegen gellen. (Kl. 18, ll. 97–100)

[I have lived for forty years less two, with raging, fighting, composing, singing so many songs; it would be high time that I hear the screaming of my own children (from a marriage) in the manger.]

The irony is obvious, and yet the poet betrays his uneasy feelings about entering married life with its obligations and duties. He uses the negative image in order to contrast his present life with adventures in his youth and thus follows the old topos of *laudatio tempus acti*. Nevertheless these lines are, as far as I know, the first reference to concrete family life and screaming babies torturing the poet-father in German literature. The burden on Oswald of his role as estate manager, warlord, and father taints his perception of his wife. When we accept the irony in his songs, however, as a deliberate strategy, then the poetic statement about his private life assumes a different perspective: the singer acknowledges both that he is married and living with his wife on their estate, and that he has children whom he does not treat well.

On the other hand, Oswald composed a number of beautiful songs, such as "Simm Gredlin, Gret" (Kl. 77), and "Ich hör, sich manger freuen lat" (Kl. 110), glorifying his wife Margarete and depicting the joys of his married life with her. Oswald changes his attitude toward marriage and family depending on his personal situation at the time of the writing.[50] Apparently, his wife and children are scapegoats at times for his personal misery, such as in "Von trauren möcht ich werden taub" (Kl. 104). At other times, when Oswald elaborates on his love experiences both during the wedding night (Kl. 70) and later as husband (Kl. 75, Kl. 83), Margarete emerges as the deeply beloved wife.[51] In "Wol auff, wol an" (Kl. 75) especially, we hear of the couple taking a bath together and enjoying the physical pleasures of conjugal love.[52]

Finally, in such poems as "Sich manger freut" (Kl. 102), Oswald does not shy away from confessing adultery, which proves to have disastrous results for his whole life in political, economic, and personal terms.[53] Although it is impossible for us today to disentangle the web of fiction and facts in Oswald's œuvre, since he is playing with both fiction and fact in a highly sophisticated manner,[54] the play itself offers significant insight into the poet's awareness about the new relevance of the family for personal well-being and success in the increasingly complex world of the Late Middle Ages. Whereas the traditional *Minnesang* was basically only concerned with adultery, Oswald has moved away from his literary theme and reflects instead on the multiple aspects of married life, love affairs, and conjugal love.

Undoubtedly, early traces of more realistic and diversified views can be found in Wolfram von Eschenbach's and Walther von der Vogelweide's poetry, but only with Oswald von Wolkenstein do we actually encounter serious reflections on marriage and its relevance to erotic love.[55] The same applies, although to a lesser degree, to the lyric œuvre of the Styrian poet Hugo von Montfort (1357–1423). I refer to a song that stands out among his texts for its unusual setting. In "Ich gieng ains morgens frü am tag" (No. 25), the narrator walks into a charnel house one morning and overhears several conversations between skeletons who reflect on their previous lives.[56] Whereas some confess committing adultery and leading lewd lives, others, who soon gain preponderance, stress their virtues and marital loyalty. The last voice is from a man who emphasizes:

> wolauff und wach und gang zü mir
> recht tün und fröd die sag ich dir
> ich was ain herr gar stoltz von leib
> und hett ich gesehen tausent weib
> ich hett mein ee nicht gebrochen (25, ll. 149–53)

> [Get up, wake up, and come to me; I will teach you how to act honorably and to have happiness. I was a man with an attractive body, and even if I had seen a thousand women, I would not have broken up my marriage.]

A number of other examples can be found in which Hugo idealizes marriage and condemns adultery and other forms of extramarital love.[57] Although of aristocratic background, he strongly defends a value system often associated with the world of the bourgeoisie.

Oswald, however, expresses his appreciation of marriage in much more explicit and sensual terms than Hugo. In this regard, this Tyrolean singer has correctly been associated with the Bohemian-German writer Johannes von Tepl, who created the famous dialogue poem *Der Ackermann aus Böhmen* (ca. 1401).[58] The latter is one of the first major prose texts in the history of German literature in which Everyman—namely, the Ploughman—and Death argue about the value of life. The debate begins with Ackermann's bitter complaints about Death's unfair, cruel and mean-spirited actions against man. The Ploughman's own wife has been taken, and he is deeply saddened by her death. In clear contrast to all previous misogynist treatises, the Ploughman declares: "Ja, herre, ich was ir friedel, sie mein amei" (V:104). [Yes, my lord, I was her lover, and she was my mistress.] Moreover, he praises her as his sun, his guiding star, his Venus, and as the eternal source of his joy and his banner of happiness. Because Death does not seem to understand this, the Ploughman continues with his praise of his deceased wife:

> wan sie was edel der geburte, reich der eren, schöne,
> frut über alle ire gespilen, gewachsener persone,
> warhaftig und züchtig der worte, keusche des leibes,
> guter und frölicher mitwonung. (VII:106)

[She was of noble birth, rich with honor, a more beautiful fruit than all other her friends, honest and chaste in her words, chaste with her body, a good and happy companion.]

The dead woman is characterized as the loyal hen that took care of her chicks and as a God-given gift for her husband. As a consequence, the mourner elevates her above all other creatures and advocates the virtues of marriage in the highest terms possible:

> wen Got mit einem reinen, züchtigen und schönen
> weibe begabet, der ist volkomenlich begabet, und
> die gabe heißet gabe und ist ein gabe vor aller
> irdischer auswendiger gabe. (VIII:108)

[He whom God gives a pure, chaste, and beautiful wife has received a perfect gift. And this gift is called a gift, and is the highest gift that can be bestowed.]

Although it is apparent from a letter the poet wrote to his friend Petrus Rother and dated 1401 that Johannes von Tepl's dialogue poem resulted from an interest in rhetoric, it would be erroneous to proceed from here to declare the whole work to be merely an exercise *in hoc idiomate indocili*.[59] Whatever purpose prompted the writer to compose this powerful text, he certainly documented a shift in man's appreciation of women, especially of married life. André Schnyder applies the term "Trauerarbeit," derived from Sigmund Freud's psychoanalytic studies, to the interpretation of *Der Ackermann*, and thus indicates a possible avenue for an appropriate understanding of this text on a deeper level. The narrative voice evokes the pain that he experienced because of his wife's death, and in order to compensate for this pain, he projects an ideal image of his deceased wife, which offers him, simultaneously, the realization that she is actually gone.[60] Memory replaces the actual person, and her posthumous adulation elevates her to the level of a supreme ideal:

Bei Got, unvolsagenlich herzeleid ist mir geschehen,
do mein züchtige, treue und stete hausere mir so
snelle ist enzücket, sie tot, ich witwer, meine kinder
weisen worden sint. (XXI:122)

[My God, ineffable heartfelt pain has struck me when my chaste, loyal, and constant honor of my house has been snatched away so quickly. She is dead, I have become a widower, and my children are orphans.]

Although the catalogue of marital values and ideals is repeated, the insistence on the unique character and quality of his wife gains such weight that, at the end, the concepts of marriage and woman begin to assume a new dimension—one that definitely removes this poem from the Middle Ages and makes it, if we may say so, the first German Renaissance text.[61] The Ploughman successfully defends his viewpoint about human existence, the human body, and in close conjunction, the value of marriage; he thus idealizes the notion of family life as it has come to typify the modern age: "Ich bin vormals in der lieben lustigen e gewesen; warzu sol ich mich nu wenden?" (XXVII:130). [I used to live in the dear, happy marriage; where should I go from here?] Interestingly, the Ploughman supports his attack against Death (which represents the medieval way of thinking) by referring back to the late antique philosopher Boethius, according to whom "wan weibes und kinder habe ist nicht das minstre teil der irdischen selden" (XXIX:132) [to be married and to have children is not the least form of earthen happiness]. He also emphasizes several times in his speech that women have the positive power of introducing and maintaining peace, harmony, and happiness; that they instill in men virtue and love for honor; and that they are of supreme importance for the continuation of joyful human existence. With this text, we have firm documentation that, with the beginning of the fifteenth century, the attitude toward women and the family experienced a dramatic transformation.[62] Johannes von Tepl is certainly one of the strongest defenders of marital bliss, but he did not remain the only one.

Heinrich Wittenwiler incorporated a highly dialectic debate on marriage (with all its advantages and disadvantages) in his famous didactic poem *Der Ring* (ca. 1400).[63] A multitude of opinions clash with one another, and although the question is finally decided by only one counselor in favor of marriage, encouraging the male protagonist to proceed with his plans to establish a family, the whole issue remains open for debate. Wittenwiler is never quite interested in straightforward statements and has allowed his poem to be permeated by a plethora of contradictory statements. He is a satirist and ridicules the dominant values of his time. Nevertheless, the fact that marriage and its values are discussed publicly indicates a renewed interest in this social institution and supports our thesis about the particularly positive evaluation of marriage in fifteenth-century literature.[64]

Oswald von Wolkenstein seems to vacillate in his qualification of marriage and family, yet demonstrates an obvious interest in his personal life with Margarete von Schwangau. Finally, prose novels (chapbooks) such as Thüring von Ringoltingen's *Melusine* (1456) offer significant evidence that the changes brought about or at least reflected by Johannes von Tepl, Heinrich Wittenwiler, and Hugo von Montfort, among others, began to have their effect.

Based on an international *Stoff* that had found a wide and international dissemination in the Middle Ages (such as in Walter Map's *De nugis curialium*, Gervasius of Tilbury's *Otia imperialia*, and possibly Marie de France's *lais* "Lanval"),[65] and using the fourteenth-century French version by Jean d'Arras as his immediate source, the Swiss writer Thüring von Ringoltingen's *Melusine* is one of the most intriguing and popular German prose novels representative of the late-medieval *Volksbuch*.[66] In contrast to any other medieval romance or courtly love poem, the protagonist—a magical woman, part human being, part snake—approaches the male hero, Reymund, and offers to marry him in order to help him escape imminent danger. He has killed his lord by accident and does not know how to help himself. She points out the steps he must take to divert any suspicion and advises how to arrange their marriage.[67] Once the marriage has been concluded, the couple goes to bed, and that same night, Melusine becomes pregnant (43). After the wedding festivities, the wife embarks on an ambitious building program which includes a castle, churches, and a monastery. Subsequent chapters explain how many children she bore and what physical characteristics they had—everything seen from the woman's perspective.

Next, the narrator turns his attention to the chivalric adventures that her sons later experience and describes how they acquire kingdoms. Many chapters deal with world historical events; others discuss the achievements of Melusine's offspring and elaborate upon events in the family history. In other words, instead of showing the expected agnate power distribution and family tree, Thüring's *Melusine* reflects archaic cognatic family structures in which the woman was the dominant force.[68]

The real tragedy, and the highlight of this Volksbuch, evolves when Reymund begins to feel uncertain about his wife's nature and her mysterious disappearances on Saturdays. His brother encourages him to investigate the secret, hinting that Melusine might be committing adultery: "Vnd rat eüch das ir gedenckent züwissen was ir gewerb sey </> das ir nit zü einem toren gemacht werdent / vnd ir von ir nit geeffet werdent" (96). [And I advise you to try to find out what she is doing so that you are not made to be a cuckold or a fool.] With this text, we have moved into the world of the late medieval bourgeoisie, who harbored great fear of adultery as a factor threatening the social and economic status of the cheated wife or husband.[69] To Reymund's great dismay, he discovers that his wife is, in fact, not a human being but half-snake and half-woman. However, after a moment filled with anxiety and distress, he resolves to ignore this fact and to live with his wife as happily as before. At the same time, he severely rebukes his brother for slandering his wife: "nvd sagent mir von meinem gemahel nit arges. dann sy ist frumm vnd aller schand vnschuldig" (99) [and never say anything negative about my wife, because she is virtuous and free from any vice].

Since Reymund has broken his promise never to investigate his wife's activities on Saturdays, he is now deeply worried that she might end their marriage and disappear from his life. He decides that if this happens, he will withdraw from the world and become a hermit (100), an interesting indication of the importance placed on marriage as a social institution and, above all, on his intense personal relationship with his wife. Melusine forgives him in this case and proves to be a loyal, loving companion, her husband's trustworthy and supportive friend: "Sy vmbfieng vnd hielß vnd kust in gar liplich. des frewet er sich gancz vnd wart pald gesunt" (101). [She hugged and necked and kissed him dearly. He enjoyed it very much and soon became healthy again.]

But his suspicions about Melusine's true nature are not eliminated entirely, and soon thereafter, Reymund commits the same transgression as before. This time, however, he tells the public about what he saw the previous time. His rage is stirred up by his son Geffroy's criminal act against another son; when Melusine meets him at court, Reymund publicly slanders her and thereby transgresses the basic contract between the couple. He then must helplessly witness her expulsion from human society. All his pleas are in vain; he is excessively remorseful over the collapse of his marriage:

> vnd er mocht vor iamer vnd herczenleit nicht ein wort gesprechen
> </> dann in bedaucht das sein hercz alle augenplick von grossen

schmerczen vnd leid pillich prechen sölt. . . . Reymund stünd auff vnd
gieng zü Melusine mit gar iämerlichen geperden. vnd vmbfieng vnd
kust sy mit grossen betrübtnussen vnd weinet pitterlichen / vnd von
grossem vnd vnaußsprechenlichem herczen leide so sy beide hetten /
des scheidenshalb. viellen sy beide stracks nyder auf die erden. (120)

[For all his misery and heart pains he could not speak one word, and
he thought that his heart would have to break for the great pain and
suffering. . . . Reymund stood up and went to Melusine with griev-
ous gestures and hugged and kissed her with deep sadness and cried
bitterly because of his deep and ineffable heart pain which both felt
because of the departure. Both fell right on the ground.]

The events take an irreversible turn, since Melusine will never rejoin
her husband in marriage. She must live as a ghost from then on, still suffering from her mother's curse, and she only appears in the castle on several
nocturnal occasions to secretly breast-feed her youngest child. When he
learns about these sightings, Reymund hopes that his wife might forgive him,
but alas, as the narrator stresses, "das aber leyder nit gesein mocht" (126)
[unfortunately this could not be].

With this, we can try to offer an interpretation of how marriage and
family are viewed in Thüring von Ringoltingen's remarkable adaption of the
French romance. To some extent, Reymund accepts Melusine's offer to marry
her because of his fear of prosecution. Conjugal life with Melusine appears
to offer security. Second, she proves to be immensely rich and thus provides
infinite wealth for her husband. Moreover, she is a very fertile woman, although all her children are born with some strange feature that marks them
as descendants of a fairy godmother. Nevertheless, the personal and emotional relationship between the couple is described in very positive terms;
the disruption and break-up are painted in exceedingly negative language.
Although Reymund's own brother tries to talk him into distrusting his wife,
he eventually rejects these manipulations and ignores the uncanny aspects
of Melusine in favor of his happy partnership with her. Reymund's deep sorrow and abjection because of her disappearance strike a tender emotional
cord and indicate that married life has assumed, at least for the Bernese author Thüring, a social and personal value of highest importance. This extraordinary appreciation of conjugal love seems to run in the family, because
when Geffroy finally learns about his grandparents, he encounters a story
similar to the one that had befallen Melusine and Reymund. His grandmother Presine, also a member of the world of fairy figures, is married to a

human being, King Helmas. In their marriage contract, Presine stipulates that Helmas is never to try to make love to her while she is lying in childbed recovering from a delivery—certainly a very understandable and not very harsh limitation imposed on the husband. Nevertheless, Helmas transgresses this law just as Reymund would later transgress his own law, and thus loses his family. After the birth of her three daughters (among them, Melusine), Presine takes her children and leaves her husband. Once the daughters reach the age of 15, their mother informs them about their father. Filled with rage over their father's "crime," all three plot against him and banish him to a mountain (138ff). But Presine reveals her unbroken love for her husband when she punishes her three daughters for their act. She condemns Melusine to assume a half-snake, half-human form. Meliora is forced to become a ghost who must wait for liberation by a relative who is bold enough to undergo a test. Palentina is forced to protect a treasure until the gates are broken by a knight.

Grieving over the loss of her husband, Presine thus initiates the historical events leading directly to Melusine's marriage with Reymund. Her action also precipitates such future events as the attempts of Melusine and Reymund's children to commit incest with their aunts Meliora and Palentina. Ultimately, the three sisters are banned until the Judgement Day. Geffroy discovers the text of his family history engraved on his grandfather's tombstone in the middle of a mountain (his prison) and thus also learns that the relationship between his grandparents was one of conjugal love:

> Dann wiewol er sich ser an mir übergriffen hette. dennoch was ich im von herczen günstig / das ich die rach so mein tochter vorgenant von meinem wegen an im begiengen nit mocht noch wolt vngerochen lassen. (140f)

> [Because, although he had transgressed against me badly, I still felt strongly for him in my heart. Therefore, I could not and did not want to let the revenge that my daughters had carried out against him on my behalf be left unrevenged.]

This indicates that, although the relationship between husband and wife is deeply troubled because of "cultural"—or should we say "ethnic"—differences, their love is given a high value; and consequently, the family as a form of coexistence gains greater esteem.

Other Volksbücher do not follow the same example and tend to focus primarily on the efforts of protagonists to find each other. In Veit

Warbeck's *Die Schön Magelone* or in Elisabeth von Nassau-Saarbrücken's *Hug Schapler*, the narrative is limited to the lifespan before the marriage and breaks off either with the marriage or shortly thereafter, summarizing the hero's married life in a few pages.[70] *Fortunatus*, on the other hand, includes marriage and family life only because it appears to be the natural consequence for a respected member of society. In other words, Fortunatus chooses a wife not out of love but because he wants to establish a family. Family life in itself, however, does not especially attract him, although his wife laments dearly when he embarks on a second world trip through the countries of the Orient.[71]

We may safely argue that in some texts of late medieval German literature, the concept of family and marriage has undergone a considerable transformation. It is a different question, of course, whether this new perception of the marriage partner as a friend and lover, supporter and confidant, found its reflection in the social reality of the time. But it would be strange to assume that literary texts have little or no relevance to our understanding of mental history.[72] Letters by German and English women to their husbands might prove to be a valuable avenue for further study.[73]

Courtly poets from the High Middle Ages did not denigrate the value of marriage altogether. We have observed an intriguingly positive image of conjugal love between Rual and Floraete in Gottfried von Strassburg's *Tristan* and between Parzival and Condwiramur in Wolfram von Eschenbach's *Parzival*. But these allusions to a happy family life can be traced only in the margins; they have not assumed center stage.

This attitude does not begin to change significantly[74] until the fifteenth century. The twelfth-century poet Wolfram von Eschenbach made the first attempts to advocate that mistress and lover should be married (though he did this in very tentative terms within the framework of one of his dawn songs).[75] By contrast, the fourteenth- and fifteenth-century composers Hugo von Montfort and Oswald von Wolkenstein harbored a very explicit concept of a fulfilled marriage, which is supposed to provide man and woman with conjugal happiness despite having some negative features that von Wolkenstein also incorporated into his songs. Many of their texts contain unequivocal messages that marriage and family are important for both sexes and deserve great respect as social institutions. Johannes von Tepl goes full steam toward idealization of marriage and the married life. Thüring von Ringoltingen, finally, presents a mysterious and inexplicable relationship between a man and a woman from the world of fairies, and herewith portrays an ideal form of family life that could have been adapted both by noble and bourgeois audiences.[76]

German literature does not begin to discuss marriage openly in an idealizing fashion on a broad scale until the eighteenth century, but this does not undermine my hypothesis. In the sixteenth century, the Reformation radically altered public discussion about marriage and family. Martin Luther supported marriage in strong terms, but his theological perspective did not incorporate the same emotional dimension for both husband and wife as did fifteenth-century German literature. Instead, Luther saw women as men's caretakers—as mothers, housewives, and even companions. Yet for him, marriage was a natural consequence of the existence of two sexes, and he denied people a choice: because the Bible requires people to have progeny, they had to marry. Divorce or the refusal to marry were only acceptable under very specific circumstances.[77]

Due to Luther's tremendous influence, German poets mostly removed themselves from any further discussion about conjugal love and thus altogether abandoned the basic concepts that had been boldly developed by Hugo von Montfort, Oswald von Wolkenstein, Johannes von Tepl, and Thüring von Ringoltingen.[78] Instead, we observe a functional, pragmatic perception of marriage and the family as the foundation of a new bourgeois society. This assigns fifteenth-century German literature, which was still dominated by aristocratic writers and audiences, a special role within medieval history. In terms of marriage and family, it seems to have been a period in which new models of social interaction could be freely discussed within the traditional framework. Moreover, these models were capable of experimentation. Once the transition from the Middle Ages to the Reformation was completed, the family was relegated again to a subordinate position, and it had to conform to the new dominant bourgeois value system. Perhaps this might explain why most of the major sixteenth-century German literary texts refrain from examining the family from a social perspective; it might also elucidate why the texts no longer elaborate upon conjugal love in poetic treatments. For example, the total absence of love, marriage, and sex in the notorious collection of farcical tales *Till Eulenspiegel* (first printed in 1510/11)[79] might be explained by the fact that the idea of the family had been formalized to such an extent through the Reformation that it lost all its attractiveness for contemporary readers. Other sixteenth-century literary works by German writers confirm the general impression that the social institution of the family was no longer of major significance for the reading public, Johannes Fischart with his *Ehezuchtbüchlein* being a noteworthy exception.[80]

The *Historia von D. Johann Fausten*, the devil books, or religious drama, focus on a wide variety of themes but never demonstrate real interest in the family. Some of the Shrovetide plays by Hans Sachs or Hans Folz (to mention only two names among the many *Meistersinger* and other dramatists) locate their protagonists in families but center on human folly, human stupidity, or political problems, not on the erotic element determining the relationship between a couple. In this sense, again, fifteenth-century German literature represents a unique body of texts in which the family assumes a major role, since it had not been functionalized as it would be in the following century and since poets such as Johannes von Tepl or Oswald von Wolkenstein strove to project an idyllic image of their marriages or to present themselves as members of a very intimate family, almost in the modern sense of the word.

NOTES

1. An early version of this paper was presented at the annual convention of the Rocky Mountain Medieval and Renaissance Association, Flagstaff, Ariz., April 8–10, 1993. I thank the audience and co-panelists for their valuable comments.

2. *The Letters of Abelard and Heloise*, translated with an introduction by Betty Radice (Harmondsworth: Penguin, 1974/75), 114.

3. See, for a comprehensive overview, Frances Gies, *Marriage and the Family in the Middle Ages* (New York: Harper & Row, 1987); Michael Anderson, *Approaches to the History of the Western Family, 1500–1914*, Studies in Economic and Social History (London-Basingstoke: The Macmillan Press, 1980); Theodore K. Rabb and Robert I. Rotberg, *The Family in History: Interdisciplinary Essays* (New York: Harper & Row, 1971); Michael Schröter, *"Wo zwei zusammenkommen in rechter Ehe. . . ,"* *Sozio- und psychogenetische Studien über Eheschließungsvorgänge vom 12. bis 15. Jahrhundert*. Mit einem Nachwort von Norbert Elias (Frankfurt a. M.: Suhrkamp, 1985). Closely related is the significant study by Christopher N.L. Brooke, *The Medieval Idea of Marriage* (Oxford/New York: Oxford Univ. Press, 1989).

4. Diane Bornstein, "Family, Western Europe." In *Dictionary of the Middle Ages*, edited by Joseph R. Strayer, vol. 4 (New York: Charles Scribner's Sons, 1984), 599–605: "The concept of the conjugal family did not develop until the sixteenth and seventeenth centuries." See also H.-W. Goetz, "Die Familie in der Gesellschaft des Mittelalters," *Lexikon des Mittelalters*, vol. 4/2 (Munich-Zurich: Artemis, 1987), cols. 270–75.

5. Hanna Schissler, "Geschlechtergeschichte. Herausforderung und Chance für die Sozialgeschichte," *Was ist Gesellschaftsgeschichte: Positionen, Themen, Analysen*, ed. Manfred Hettling, Claudia Hierkamp, Paul Nolte, Hans-Walter Schmuhl (Munich: Beck, 1991), 22–30; Ute Frevert, "Männergeschichte oder die Suche nach dem 'ersten' Geschlecht," ibid., 31–43; Peter Dinzelbacher and Hans Dieter Mück, eds., *Volkskultur des europäischen Spätmittelalters*, Böblinger Forum 1 (Stuttgart: Kröner, 1987).

6. Rolf Sprandel, *Verfassung und Gesellschaft im Mittelalter*, Uni-Taschenbücher 461 (Paderborn: Schöningh, 1975), 33f.

7. Karl Bosl, "Die 'Familia' als Grundstruktur der mittelalterlichen Gesellschaft," *Zeitschrift für bayerische Landesgeschichte* 38 (1975): 403–24.

8. Heinz Reif, ed., *Die Familie in der Geschichte*, Kleine Vandenhoeck-Reihe 1474 (Göttingen: Vandenhoeck & Ruprecht, 1981); Erich Maschke, *Die Familie in der deutschen Stadt des späten Mittelalters*, Sitzungsberichte der Heidelberger Akademie der Wissenschaften, Philosophisch-historische Klasse, 1980, 4. Abhandlungen (Heidelberg: Winter 1980); Michael Mitterauer and Reinhard Sieder, *Vom Patriarchat zur Partnerschaft: Zum Strukturwandel der Familie*, 2nd ed. (Munich:

Beck, 1980); H. Reif, ed., *Die Familie in der Geschichte* (Göttingen: Vandenhoeck & Ruprecht, 1982); A. Burguière et al., *Histoire de la famille*, vol. I (Paris: Armand Colin, 1986); P. Schuler, ed., *Die Familie als historischer und sozialer Verband: Untersuchungen zum Spätmittelalter und zur frühen Neuzeit* (Sigmaringen: Thorbecke, 1987).

9. Ingeborg Weber-Kellermann, *Die deutsche Familie: Versuch einer Sozialgeschichte*, Suhrkamp Taschenbuch 185 (Frankfurt a. M.: Suhrkamp, 1974/75), 38ff.; J.W. Milden, *The Family in Past Time* (New York: Garland, 1977); David Herlihy, "Land, Family and Women in Continental Europe, 1101–1200," *Traditio* 18 (1962): 89–120; David Herlihy, "The Making of the Medieval Family: Symmetry, Structure, and Sentiment," *Journal of Family History* 8 (1983): 116–30; David Herlihy, *Medieval Households*, Studies in Cultural History (Cambridge, Mass.: Harvard Univ. Press, 1985).

10. For a summary of family research, see M.M. Sheehan and K.D. Scordellato, *Family and Marriage in Medieval Europe: A Working Bibliography* (Vancouver: Univ. of British Columbia Press, 1976); H.-W. Goetz, "Die Familie in der Gesellschaft des Mittelalters," *Lexikon des Mittelalters*, vol. 4/2 (Munich-Zurich: Artemis, 1987), cols. 270–75.

11. Peter Dinzelbacher, "Gefühl und Gesellschaft im Mittelalter: Vorschläge zu einer emotionsgeschichtlichen Darstellung des hochmittelalterlichen Umbruchs," *Höfische Literatur, Hofgesellschaft, Höfische Lebensformen um 1200*, ed. Gert Kaiser and Jan-Dirk Müller. Studia humaniora 6 (Düsseldorf: Droste, 1986), 213–41. He goes so far as to characterize the emergence of courtly literature as an expression of the discovery of love between man and woman in the early High Middle Ages.

12. It is a problematic approach to use literature as a vehicle for social-historical studies, yet not an unfruitful one, if properly considered. See Jan-Dirk Müller, "Aporien und Perspektiven einer Sozialgeschichte mittelalterlicher Literatur: Zu einigen neueren Forschungsansätzen," Albrecht Schöne, ed., *Kontroversen, alte und neue. Akten des VII. Internationalen Germanisten-Kongresses Göttingen 1985* (Tübingen: Niemeyer, 1986).

13. For a summary analysis based on French sources, see Danielle Régnier-Bohler, "Imagining the Self," Georges Duby, ed., *Revelations of the Medieval World*, Arthur Goldhammer, trans., A History of Private Life II (Cambridge, Mass.-London: The Belknap Press of Harvard Univ. Press, 1988), 311–94, here 335–56.

14. Helmut Brall, "Familie und Hofgesellschaft in Wolframs *Parzival*," *Höfische Literatur, Hofgesellschaft, Höfische Lebensformen um 1200*, 541–83.

15. Several interesting approaches to familial relationships are developed in *Les relations de parenté dans le monde médiéval. XIVe colloque du Centre Universitaire d'Etudes et de Recherches Médiévales d'Aix*. Sénéfiance 26 (Aix-en-Provence: Université de Provence, CUERMA, 1989). However, they do not touch specifically on the topic discussed here.

16. Wolfram von Eschenbach, *Parzival*, trans. with an introduction by Helen M. Mustard & Charles E. Passage (New York: Vintage Books, 1961); for the histori-cal-critical ed., see *Wolfram von Eschenbach*, Karl Lachmann, ed., Siebente Ausg. von Eduard Hartl (Berlin: de Gruyter, 1952). References will be to this edition, with numbers for the chapters (each chapter contains thirty verses) and the lines.

17. The same applies to many other medieval romances, for instance, if we consider French literature (*Gormont et Isembart, Doon de la Roche, Baudoin de Sebourc, Florent et Octavien*), where the search for the father often leads to patricide; see D. Régnier-Bohler, 336f.

18. Ann-Marie Eva Nilsson, "Amour et Maternité dans *Tristan et Yseut*," forthcoming in *Tristania*.

19. Siegfried Richard Christoph, *Wolfram von Eschenbach's Couples*, Amsterdamer Publikationen zur Sprache und Literatur 44 (Amsterdam: Editions Rodopi, 1981).

20. For a good English translation, see Marion E. Gibbs and Sidney M. Johnson, *Wolfram von Eschenbach: Titurel and the Songs*, texts and translations with introduction, notes, and comments. Garland Library of Medieval Literature, Series A, 57 (New York-London: Garland, 1988), stanzas 19–23.

21. Joachim Bumke, *Wolfram von Eschenbach*, 6th ed. Sammlung Metzler 36 (Stuttgart: Metzler, 1991); Michael Curschmann, "Das Abenteuer des Erzählens. Über den Erzähler in Wolfram's 'Parzival,'" *Deutsche Vierteljahresschrift für Literaturwissenschaft und Geisteswissenschaft* 45 (1971), 627–67.

22. Regarding Wolfram's *Parzival*, see C.N.L. Brooke, *The Medieval Idea of Marriage* (New York: Oxford Univ. Press, 1989), 199: "it is the union of husband and wife, at bed and board, their pleasure in one another, pleasure in each other's company, pleasure in sleeping together, which makes marriage so joyous a thing in Wolfram's eyes." This is much too positive an interpretation and ignores the structural orientation of Wolfram's work, in which love and marriage are presented as victims of a world in which chivalry dominates.

23. For a comprehensive survey of Hartmann scholarship, see Peter Wapnewski, *Hartmann von Aue*, 5th ed., Realien zur Literatur. Abteilung D. Sammlung Metzler, M 17 (Stuttgart: Metzler, 1972); Lambertus Okken, *Kommentar zur Artusepik Hartmanns von Aue*. Im Anhang: Bernhard Dietrich Haage, "Die Heilkunde und Der Ouroboros." Amsterdamer Publikationen zur Sprache und Literatur 103 (Amsterdam-Atlanta: Editions Rodopi, 1993).

24. Hartmann von Aue, *Erec*, trans. with an introduction and commentary by Michael Resler. Middle Ages Series (Philadelphia: Univ. of Pennsylvania Press, 1987).

25. The attempts of Jean-Marc Pastré, "Les marques de la filiation dans le *Parzival* de Wolfram von Eschenbach," 233–45, and Daniel Rocher, "La femme mariée entre deux familles dans la littérature narrative allemande au moyen âge," 247–55, *Les relations de parenté dans le monde médiéval* (1989), lead only to a repetition of our present knowledge about the role of family and marriage in the "classical" Middle High German literature.

26. Quoted from *Iwein*, trans. Patrick M. McConeghy, Garland Library of Medieval Literature 19 (New York-London: Garland, 1984).

27. Volker Mertens, *Laudine: Soziale Problematik im "Iwein" Hartmanns von Aue* (Berlin: E. Schmidt, 1978); Herbert Ernst Wiegand, *Studien zur Minne und Ehe in Wolfram's "Parzival" und Hartmann's Artusepik*, Quellen und Forschungen zur Sprach- und Kulturgeschichte der germanischen Völker, N.F. 49, 173 (Berlin-New York: de Gruyter, 1972). Achim Masser, "'Ir habt den künec Ascalon erslagen,'" *Uf der mâze pfat: Festschrift für Werner Hoffmann zum 60. Geburtstag*, ed. Waltraud Fritsche-Rößler and Liselotte Homerin, Göppinger Arbeiten zur Germanistik 555 (Göppingen: Kümmerle, 1991), 183–204, makes a valiant attempt to connect the literary text with the historical reality. If his thesis can be upheld, we would have an additional supporting argument for the relatively low level of amatory bonding between husband and wife in the upper social classes of the medieval world.

28. Quoted from *German Medieval Tales*, ed. Francis G. Gentry, forward by Thomas Berger, The German Library 4 (New York: Continuum, 1982), 1–21, here 5.

29. Otfried Ehrismann, *Nibelungenlied: Epoche—Werk—Wirkung*, Arbeitsbücher zur Literaturgeschichte (Munich: Beck, 1987), 153, 179f. *Das Nibelungenlied*, Nach der Ausgabe von Karl Bartsch hg. von Helmut de Boor, 13th ed. (Wiesbaden: Brockhaus, 1956).

30. W.P. Ker, *Epic and Romance: Essays on Medieval Literature* (New York: Dover, 1957), 7ff.

31. Quoted from *Kudrun*, trans. Marion E. Gibbs and Sidney M.M. Johnson, Garland Library of Medieval Literature, Series B, 79 (New York-London: Garland, 1992); see also *Kudrun*, ed. Karl Bartsch. 5th ed. rev. and with a new introduction by Karl Stackmann (Wiesbaden: Brockhaus, 1965).

32. Winder McConnell, *The Epic of Kudrun: A Critical Commentary*, Göppinger Arbeiten zur Germanistik 463 (Göppingen: Kümmerle, 1988); Barbara Siebert, *Rezeption und Produktion: Bezugssysteme in der "Kudrun,"* Göppinger Arbeiten zur Germanistik 491 (Göppingen: Kümmerle, 1988).

33. Winder McConnell, "Marriage in Nibelungenlied and Kudrun," William C. McDonald, ed., *Spectrum Medii Aevii: Essays in Early German Literature in Honor of George Fenwick Jones*, Göppinger Arbeiten zur Germanistik 362 (Göppinger: Kümmerle, 1983), 299–320; further references can be found in the translation by M.E. Gibbs and S.M. Johnson, xxxix ff.

34. *Morîz von Craûn*. *Mittelhochdeutsch/Neuhochdeutsch*, Übersetzung, Kommentar und Nachwort von Albrecht Classen, Universal-Bibliothek 8796 (Stuttgart: Reclam, 1992).

35. A very clear example is the novelistic tale *Tristan als Mönch*, in the tradition of Gottfried von Strassburg's *Tristan* and Eilhart von Oberg's *Tristrant*; cf. Danielle Buschinger, "'Tristan le Moine,'" *Tristan et Iseut: mythe européen mondial, Actes du Colloque des 10, 11 et 12 janvier 1986*, publiés par les soins de Danielle Buschinger, Göppinger Arbeiten zur Germanistik 474 (Göppingen: Kümmerle, 1987), 75–86, here 79.

36. Gottfried von Strassburg, *Tristan*, trans. in its entirety for the first time with the surviving fragments of the *Tristan* of Thomas, with an introduction by A.T. Hatto (Harmondsworth: Penguin, 1984). See also *Das Tristan-Epos Gottfrieds von Strassburg. Mit der Fortsetzung des Ulrich von Türheim*, nach der Heidelberger Handschrift cod. pal. germ. 360 hg. von Wolfgang Spiewok, Deutsche Texte des Mittelalters LXXV (Berlin: Akademie-Verlag, 1989).

37. Rüdiger Krohn, "Erotik und Tabu in Gottfrieds *Tristan*: König Marke," *Stauferzeit: Geschichte, Literatur, Kunst*, ed. R.K. Bern Thum and Peter Wapnewski, Karlruher Kulturwissenschaftliche Arbeiten 1 (Stuttgart: Klett-Cotta, 1977), 362–76.

38. Gisela Hollandt, *Die Hauptgestalten in Gottfrieds Tristan: Wesenszüge, Handlungsfunktion, Motiv der List*, Philologische Studien und Quellen 30 (Berlin: Schmidt, 1966).

39. Peter Moraw, *Von offener Verfassung zu gestalteter Verdichtung: Das Reich im späten Mittelalter, 1250 bis 1490*, Propyläen Geschichte Deutschlands 3 (Berlin: Propyläen, 1985), 59ff; Jean Gaudemet, *Le mariage en occident: Les moeurs et le droit* (Paris: Les éditions du CERF, 1987).

40. Jutta Goheen, *Mensch und Moral im Mittelalter: Geschichte und Fiktion in Hugo von Trimbergs "Der Renner,"* (Darmstadt: Wissenschaftliche Buchgesellschaft, 1990), 144ff.

41. For a critical commentary, see Ulrich Seelbach, *Kommentar zum "Helmbrecht" von Wernher dem Gartenaere*, Göppinger Arbeiten zur Germanistik 469 (Göppingen: Kümmerle, 1987).

42. Wernher der Gartenaere, *Helmbrecht*, 8th rev. ed. by Kurt Ruh. Altdeutsche Textbibliothek 11 (Tübingen: Niemeyer, 1968).

43. A. Classen, "Misogyny and the Battle of Genders in the Stricker's *Maeren*," *Neuphilologische Mitteilungen* XCII, 1 (1991): 105–22.

44. Walter Blank, "Zur Paarbeziehung in deutscher Märendichtung: Sozialer Kontext und Bedingungen," *The Making of the Couple: The Social Function of Short-Form Medieval Narrative, A Symposium*, ed. Flemming G. Andersen and Morten Nøjgaard (Odense: Odense Univ. Press, 1991), 67–87, here 76f.

45. Joachim Bumke, *Geschichte der deutschen Literatur im hohen Mittelalter* (Munich: Deutscher Taschenbuch Verlag, 1990), 233ff; James A. Schultz, *The Shape of the Round Table: Structures of Middle High German Arthurian Romances* (Toronto: Univ. of Toronto Press, 1983).

46. Anton Schwob, *Oswald von Wolkenstein: Eine Biographie*, 3rd ed., Schriftenreihe des Südtiroler Kulturinstitutes 4 (Bozen: Athesia, 1979); Anton Schwob, "Die Edition der Lebenszeugnisse Oswalds von Wolkenstein und neue Funde zum

realen Erlebnishintergrund seiner Lieder," *Ex Ipsis Rerum Documentiis, Beiträge zur Mediävistik: Festschrift für Harald Zimmermann zum 65 Geburtstag*, ed. Klaus Herbers, Hans Henning Kortüm, and Carlo Servatius (Sigmaringen: Thorbecke, 1991), 159–72.

47. A. Classen, *Die autobiographische Lyrik des europäischen Spätmittelalters: Studien zu Hugo von Montfort, Oswald von Wolkenstein, Antonio Pucci, Charles d'Orléans, Thomas Hoccleve, Michel Beheim, Hans Rosenplüt und Alfonso Alvarez de Villasandino*, Amsterdamer Publikationen zur Sprache und Literatur 91 (Amsterdam-Atlanta: Editions Rodopi, 1991).

48. Quoted from *Die Lieder Oswalds von Wolkenstein*, 3rd ed., Hans Moser, Norbert Richard Wolf, and Notburga Wolf (Tübingen: Niemeyer, 1987).

49. For the history of misogyny, see *Woman Defamed and Woman Defended: An Anthology of Medieval Texts*, ed. Alcuin Blamires with Karen Pratt and C.W. Marx, (Oxford: Clarendon Press, 1992).

50. A. Classen, "Love and Marriage in Late Medieval Verse: Oswald von Wolkenstein, Thomas Hoccleve and Michel Beheim," *Studia Neophilologica* 62 (1990): 163–88.

51. Norbert Mayr, "Das Vogelfängerlied Oswalds von Wolkenstein," *Der Schlern* 56 (1982): 35–40.

52. Dirk Joschko, *Oswald von Wolkenstein: Eine Monographie zu Person, Werk, und Forschungsgeschichte*, Göppinger Arbeiten zur Germanistik 396 (Göppingen: Kümmerle, 1985), 134ff.

53. A. Classen, "Representation of Reality: Oswald von Wolkenstein's Lyric Poetry and Contemporary North Italian and South Tyrolean Frescoes and Book Il-lustrations," *Arcadia* 24, 2 (1989): 113–30.

54. Ulrich Müller, *"Dichtung" und "Wahrheit" in den Reiseliedern Oswalds von Wolkenstein: Die autobiographischen Lieder von den Reisen*, Göppinger Arbeiten zur Germanistik 1 (Göppingen: Kümmerle, 1968).

55. W.T.H. Jackson, "Faith Unfaithful—The German Reaction to Courtly Love," *The Meaning of Courtly Love*, ed. F.X. Newman (Albany: State Univ. of New York Press, 1972), 55–76.

56. Quoted from *Hugo von Montfort II: Die Texte und Melodien der Heidelberger Handschrift cpg 329*, Transkription von Franz V. Spechtler, Litterae 57 (Göppingen: Kümmerle, 1978); for the motif of the charnel house, see William C. McDonald, "On the Charnel House as a Poetic Motif: Villon and German Poetry on Death," *Fifteenth-Century Studies* 19 (1992), 101–45.

57. A. Classen, *Die autobiographische Lyrik*, 127ff.

58. There are several versions of the text; here quoted from Johannes von Tepl, *Der Ackermann*, ed. Willy Krogman. Deutsche Klassiker des Mittelalters, Neue Folge 1 (Wiesbaden: Brockhaus, 1964). See Fritz Martini, "Dichtung und Wirklichkeit bei Oswald von Wolkenstein," *Dichtung und Volkstum* 39 (1938): 390–410, here 400.

59. For a summary overview of *Ackermann* scholarship, see Thomas Cramer, *Geshichte der deutschen Literatur im späten Mittelalter* (Munich: Deutscher Taschenbuch Verlag, 1990), 356ff. Josef Heilig discovered this letter in the library of Fribourg, Switzerland, in 1933.

60. André Schnyder, "Die Trauerarbeit des Witwers: Vorläufiger Versuch, ein altbekanntes Werk neu zu sehen," *Jahrbuch der Oswald von Wolkenstein Gesellschaft* 4 (1986/1987), 25–39.

61. A. Classen, "Der 'Ackermann aus Böhmen'—Ein literarisches Zeugnis aus einer Schwellenzeit: Mittelalterliches Streitgespräch oder Dokument des deutschen Frühhumanismus," *Zeitschrift für deutsche Philologie* 110, 3 (1991): 348–73.

62. Monika Londner, *Eheauffassung und Darstellung der Frau in der spätmittelalterlichen Märendichtung: Eine Untersuchung auf der Grundlage rechtlich-sozialer und theologischer Voraussetzungen*, Ph.D. thesis, West Berlin, 1973.

63. Rainer Helfenbein, *Zur Affassung der Ehe in Heinrich Wittenwilers*

"Ring," Ph.D. thesis, Bochum, 1976; Rolf R. Müller, *Festival and Fiction in Heinrich Wittenwiler's "Ring": A Study of the Narrative in Its Relation to the Traditional Topoi of Marriage, Folly, and Play,* German Language and Literature Monographs 3 (Amsterdam: Benjamins, 1977); see also, despite its early publication date, the useful study by Charles Gervaise Fehrenbach, *Marriage in Wittenwiler's Ring,* The Catholic University of America Studies in German 15 (Washington: The Catholic University of America Press, 1941; rpt. New York: AMS Press, 1970).

64. Heinrich Wittenwiler, *Der Ring,* Frühneuhochdeutsch/Neuhochdeutsch, nach dem Text von Edmund Wießner ins Neuhochdeutsche übersetzt und herausgegeben von Horst Brunner, Universal-Bibliothek, 1991 (Stuttgart: Reclam, 1991), 154–205.

65. Bea Lundt, "Schwestern der Melusine im 12. Jahrhundert. Aufbruchs-Phantasie und Beziehungs-Vielfalt in Texten von Marie de France, Walter Map und Gervasius von Tilbury," Bea Lundt, ed., *Auf der Suche nach der Frau im Mittelalter: Fragen, Quellen, Antworten* (Munich: Fink, 1991), 232–53.

66. I have critically examined the entire *Melusine* scholarship in my forthcoming monograph *The German Volksbuch: Critical History of a Late Medieval Genre* (Lewiston, NY: Edwin Mellen Press, 1995).

67. Here quoted from *Romane des 15. und 16. Jahrhunderts. Nach den Erstdrucken mit sämtlichen Holzschnitten,* ed. J.-D. Müller, Bibliothek der frühen Neuzeit 1 (Frankfurt a. M.: Deutscher Klassiker Verlag, 1990), 23ff. Her active role in pursuing him is a remarkable feature, 25: "Reymond so solt du mir zü dem ersten schween bey gott vnd seinem leichnam das mich zü einem eelichen gemahel nemen vnd an keinem samstag mir nymmer nachfragen noch mich ersüchen wöllest." [Reymond, first you should give me your oath by God and his Corpus that you will marry me and that you will never question on Saturdays where I am or search for me.]

68. H.-W. Goetz, "Die Familie," 272, observes that the change from cognatic to agnate family structure occurs in medieval Europe during the tenth and eleventh centuries. Thüring's fascination with the archaic fairy tale indicates, however, that some undercurrents of matriarchal elements were still present in the fifteenth century.

69. For a broad survey of fifteenth-century marriage teachings, see Walter Blank, "Ehelehren in mittelhochdeutscher Dichtung: Nürnberger Fastnachtspiele des 15. Jahrhunderts," *Liebe in der deutschen Dichtung des Mittelalters: St. Andrews-Colloquium 1985,* ed. Jeffrey Ashcroft, Dietrich Huschenbett, and William Henry Jackson (Tübingen: Niemeyer, 1987), 192–203.

70. Both texts can be found in J.-D. Müller's edition, *Romane des 15. und 16. Jahrhunderts.* See also his critical overview "Volksbuch/Prosaroman im 15./16. Jahrhundert—Perspektiven der Forschung," *Internationales Archiv für Sozialgeschichte der deutschen Literatur.* 1. Sonderheft: *Forschungsreferate* (Tübingen: Niemeyer, 1985), 1–128.

71. Quoted from J.-D. Müller, ed., 482.

72. We have at least one confirmation for this hypothesis. Margareta von Schwangau, wife of the poet Oswald von Wolkenstein, has left us a number of very moving letters to her husband in which she expresses her worry about his well-being. See A. Classen, "Margareta von Schwangau: Epistolary Literature in the German Late Middle Ages," *Medieval Perspectives,* ed. Pedro F. Campa, Charles W. Connell, and Robert J. Vallier, vol. 1/1 (SEMA: 1987), 41–53.

73. Stephan Kohl, *Das englische Spätmittelalter: Kulturelle Normen, Lebenspraxis, Texte,* Studien zur englischen Philologie, N.F., 24 (Tübingen: Niemeyer, 1986), 98ff.

74. Richard Koebner, *Die Eheauffassung des ausgehenden deutschen Mittelalters* (Breslau: Nischkowsky, 1911).

75. Wolfram, "Der helnden minne ir klage," in Wolfram von Eschenbach, *Titurel and the Songs,* texts and translations with introduction, notes, and comments by Marion E. Gibbs and Sidney M. Johnson. Garland Library of Medieval Literature,

Series A, 57 (New York-London: Garland, 1988), 82ff.

76. Philippe Braunstein, "Toward Intimacy: The Fourteenth and Fifteenth Centuries," *A History of Private Life: Revelations of the Medieval World*, 535–630, here 563f., using pictorial evidence to support the argument, which runs parallel to mine.

77. See my discussion, together with Tanya Amber Settle, in "Women in Martin Luther's Life and Theology," *German Studies Review* XIV, 2 (1991): 231–60.

78. If we had some testimony from late medieval German women writers, perhaps the general picture might have been different. One case might be alluded to, however. The anonymous *Frau Tugendreich* from ca. 1520 could have been written by a woman, and here we have a very negative description of the effects of male machinations to marry women away. Elisabeth Lienert, *"Frau Tugendreich": Eine Prosaerzählung aus der Zeit Kaiser Maximilians I. Edition und Untersuchung*, Münchener Texte und Untersuchungen zur deutschen Literatur des Mittelalters 92 (Munich-Zurich: Artemis, 1988).

79. Quoted from *Deutsche Volksbücher in drei Bänden*, vol. 2: *Tyl Ulenspiegel, Hans Clauerts werkliche Historien, Das Lalebuch*, selected and with an introduction by Peter Suchsland, 2nd ed., Bibliothek Deutscher Klassiker (Berlin-Weimar: Aufbau-Verlag, 1975). For a critical discussion of *Till Eulenspiegel*, see my recent study, *The German Volksbuch*.

80. Wolfgang Beutin, *Sexualität und Obszönität: Eine literaturpsychologische Studie über epische Dichtungen des Mittelalters und der Renaissance* (Würzburg: Königshausen & Neumann, 1990), 335f.

For Better and Worse

Women and Marriage in *Piers Plowman*

Kimberly Keller

William Langland's *Piers Plowman* is so complex a poem, with so many variations wrought upon a single word or idea, that the reader may occasionally (or perhaps more often than that) sense contradictions. Sometimes these contradictions are resolved ingeniously at a later point in the poem, and the reader is amazed at the poet's absolute awareness and graceful hand. At other times, however, apparent contradictions are never resolved or even matched in battle. They lurk beneath the surface, written but perhaps unrealized by Langland himself. One such conflict is played out between Langland's advocacy of marriage, voiced through characters like Wit and Faith, reinforced by depictions of wives like Dame Study and Dame Holy Church, and the opposing antifeminine, even antimatrimonial, material acted out by the negative depiction of Meed as a villainous potential wife.

As a member of medieval English society, Langland was exposed to misogynist ideologies. R. Howard Bloch argued that he was most often faced with a mainstream value system in which "woman" was both objectified and exalted as a "bride of Christ" or seen as a potential "devil's gateway" to lust and depravity.[1] The wife was more narrowly viewed. She could no longer be the virginal "bride of Christ" but, instead, often embodied the topos of the "devil's gateway," and her stereotypical behavior was lamented by husbands and churchmen alike as "contentious, prideful, complaining, foolish, uncontrollable, unstable, and insatiable."[2] Husbands were obliged to control these female deviants, and were given the legal means to do so, as Barbara D. Palmer has shown: "A wife was a legal minor to her husband; the husband had civil and clerical authority to correct her, by beating if necessary."[3] Although Langland could not have been far removed from this ideology and the very real physical actions arising from it, this did not keep him from consciously seeing woman as a partner to be loved rather than as a minor to be chastised and controlled.

Throughout much of *Piers Plowman*, Langland elevates the status of woman and wife by promoting a positive view of marriage. Rather than warning men away from marriage and women, rather than favoring clerical celibacy, he emphasizes the redemptive and sacramental value of marriage. Langland, writing in the late fourteenth century, was ahead of the Church in declaring marriage a sacrament: it was not officially deemed the seventh sacrament until the Council of Florence in 1439.[4] Langland was part of an emergent group of thinkers and theologians in the later Middle Ages for whom "the union of marriage came to be much more sacramental,"[5] in spite of the concurrent popularity of much antimarriage, antifeminine writing.

The allegorical personification Wit is the first to emphasize the sacramental character of marriage. He arrives at his conclusion by emphasizing the almost universally acclaimed goods of marriage, procreation, and safety from the sin of fornication, and by refuting two major obstacles thrown up by those who sought to discourage the sacramentality of marriage: financial profit and the inherent sinfulness of sexuality. His praise of procreation is generous. He reminds the reader and the skeptic that all societal and ecclesiastical roles are ultimately filled by people who are the progeny of marriage:

> In this world is Dowel trewe wedded libbynge folk,
> For thei mote werche and wynne and the world sustene.
> For of hir kynde thei come that Confessours ben nempned,
> Kynges and knyghtes, kaysers and clerkes,
> Maidenes and martires—out of o man come.[6]

> [Do-Well in this world is wedded people who live truly,
> For they must toil to take their bread and to sustain the world.
> For those who are called confessors come of their kind,
> Kings and kaisers, clerks and knights;
> Maidens and martyrs from one man have their being.]

Wit goes on to emphasize the wisdom of choosing marriage over sinful fornication. Only in marriage can the sexually active (or interested) find salvation. Wit advises:

> And every maner seculer that may noght continue,
> Wisely go wedde, and ware hym fro synne;
> For lecherie in likynge is lymeyerd of helle. (9.179–181)

> [And every manner of secular man that cannot remain continent

Wisely go wed and ward off sin,
For fantasies of the flesh are the Fiend's lures.] (9.182–4)

Thus Wit puts forth a virtuous picture of marriage. In this marital union, the wife does not represent temptation to sin but the possible redemption of sexuality.

Even the strictest canonists could not deny that procreation was, at the very least, a most necessary evil, and none would claim that fornication was in any way permissible. The saving graces of marriage, as Wit points out, were then procreation and freedom from certain sexual sins. Although some members of the contemporary church held a generally positive view of marriage, not everyone was convinced that these advantages made marriage worthy of sacramentality.

One reason used to oppose the sacramentality of marriage was financial, since money was often associated with unions between families:

> The canonists knew that money frequently changed hands during marriage negotiations whether in the form of a dowry or as a stipend for the nuptial benediction. If matrimony were to confer grace, the contracting parties would be guilty of simony.[7]

Wit tries to sanctify marriage by encouraging people to become less involved with the financial issues surrounding marriage. He persuades people to marry for love, not riches or lands:

> Forthi I counseille alle Cristene coveite noght be wedded
> For coveitise of catel ne of knyrede riche;
> Ac maidenes and maydenes macche yow togideres;
> Wideweres and wodewes, wercheth the same;
> For no londes, but for love, loke ye be wedded,
> And thanne gete ye the grace of God, and good ynough to live
>   with. (9.173–8)

> [Therefore I counsel all Christians not to crave to be married
> For a fat fortune or family connections.
> But virgins and virgins should make vows with one another,
> And widowers and widows should wed in the same way.
> For no lands but for love look to it that you marry,
> And then you'll get the grace of God and goods enough to live
>   with.] (9.176–81; pp. 86–7)

The other, more often argued reason against the sacramentality of marriage was the fundamental belief in the sinfulness of the sexual act. Augustine did not see physical sexuality as essentially corrupt, but Jerome and a number of others did. The more rigorous contempt of human sexuality rose and fell during the later Middle Ages. Wit does not explicitly validate the sexual act, but his declaration that marriage was created by God himself seems to undercut the idea that it is unconditionally sinful. He reasons:

> Ac if thei leden thus hir lif, it liketh God almyghty,
> For he made wedlok first and hymself it seide:
> Bonum est ut unusquisque uxorem suam habeat propter
>   fornicacionem. (9.190–191a)

> [But if they lead their lives thus, it delights God almighty,
> For he first devised marriage and referred to it himself:
> "It is good for every man to have his own wife on account of forni
>   cation."] (9.192–4; p. 87)

It is good to avoid fornication, especially if in doing so one participates in the state of the first couple, as they were created by God.[8]

If marriage is a necessary good and even a blessing of God, then woman cannot be completely evil because she is bound with man in marriage. Like Wit, Faith emphasizes the sacramentality of marriage. He discusses it in terms of the Holy Trinity and, in a move that seems awkward and obvious, praises woman for her role in marriage, childbearing, and widowhood. This unusual praise begins:

> As widewe withouten wedlok was nevere yit yseyghe,
> Na moore myghte God be man but if he moder hadde.
> So widewe withouten wedlok may noght wel stande,
> Ne matrimoyne withouten muliere is noght muche to preise:
> Maledictus homo qui non reliquit semen in Israel.
> Thus in thre persones is parfitliche pure manhede—
> That is, man and his make and mulliere hir children. (16.216–222)

> [As a widow without wedlock was never yet seen,
> No more might God be man unless a mother bore him.
> So widow without wedlock may not well be,
> Nor matrimony without children is not much to be praised.

"Cursed is the man who has not left his seed in Israel."

Thus manhood separate, as a thing by itself, subsists in three
   persons,

That is man and his mate and from marriage their children.]

(16.216–222; p. 187)

As M.T. Tavormina suggests, "Langland justifies the whole institution of marriage on the basis of its fecundity. We should remember here that the first command given to man was 'increase and multiply' and that this command cannot be lawfully fulfilled without marriage."[9] If woman and wife is necessary for the perfected state of humanity, then the feminine—as a gender—cannot be the embodiment of sin. Faith goes to great lengths to praise the woman's role in marriage and to defend her status from any possible detractors. This idea promotes the status of woman while emphasizing the possibilities of a truly good wife.[10]

This pro-marriage philosophy drives the interaction of Dame Study and her husband, Wit. When the reader first encounters Dame Study, she is in a fury over Wit's foolish disclosure of knowledge to Wille. She may, at first, seem to illustrate Bloch's topos of "woman as riot"[11] as she delivers her long diatribe, but the content of her argument and her interaction with Wit reveal that she is a good wife.

Dame Study's words make it clear that she is trying to control Wit's disclosures not for her own benefit but for his. She explains to Wit that indiscriminate gifts of knowledge could lead to a misuse of the faculty he represents. As examples, she brings up three types of people who often misuse their wits: the wealthy, minstrels, and clergy. She logically and clearly explains to Wit the dangers inherent in his lack of circumspection.

An important aspect of Study's speech is her favorable use of the power of oft-denigrated feminine speech. Britton Harwood identifies her oral style with that of a medieval master whose student is nourished with wise words and also by the immediacy of the spoken word itself.[12] Study not only resembles a teaching master but is also presented as a persuasive wife. Sharon Farmer examines a group of clerics who beseech wives to reform their husbands. She reveals several examples of clerics in the eleventh through thirteenth centuries who "agreed that wives could, and should, employ their feminine characteristics in order to tame their husbands."[13] Study is not only a vocally powerful, and positive, feminine character, but she also overturns the prevalent negative stereotype of the garrulous, frustrating wife.

Study uses wifely persuasion, and her superior knowledge of the faculty she represents, to alert Wit to the potential downfall that could be caused by his behavior. The marriage of Wit and Study is a partnership in which neither partner is perfect but at least one of the spouses is looking after the well-being of the other. The depiction of the personifications is molded on positive aspects of marital relationships in Langland's society. After examining remaining records surrounding medieval marriages, Barbara Hanawalt concludes: "*Partnership* is the most appropriate term to describe marriage in medieval English peasant society. The partnership was both an economic and an emotional one."[14] She goes on to list the many aspects of married life that made this sort of partnership necessary and desirable. In this brief scene in which their roles as a married couple are highlighted, Study and Wit act as partners, advising and relying upon one another.

The possibility of a wife who is more ideal than the argumentative but helpful Dame Study is borne out in a simile that Patience creates to illustrate the benefits of Christian poverty:

> Muche hardier may he asken, that here myghte have his wille
> In lond and in lordshipe and likynge of bodie,
> And for Goddess love leveth al and lyveth as a beggere.
> And as a mayde for mannes love hire moder forsaketh,
> Hir fader and alle hire frendes, and folweth hir make—
> Muche is that maide to love of [a man] that swich oon taketh,
> Moore than a maiden is that is maried thorugh brocage,
> As by assent of sondry parties and silver to boote,
> Moore for coveitise of good than kynde love of bothe—
> So it fareth by ech a persone that possession forsaketh
> And put hym to be pacient, and poverte weddeth,
> The which is sib to God hymself, and so neigh is poverte.
> (14.261–272)

> [Much more confidently may he claim it that could have his will
>   here
> In land and in lordship and in delights of the body
> And leaves it all for God's love and lives like a beggar.
> And as a maid forsakes her mother for a man's love,
> Her father and all her friends, and follows her mate—
> Much is that maid to be loved by the man who weds her,
> More than a maiden is who is married through brokerage
> As by assent of sundry parties, and silver thrown in,
> More for the sake of money than the mutual love of the pair—
> So it proves with every person who forsakes possession

And applies himself to be patient, and weds Poverty,
Who is sib to God himself—so close is Poverty.]
(14.262–73; p. 156)

Patience examines two sorts of wives, both examples of more abstract principles. First there is the good wife, beneficial to her mate, who forsakes all comforts and follows him for love alone. The second sort of wife is married through her parents, who are interested in her future bridegroom for the sake of money and status.

Patience is obviously not claiming that all wives and all marriages are good. However, Langland does expect the reader to agree with him that some marriages and some women are truly beneficial. If he did not believe this, and if he did not expect many members of his audience to already believe this or to have been persuaded to accept it by this point in the poem, he would have chosen a more acceptable simile to illustrate the important concept of patient poverty. In this simile, Langland equates the love of a good woman with the benefits of patient poverty. This is a great endorsement of marriage and women, because Langland believes that patient poverty is so great a virtue that it entitles one to the kingdom of heaven not through God's mercy but by true right.[15]

If Wit and Dame Study represent a harmonious union of human beings, then Dame Holy Church represents the sort of ideal wife whom Patience compares to patient poverty. Dame Holy Church is, of course, the bride of Christ. In this poem, she is also the "lemman" of Leaute, or justice. Neither of these potential "husband" figures appears in the poem in direct relation to Dame Holy Church. However, she is able to act responsibly and in accord with both, without their control or aid. Study and Wit need mutual correction, but Holy Church is the perfect wife, because she is so in touch with her husband's needs through her love that she needs no other aid.

Dame Holy Church speaks of her love for God:

I do it on *Deus caritas* to deme the sothe;
It is as dereworthe a drury as deere God hymselven. (1.86–7)

[I call on "Deus caritas" to declare the truth;
It's as glorious a love-gift as dear God himself.] (1.86–7; p. 11)

Dame Holy Church is an ideal example of the good wife. She is so full of love that she is in natural harmony with both God and justice. In many ways she transcends stereotypical feminine weaknesses, but in her anger toward

73

Meed and in what could be seen as her self-righteousness, she remains fallible and human, not an impossible, idealized figure but a feminine character who elevates herself through love and desire.

These examples of favorable feminine personifications and the endorsement of marriage and partnership, as important as they are, are not without a sort of implicit critique in the poem. The dominant literary tradition, in which women are often choice representatives of corrupted humanity, underlies important parts of *Piers Plowman*. These antifeminine ideas are quoted and supported by Langland's personifications and fuel the creation of Meed, a dangerous feminine personification and a terrifyingly negative potential wife.

It is not surprising that the dominant misogynistic view is stated most strongly in a paraphrase of scriptural authority. In Passus XVII, borrowing an analogy from Proverbs 21:19 and 27:15, the Samaritan illustrates the misogynistic view of women in his discussion of the ways in which the mortal, human condition itself makes perfection a difficult goal:

> Thre thynges ther ben that doon a man by strengthe
> For to fleen his owene hous, as Holy Writ sheweth.
> That oon is a wikkede wif that wol noght be chastised:
> Hir feere fleeth hire for feere of hir tonge.
> . . . .
> The wif is oure wikked flessh that wol noght be chastised,
> For kynde clyveth on hym evere to contrarie the soule.
> And though it falle, it fynt skiles, that "Frelete it made,"
> And "That is lightly foryyven and foryeten bothe
> To man that mercy asketh and amende thenketh." (17.318–21,
> 17.331–35)

> [There are three things that make a man by force
> To flee from his own house, as Holy Writ shows.
> The first one is a shrewish wife who will not be chastised;
> Her mate flees her for fear of her tongue.
> . . . .
> The wife is our wicked flesh that will not be chastised
> Because nature cleaves to it to contravene the soul;
> And though it falls it finds excuses that "Frailty caused it,"
> And "That is fast forgotten and forgiven too
> To a man who asks for mercy and means to amend."] (17.321–24,
> 17.334–338; pp. 199–200)

Like the Samaritan's teaching, the Proverbial analogy equates an angry woman with continual rain (Prov. 27:15) and considers homelessness in the wilderness a preferable alternative to her company (Prov. 21:19).

There are many ways in which these proverbs could be interpreted. The first idea that comes to mind after a strictly literal reading is that they are behavioral lessons to women. A "wikkede wif" will surely lose her husband, security, and status if she carries on long enough. However, the Samaritan interprets these proverbs as allegorical lessons to men rather than as practical admonitions to women. The twentieth-century commentator Carole R. Fontaine points out this age-old tendency in biblical interpretation: "As always in male-centered scripture, the positive and negative roles of women are viewed primarily from the perspective of what they provide for the men involved."[16] Jerome uses these proverbs to warn men away from marriage.[17] Langland's Samaritan goes further: he uses the woman in the proverbs not simply to warn men of the evils of marriage; he considers the allegorical type of the wicked wife as part of the masculine self, like the flesh, which demands control if one is to achieve salvation. Lechery, gluttony, and sloth are all deadly sins, for which the soul can be damned to eternal torment. Equating an unruly wife with deadly sin obliquely says that it is a damnable thing for a husband not to be able to control his wife. In fact, inability to control women and wives is as bad as committing a deadly sin.

This view is illustrated even more clearly in Reason's sermon at the beginning of Passus V. Reason points out the inappropriateness of a wife who spends a great deal of money on her own wardrobe while her husband goes about poorly clad. Reason also advocates the advantages of wife-beating:

> He warnede Watte his wif was to blame
> For hire heed was worth half marc and his hood noght worth a
> grote,
> And bad Bette kutte a bough outher tweye
> And bete Beton therwith but if she wolde werche. (5.30–33)

> [He warned Wat his wife was to blame
> That her head was worth a mark and his hood not a groat.
> He bade Bart cut a bough or two
> And beat Betty with it unless she got busy at her chores.] (5.30–33)

Reason "warns" Watte. A warning implies some sort of threat. Is Watte threatened by his wife's behavior, or are society and Reason threatened by

Watte's attitude of noninterference? Reason's concern with this behavior suggests that it is not just an individual domestic difficulty, but an example of a deep social problem. Reason's sermon is aimed at improving the moral character of the folk. His advice to another man to beat his wife with a tree limb or *two* can easily be seen as an attempt to improve both man and wife. Beton will be cured of her laziness, and Bette will now be able to exert proper control over his wife, fulfilling the obligations of a good husband.

If failing to punish one's wife is morally culpable, as Reason shows, and can be equated with sin as the Samaritan illustrates, how then does it fit in with more conventional ideas of sin and evil? Sin is generally a state in which a person is unable to control his or her animal or emotional desires through reason or faith in God. In these examples, the masculine figure is equated with the reasonable faculties, while the feminine is seen as the errant emotional or physical self. In a less allegorical, less sophisticated reading, the man becomes the one gifted with reason and charged with the discipline of the incapable wife.

Not only does the man protect woman from her own inherent sinfulness, but in the process of thinking of himself as exclusively rational, he projects his animal, sinful nature onto her, so she takes on his negative, dangerous qualities and he becomes free of them. He no longer has to exercise self-control to be worthy of salvation; instead, he is merely bound to control his wife, the projection of his sinful nature.[18]

Langland does not openly espouse this philosophy, but it makes itself apparent in both the Samaritan's interpretation of the proverbs and Reason's sermon. It exists in a more vital but less explicit way in the very large part of the *Visio* in which Meed is the focus of attention, for Meed comes to represent the consequences of the uncontrolled, unreasonable feminine nature.

In the Meed episode, the reason why the masculine characters are interested in Meed's marriage is that they want to choose the man who will be her husband, or that they wish to use this position to control her themselves. Taking Meed on a strictly allegorical level, one might say that this simply illustrates the human desire to control large sums of money. However, as in the Samaritan analogy, marriage is the vehicle used to express this desire to control, and the object at issue is portrayed as a woman. Joan Ferrante emphasizes the importance of not neglecting the gender of an allegorical personification:

> I am not suggesting that the personifications in the allegories . . . are female because of an inherent femaleness in the concepts they embody,

but rather that, because they are female and because there are various impulses to encourage the identification of the symbol with the thing symbolized, their female attributes are emphasized and their female powers exalted.[19]

Ferrante explains how the gender of a personification is related to certain characteristics of the concept represented, and urges the modern reader not to overlook the gender of the personification. Focusing on *Piers Plowman* and the possibilities opened up with the lack of grammatical gender in the English language, Helen Cooper adds that for Langland, "personification allegory was able to define the nature of the human form its concepts might take without grammatical constraint."[20] Both Meed's allegorical significance and her gender must be taken into account.

In the complex character of Meed, Langland plays on the shared characteristics of woman and money. Woman's weakness can be described as morally neutral. Her distinguishing trait, that of being easily manipulated, is not necessarily threatening but can easily become so. She is not intrinsically evil, since she is able to be neither actively beneficial nor harmful without male support and control. Money is also morally neutral. Both women and money, according to some ideologies, should be controlled by men. Any failure of a woman can be blamed on a lazy, negligent husband who cannot control his wife. Likewise, poor use of money can be blamed only on the human agent controlling the currency. However, for all their qualities of moral neutrality, both women and money are often seen as possible dangers to men. Money can easily corrupt—as Langland points out, it is tempting to take more than we need. Woman can also corrupt. Her sinful nature can rob a man of his reason; her sensuality can rob him of his soul.

Meed is briefly seen as morally neutral.[21] When first introduced, she is silent and apparently willing to do the bidding of anyone who asks. She is easily "enchaunted" by Favel's "faire speche" (2.42), and she is easily led into marriage by Liar (2.43). She is fetched from her room and brokered in marriage by Favel without so much as a sound (2.65–6). However, since Meed is weak and flexible—truly "feminine" in nature—and led into sin by the masculine personification whom she does not question, she quickly becomes corrupted.

Once this corrupted Meed reaches the king's court, he makes the mistake of not controlling her himself. The corrupted Meed imitates her former patrons, and is encouraged by the weakness of the men she encounters at court. Meed corrupts lords with money and churchmen with hopes of unearned advancement. A friar confessor is moved to absolve her for "a seem of whete" (3.40). If Meed gives money for the church window project of her friar confessor, it is only on the condition of his further corruption. She exchanges her money for the promise that he will

> . . . love lordes that lecherie haunten
> And lakketh nought ladies that loven wel the same. (3.53–4)

> [. . . love lords that practice lechery
> And don't malign ladies that love it well too.] (3.53–4; p.23)

She also corrupts the mayor with a gift of silver. As if her actions do not speak loudly enough, the narrator follows them with a lengthy diatribe on their sinfulness.

In her own self defense, Meed makes two important points. The first is that she covertly admits that even at her best, she still manipulates men. Trying to get the upper hand, she makes an offer to the critical Conscience:

> Yet I may, as I myghte, menske thee with yiftes
> And mayntene thi manhode moore than thow knowest. (3.184–85)

> [I'm still able—as I always was—to honor you with gifts
> And to maintain your manhood more than you admit.]
> (3. 184–5; p. 27)

Meed makes it clear that a woman may be capable of indulging and even supporting a man's masculinity. However, in this equation Meed puts herself first as the dominant partner, the breadwinner, so to speak.

Meed also makes the unstated assertion that she should be able to control men for their own safety and good. Here, she not only admits her power but also tries to emphasize her goodness through identification with the masculine. She praises her power through masculine associations:

> Hadde I ben marchal of his men, by Marie of hevene!
> I dorste have leyd my lif and no lasse wedde,
> He sholde have be lord of that lond in lengthe and in brede,
> And also kyng of that kith his kyn for to helpe—
> The leeste brol of his blood a barones piere! (3.201–5)

> [If I'd been marshall of his men, by Mary of Heaven,
> I'd have dared lay my life, and no less a pledge,

He'd have been lord of that land in length and in breadth,
And also king of that country to raise his kin's estate,
The least brat of his blood a baron's peer.] (3.201–5; p. 28)

She equates herself with a marshall, and phrases her comment as a traditional warrior's boast.

In order to undercut her argument, Conscience asserts that the positive qualities that Meed mentions in her defense are not even hers. He abstracts the good traits away from her and puts them into another category altogether, that of measurable hire. He first says that there are two types of "mede": earned and undeserved. At first it sounds as if both types of reward could still be embodied in the single character of Meed, although in a rather Jekyll-and-Hyde sort of way.

However, when Conscience describes the second, positive sort of "mede," he denies that it can be considered something that Meed can claim as her own. Earlier, justly earned wages were a type of "mede," but now they are subsumed under another category, that of "measurable hire."

That laboreres and lewede [leodes] taken of hire maistres,
It is no manere mede but a mesurable hire.
In marchaundise is no mede, I may it wel avowe:
It is a permutacion apertly—a penyworth for another. (3.255–8)

[What laborers and lowly folk unlearned get from their masters,
It is in no manner meed but a measurable hire.
There is no meed in merchandise, I may well assert it;
It is a plain permutation, one pennyworth for another.]
(3.255–8; p. 30)

Conscience renames positive connotations or uses of "meed" as measurable hire. In Latin, this would be *mercede*, the term Langland substitutes for "measurable hire" in the C-text. *Mercede* is from *merces*, a feminine noun.[22] Conscience is not saying that Meed is lacking in positive qualities solely because she is gendered feminine, but also because she is a female whose weak nature has been corrupted and she now refuses to repent. She has taken a masculine role, although she is incapable of rightfully filling it. Instead of being controlled by men, as money and women should be, she attempts to control them. In opposition to her, "measurable hire" and trade are ideal examples of the proper use of money and the proper place for women: they are well under the control of reasonable men.

In spite of Meed's various tactics to keep her prominence in the king's court, she is ultimately doomed to submission and silence. It rends the fabric of society when a woman dominates a man or men, and right order can only be restored by masculine control. The most clear and ironic statement of this is Conscience's assertion that Leaute should be master over Meed. Leaute is both "law," something women are often said to be without, and a masculine allegorical figure. Earlier in the poem, his relationship to Meed is described by Dame Holy Church:

> "That is Mede the mayde," quod she, "hath noyed me ful ofte,
> And ylakked my lemman that Leautee is hoten,
> And bilowen h[ym] to lordes that lawes han to kepe." (2.20–22)

> [That is Meed the maid who has harmed me very often
> And maligned my lover—Lewte is his name—
> And has told lords who enforce laws lies about him.]
> (2.20–22; p. 15)

Meed has apparently slandered Leaute and defied law. Conscience wishes to reverse the situation. Law will control Meed, male will have power over female, and the kingdom will be set to rights. Conscience proclaims:

> Shal na moore Mede be maister as she is nouthe,
> Ac love and lowenesse and leautee togideres—
> Thise shul ben maistres on moolde [trewe men] to save.
> And whoso trespaseth ayein truthe or taketh ayein his wille,
> Leaute shal don hym lawe, and no lif ellis. (3.290–4)

> [Meed shall no more be master on earth,
> But Love and Lowliness and Lewte together,
> These shall be governors on this ground to guard true men,
> And whoever trespasses against Truth and takes things against his
> will
> No living man but Lewte shall apply the law to him.]
> (3.290–4; p. 31)

Meed's feminine deviance must be controlled by masculine laws, as represented by Leaute, and there are to be no exceptions.

Meed is gendered feminine not because she is completely evil but because she must be controlled. Even her femininity is not entirely without positive potential. Theology himself calls her "muliere, a maiden of goode" (2.132). The ideal state of such a feminine personification is that represented by "measurable hire." She is controlled by men and hence free from wrong. She is no better than morally neutral herself, but in her case, the proper behavior of male guardians has allowed her to become a positive influence on society, while Meed uncontrolled, like the fleshy wife of the Samaritan's analogy, can only cause sin and wrong.

Langland, as a member of medieval English society, was constantly exposed to various ideas which ranged from fairly liberal to misogynistic. The mainstream misogyny was the subject of many books and treatises and was acted out all around him. The pervasiveness of this aspect of his culture obviously did not completely control his thought. However, in spite of Langland's liberal ideas about the sacramentality of marriage, and the possibility for good and even ideal wives, his poem is not free from the misogynistic mainstream ideology. The dominant ideology in which women represent the sinfulness of man is revealed in the Samaritan's analogy and fuels the lengthy and complex Meed episode. Terry Eagleton analyzes this process:

> The author finds himself forced to reveal the limits of the ideology within which he writes. He is forced to reveal its gaps and silences, what it is unable to articulate. Because a text contains these gaps and silences, it is always *incomplete*. Far from constituting a rounded, coherent whole, it displays a conflict and contradiction of meanings.[23]

The presence of the dominant misogynistic ideology does not stop Langland from seeking or expressing new or even counter-hegemonic ideas. However, the dominant ideology shows its strength by setting the "limits . . . within which he writes." The trope of woman as evil mirror of the male self is so common, so much a part of everyday thought and expression, that even a possibly profeminine writer like Langland can take it for granted and not challenge it. The result is that, along with his emergent ideas, Langland perpetuates the dominant ideology, in spite of the deep contradictions between the two.

R. Howard Bloch reveals that misogyny is "found potentially in almost any [medieval] work," and he adds, "including those that are overwhelmingly profeminine like *Aucassin et Nicolette*," and he wonders if it could be ascribed to any sort of "authorial intention."[24] Bloch hints at the idea that it may not be ascribable to intention at all. The question goes beyond intent or even a totalizing term like *misogyny*. A medieval "feminist" text can combine—and in many ways, must combine—the nearly inescapable antifeminine rhetoric with equally current ideas about feminine empowerment. The newer, or less hegemonic, ideas are embedded in the old and carry with them the contradictions of contemporary and residual forms. New ideas grow out of old and cannot appear, fully matured, as if in a vacuum. Profeminine ideas are clearly vocalized in the poem, and antifeminine stereotypes can be overturned. The traditional, antifeminine ideology is most often voiced in a lower key and may need to be analyzed before it becomes apparent. The poem expresses emergent feminist ideas, but many of the underlying assumptions, vital in the creation of plot and characters, are unconsciously controlled by traditional ideology. This conflict gives rise to the contradictions within the text and causes it to send a mixed and multivalent message concerning women and wives.

NOTES

I would like to thank Larry Clopper and Tess Tavormina for ideas and discussions that helped to improve and expand this paper.

1. R. Howard Bloch, *Medieval Misogyny and the Invention of Western Romantic Love* (Chicago: Univ. of Chicago Press, 1991), 65–92.

2. R. Howard Bloch, "Medieval Misogyny," *Representations* 20 (1987): 3.

3. Barbara D. Palmer, "'To Speke of Wo that Is in Mariage': The Marital Arts in Medieval Literature," *Human Sexuality in the Middle Ages and Renaissance*, ed. Douglas Radcliff-Umstead (Pittsburgh: Univ. of Pittsburgh Publications on the Middle Ages and Renaissance, 1978), 4.

4. Beatrice Gottlieb, *The Family in the Western World from the Black Death to the Industrial Age* (New York: Oxford Univ. Press, 1993), 69.

5. Christopher N.L. Brooke, *The Medieval Idea of Marriage* (Oxford: Oxford Univ. Press, 1989), 132.

6. William Langland, *The Vision of Piers Plowman*, ed. A.V.C. Schmidt (London: J.M. Dent and Sons Ltd., 1991), 9.108–112. All quotations from and references to *Piers Plowman* will be taken from this edition. All modern translations of William Langland are from *Will's Vision of Piers Plowman*, trans. E. Talbot Donaldson, ed. Elizabeth D. Kirk and Judith Anderson (New York: W.W. Norton and Company, 1990).

7. Katharina M. Wilson and Elizabeth Makowski, *"Wykked Wyves" and the Woes of Marriage: Misogamous Literature from Juvenal to Chaucer* (Albany: State Univ. of New York Press, 1990), 120.

8. M. Teresa Tavormina emphasizes the importance of marriage as the first human state created by God. She finds evidence of this in a reading of Liberum Arbitrium's C-text discussion of marriage, widowhood, and virginity in terms of the Trinity, and I believe this reference to marriage as what God made "first" reinforces her reading. "'Bothe Two Ben Gode': Marriage and Virginity in *Piers Plowman* C. 18.68–100," *Journal of English and Germanic Philology* 81 (July 1982): 320–30.

9. M. Teresa Tavormina, "Kindly Similitude: Langland's Matrimonial Trinity," *Modern Philology* 80 (Nov. 1982): 122.

10. In fact, as M.T. Tavormina points out in "Kindly Similitude," Langland elevates marriage to an even higher position, using it as a tool to explain the complexities of the Trinity in the C-text. Tavormina emphasizes Langland's appreciation of the "love that operates in both the Trinity and matrimony," 28.

11. Bloch, *Medieval Misogyny,* 17–22.

12. Britton J. Harwood, "Dame Study and the Place of Orality in *Piers Plowman*," *ELH* 57 (1990): 9–13.

13. Sharon Farmer, "Persuasive Voices: Clerical Images of Medieval Wives," *Speculum* 61 (1986): 543.

14. Barbara Hanawalt, *The Ties That Bound: Peasant Families in Medieval England* (New York: Oxford Univ. Press, 1986), 219.

15. Patience says of the patient poor:

Forthi al poore that pacient is, may [asken and cleymen],
After hir endynge here, heveneriche blisse. (14.259–60)

16. Carole R. Fontaine, "Proverbs," *The Women's Bible Commentary,* ed. Carol A. Newsom and Sharon H. Ringe (London: SPCK, 1992), 551

17. Jerome's *Libri adversus Jovinaianum duo,* trans. and excerpted in Wilson and Makowski, 48.

18. For similar ideas in modern feminist thought, see Simone de Beauvoir, *The Second Sex,* trans. and ed. H.M. Parshley (New York: Vintage Books, 1974), 74, 78, 145, 157, 210, 281–85. Also Luce Irigaray, *This Sex Which Is Not One,* trans. Catherine Porter with Carolyn Burke (Ithaca: Cornell Univ. Press, 1985), 70–74, 84–85.

19. Joan M. Ferrante, *Woman as Image in Medieval Literature from the Twelfth Century to Dante* (New York: Columbia Univ. Press, 1975), 42.

20. Helen Cooper, "Gender and Personification in *Piers Plowman*," *The Yearbook of Langland Studies* 5 (1991): 33.

21. Another reading of Meed's moral state is Roger Eaton's thesis that Meed is completely corrupt. He admits that "Lady Meed is ambiguous at first." I argue that the initially ambiguous Meed gradually becomes corrupt. See Roger Eaton, "Langland's Malleable Lady Meed," *Costerus* 80 (1991): 119–41.

22. Robert Adams emphasizes the similarity of meaning of the English word *mede* and the Latin *merces. Merces* has many of the negative connotations of *mede. Merces,* or the "mesurable hire" of the B-text, has little intrinsic superiority to *mede.* The difference is in the behavior of the designated personifications as presented by Langland rather than in replacing one stereotypical negative word with a more positive synonym. See Robert Adams, "Mede and Mercede: The Evolution of Economics of Grace in the *Piers Plowman* B and C Versions," *Medieval English Studies Presented to George Kane,* ed. Edward Donald Kennedy, Ronald Waldron, and Joseph S. Wittig (Wolfeboro, N.H.: D.S. Brewer, 1988), 217–32.

23. Terry Eagleton, *Marxism and Literary Criticism* (Berkeley: Univ. of California Press, 1976): 34–35.

24. Bloch, *Medieval Misogyny,* 5.

II. Children

WOMEN AND CHILDBEARING IN MEDIEVAL FLORENCE

Louis Haas

According to the Florentine humanist and historian Francesco Guicciardini, the desire to have children was natural. Alessandra Strozzi bore eight children between 1426 and 1436; in his *ricordanze*,[1] the diarylike account books of the merchant elite, Ugolino Martelli listed the births of his fourteen children between 1435 and 1456; Luca Landucci and his wife had twelve children; Gregorio Dati recorded that he was one of seventeen children; Catherine of Siena's mother had twenty-five children; Antonia Masi bore thirty-six children. Examples such as these could be multiplied endlessly, but they do show how prolific the merchant elite of Florence and Tuscany was. These couples wanted swarms of children, and modern historians have long recognized that premodern Tuscany teemed with children. In 1427, for instance, the richest 1,000 households contained 873 children; the poorest thousand, only 648. In Florence wealth and the number of children were positively correlated at a significant level: in general, the higher one's tax assessment, the more children living in the household. Thus, only the wealthier segment of Tuscany's population could fulfill the desire to have many children. The main thing Francesco Datini, the fantastically wealthy merchant of Prato, required from his wife Margherita was a house filled with children. She wanted this, too. Having children was a shared desire and activity for many elite Tuscan couples, and most had children because they wanted them and loved them. Benvenuto Cellini's mother and father spent eighteen long years wanting and trying to have children but failing, until they had his older sister in 1498.[2]

Certainly in as patriarchal a society as Florence, a major reason for having male children was to provide descendants for the family and heirs to the property. Sons also carried the family name into the future. Yet Alessandra Strozzi constantly urged her sons to marry and have children because she wanted descendants not so much for her husband's lineage as for the particular family she and her husband, Filippo, had built. Men likewise saw descendants as a way to perpetuate themselves. One of the goals of marriage, according to the humanist and artist Leon Battista Alberti, was to perpetuate the husband through his children. At his son's marriage, Giovanni Chellini prayed for various benefits for his son, including children to increase "my house and me."[3] On the other hand, women certainly saw daughters as a way to perpetuate themselves.

In this patriarchal society men valued sons over daughters, though not excessively, and were disappointed, though not excessively, over the birth of girls. A particular source of that disappointment was dowry inflation, a problem that Dante had early on recognized to be affecting families, particularly fathers. Margherita Datini consoled a friend who had just given birth to another girl by noting that the father loved his daughters as much as his sons. But she then added that having a boy would be nice, since it perpetuated the family name. On the other hand, the writers of ricordanze consistently recorded that they wished friends and family members would have many children, both male and female.[4]

Nevertheless, some disappointment in the birth of daughters should be expected in Florentine society, since the birth of a male heir had much riding upon it. Considering the demographic agonies of the premodern era, Florentines quite rightly feared for their lineage's survival. Infant mortality rates were high, approaching 30 percent at times, and Florentines recognized this. In addition, periodic passes of the Black Death could eliminate a family within a few short weeks, if not days, and Florentines feared this. Dante had worried about Florence's survival if families did not have enough children. In fact, Florentines had many children as one way to avoid the awful demographic consequences of the premodern era.[5]

Florentines possessed other reasons for having children. Certainly having them was viewed as a civic duty. According to the humanist Matteo Palmieri, children increased the population and provided citizens for the state. Florentine tax policy even provided exemptions (200 florins in 1427) for each child in the household, in an attempt to promote a larger population. Having children was also a Christian duty. A woman who became pregnant acquired a soul for Christ, so Niccolò Machiavelli observed. According to Giovanni Dominici, parents made children in the flesh and spiritually in the faith. From this stemmed the attitude that children were a loan from God to the parents, and many ricordanze writers specifically stated this. Having children also helped gain salvation for one's soul, since children had a duty to pray for their parents after death, and many Florentine sons wrote prayers to God in the ricordanze, asking for forgiveness for their fathers and mothers.[6]

Florentines perceived having children, and especially many children, as an accomplishment of sorts, even a source of honor. Alberti thought that excellent children were proof of a father's diligence and honored him. Lapo Mazzei was told he should love and honor his wife because she had given him so many children. In fact, in their announcements of the death of their wives, writers of ricordanze consistently made sure to list the number of children they had had. They did the same for their daughters and even daughters-in-law.[7] At his mother's death on 20 June 1522, Piero Bonacorso noted that among her accomplishments, or legacies ("ristiano doppo lei"), were her children, including "io Piero."[8] Moreover, in noting the deaths of their male relatives, particularly those of their fathers, ricordanze writers made sure to list the number of children the deceased had had.

This accounting was not just a statement of fact but an evaluation of worth. Writers of ricordanze also recorded who had died "sanza figliuoli." Giovanni Morelli noted that before the death of her husband in 1384, his sister Sandra had one child but no more. Again, this is more than just a statement of fact; in this instance it is almost an insult, as if she had somehow failed. Undoubtedly, society put considerable pressure on couples, especially wives, to have children. At times, Francesco and Margherita Datini's friends and family criticized them and even made fun of them because they had not had any children together.[9] Having children was a source of accomplishment; and Florentines had pride in their children and in the number of them that they had. In his ricordanze Valorino Curianni identified himself first as the son of his father, Lapo, and then as a man who had two children, a boy and a girl, with a wife who was pregnant.[10] No wonder neighborhood gossip networks buzzed with information about who was pregnant and who had given birth. Margherita Datini's friends and relatives constantly communicated news of her impending pregnancies, none of which ever materialized. Despite her desire for children, she never conceived, and this fact exasperated her.[11]

Florentine society possessed many remedies for childless couples like the Datinis and many solutions for those who just wanted to increase their fertility. Some writers prescribed the proper time for intercourse in order to have children. Alberti, for instance, advised late May, at night, and specifically the hour after supper as the best time for procreation.[12] Most of this advice, however, was directed at women, which implies that men thought women had more control over the process of conception than they had.

The most visible remedy was the ritual of a new bride holding a small child in her arms during the wedding ceremony, just as Datini's illegitimate daughter had done during her wedding. When his son Tommaso married

Bartolomea Sacchetti on 2 July 1452, Giovanni Chellini recorded that Gino Capponi's little boy, Tommaso, was placed in her arms during the ceremony. The little boy was four months old at the time. Sometimes the new bride was supposed to kiss the child as part of the ritual. Certainly the idea behind this ritual was that close association to the thing desired would lead to it being realized. But the ritual could also become an occasion for display if one chose the small children of important Florentines, and the communal government tried to prevent this by prohibiting the ritual in its 1388 sumptuary statutes.[13]

Many women and men prayed for children. Florentine couples prayed for children before going to bed; others went to sacred sites and prayed for children. St. Margaret of Antioch was a favorite patron saint of childless women who wanted to remedy that condition. Florentine women who wanted to have children visited the picture of the Annunciation at Santissima Annunziata. In Machiavelli's *Mandragola*, a play that revolves around a couple's attempt to conceive a child, a character recalls a neighbor's advice that if a woman hears first mass forty days in a row at Santissima Annunziata, she would become pregnant. Reverence of and worship before an image of the most important birth announcement in history would help women attain and experience the same joy and glory that Mary had at the announcement of the conception of her child. This must have been a powerful ritual belief, since Florentine brides today still leave their wedding bouquets before the painting of the Annunciation at Santissima Annunziata.[14]

Some thought that heavenly powers needed other supernatural aid to ensure pregnancy. Francesca Tecchini, Margherita Datini's sister, told her that many women she knew had become pregnant because they had worn a certain foul-smelling poultice that had writing on it and was made by a certain woman. She told her the poultice cost very little to make and then added that with this and God, the Virgin Mary, and St. John the Baptist, she would have a child.[15] Florence, in fact, was filled with fertility devices. Witches and sorcerers provided women and men with amulets for having children. Niccolò dell'Ammannato told Francesco Datini that his wife knew of a magic belt that, if placed on a woman by a virgin boy after three repetitions of the Lord's Prayer and the Hail Mary, would ensure pregnancy. But he then added that Margherita Datini would have a better chance of getting pregnant if she fed three beggars on three successive Fridays.[16] Thus Christian and other supernatural beliefs existed side by side and even intermingled in the attempts to have children.

Figures of the Christ child (the so-called *bambini*), which represented all babies and the most important baby at the same time, and even figures of Mary Magdalene served as fertility devices. These could be made of wax, sugar, plaster, or wood. Again, these must have been powerful tools for fertility, since in Italy today, women still receive dolls at their weddings.[17]

Florentines believed that certain foods aided in fertility; consuming potions made from the mandrake or eating elder leaves supposedly increased fertility. Eating bread stored away on New Year's Day, which in Florence was the day of the Annunciation (25 March), brought fertility. Margherita Datini sent a friend a barrel of Venetian wine, telling her that drinking it would produce boys.[18] As mentioned above, not only did Florence teem with children, but it also buzzed with gossip about having them and how to have them.

Although it is obvious that the biological process of birth itself is female-centered in the mother, the social process or formulation of birth in premodern Florence was likewise female-centered, as well as female-oriented and female-controlled. Unfortunately, we know little about what went on inside the room in which birth occurred, since our writers of ricordanze were kept outside. Renaissance paintings depicting the birth of the Virgin or St. John the Baptist commonly place the expectant father outside the room in which the birth has occurred. Benedetta Carlini, the daughter of Midea and Giuliano Carlini, was born in a difficult birth in 1590. At one point during the labor, the midwife came out and told Giuliano that both mother and daughter were in peril. At that moment he fell to his knees, praying for God to spare their lives. So, even when a mother and child hovered between life and death during birth, the father was kept outside the room itself. Some Florentine homes even had separate bedrooms for husband and wife, where either could retire from the rest of the household or, in the mother's case, for pregnancy and delivery.[19] Most Florentine fathers probably spent the time outside the birthing room perhaps pacing, perhaps sitting, but certainly excluded, waiting for the arrival of their children.

As could be expected, birth at home for the Florentine merchant elite during the late Middle Ages and Renaissance could be a hectic affair, with servants running hither and yon fetching things, with the wife's and husband's friends and relatives circulating about, and with people arriving to assist in the delivery. In fact, there was a special cohort of female birth professionals present at births: midwives, *guardadonne*, and sometimes wet nurses.

Midwives were the most visible of these female birth professionals present at a birth, since they were in charge. More than one midwife could be employed at a time, especially for a difficult birth. How one became a midwife is just as unclear as what actually happened in the female-centered birthing room. Certainly, there was no formal training, and women may have just fallen into the profession by accident. In 1272 the young Margaret of Cortona became a servant to the patrician Moscani family; she soon began to assist at the births of Cortona's patricians, and eventually patrician families specifically singled her out from her colleagues as the midwife to have. They rewarded her not only monetarily but spiritually by having her stand as godmother to the children she had delivered. Moreover, she could always count on taking meals with her patient's family during the birth.[20] In medieval England, medical advice books stated that it was the mother's duty to hire the midwife.[21] Women did this in Florence as well. On 26 May 1490, Tribaldo dei Rossi recorded that his wife, Nanina, paid the midwife for delivering their child three days before. In Florence men also did this, and considering the rigors of premodern birth for women, this is to be expected. Previous service could ensure a repeat performance. Matteo Strozzi recorded that his son Piero and his daughter Andruola both had the same midwife.[22] No doubt, considering how prolific the merchant elite were, a competent and successful midwife in Florence could make an adequate living at this.

Aside from the delivery itself, midwives could and did do other things associated with the birth. As we saw above in the description of Benedetta Carlini's difficult birth, the midwife could be the first person to convey bad news to the father. At Cellini's birth the midwife was the first person to convey the good news to the father, as midwives probably did for most Florentine births. Nevertheless, for an expectant father the appearance of the midwife next to him at any point in the birthing process could provoke all sorts of emotions ranging from fear to joy. In addition, this role of the midwife as conveyer of news highlighted even more how much women were in control of the birth process and how men formed an almost passive audience, not even spectators in the true sense of the word. Midwives, too, might perform a more heartrending task. Agostino Capponi sent the twin daughters of his slave girl, Polonia, to the Innocenti, the Florentine foundlings hospital. The midwife was the one who took them there. In addition, because midwives were so intimately associated with birth, they were often called upon to treat newborns and mothers who had just given birth if and when they became ill.[23]

Another woman, called the *guardadonna*, helped at the birth, yet her duties are not quite as clear as the midwife's, even though she too was a paid specialist. From her title she must have been present at birth specifically for the mother's benefit, since she is listed simply as the woman who looks after the mother during the birth. Her role seems similar to that of the lying-in nurse whom the English aristocracy hired in the eighteenth century, whose duty it was to ease the mother's travail, give medicine, and help the doctor during birth. Apparently some guardadonne in Florence aided the midwife, since writers of ricordanze noted that guardadonne at times helped deliver children. And both midwives and guardadonne were mentioned in the same records as having been present for the same births.[24] Sometimes the guardadonne were retained for a period after the birth, to help the mother recover.

In fact, a guardadonna may have been more a servant than a birth professional such as the midwife. Renaissance paintings of birth consistently show the scene of the mother in bed being tended after the birth by a servant. On 31 July 1478, Bernardo Machiavelli recorded that the sister of two of his sharecroppers was employed in his house as a servant specifically to tend to his wife and children. He also noted that she had been in the household since the first of the month, when she had originally functioned as a guardadonna. Whatever the guardadonna did in relation to the midwife, they both seemed to have been paid about the same amount for their services. Niccolo Strozzi paid the midwife five lire, five soldi for his son Carlo's birth in 1471. The guardadonna received the same amount.[25]

Male physicians rarely attended births; and in the cases in which a physician was called, either the child, the mother, or both had died or were in grave peril. Perhaps the doctor was the birth professional of last resort, only used when things were going badly, though he was not fully trusted. Otherwise, things were left to the midwife and guardadonna, again indicating that in normal situations women controlled the birth process.

Aside from these female birth professionals, other women attended and assisted at births. Boccaccio tells a story of how a lover, one Messer Gentile, arranged the lying-in for his lady by having his mother attend the birth. Mothers of adult children, because of their own experiences of birth, would have been logical attendants in the birthing room. Female servants, too, could aid in birth, not only for their own mistress but also for others. Bernardo Strozzi, for instance, sent his servant girl to at least six different women to help them in their childbirth. Perhaps like Margaret of Cortona, she later became a midwife. Renaissance paintings of the birth of the Virgin or St. John the Baptist, for which there was not as complete a record of who was in attendance as for Christ's birth, all show swarms of women around the mother. While these paintings depict the time just after the child had been born, they certainly hint at the hustle and bustle that was present during labor. In a letter to Francesco Datini on 7 November 1388, a Saturday, Niccolò del Ammannato mentioned that six women had been attending Francesco's maid, who had been in labor since Tuesday.[26]

Female saints were even in attendance. The legend of St. Margaret was read aloud to women in childbirth, especially if the labor was difficult. At times the copy would even be placed on the woman's stomach, where it served literally as medicine. Telling the legend could help the mother identify with St. Margaret (who had been swallowed by a dragon but emerged later unharmed, as one hoped the child would) and thereby concentrate on her own body during labor. This would effect a talking cure in an anthropological sense, in which a ritual communicates with a patient hence helping her. There were other, less spiritual but more practical aids. A 1513 German treatise on midwifery describes a special birthing chair, which the author noted was very popular in Italy. As late as the nineteenth century in England, wine was still used to ease a mother's labor. In fact, she shared it with her friends and relatives who were attending her.[27] In many of the birth paintings of the Renaissance, servants bring wine to the new mother.

Surrounded by female servants, friends, relatives, and the guardadonna, all under the midwife's direction, the mother delivered a child. The guardadonna helped the mother here, soothing and encouraging her. The role of the guardadonna was essential at this point, considering the lack of anesthesia in the premodern world and especially considering the fact that premodern women dreaded the pain of labor and delivery, a dread that many men recognized as well.[28]

After the delivery, the birth professionals had other duties. The midwife washed away the blood from the child, soothed it with salt and honey on its limbs, and then covered it.[29] A prominent feature depicted in Renaissance paintings of birth is a round basin full of water, for the washing of the child. And these paintings usually show this activity: the child is either about to be bathed, is being bathed, or has just been bathed. Elisabetta Cellini's midwife washed and wrapped Benvenuto before taking him to his father.

After the child had been delivered, it was time to comfort and congratulate the new mother. Here is where Renaissance paintings of birth present a bit of colorful exactitude, since this was the moment depicted, right after the birth. Women surround the infant; women tend the mother; women visit the mother and infant. Men, if they are depicted, are placed outside the room. In premodern times, when privacy was at such a premium, especially privacy within the family, a wife did escape from her husband during childbirth.[30]

We must also remember that birth in the premodern era could be a hazardous affair, for either the mother or the child. About 20 percent of all married women's deaths at Florence were attributed to the rigors of childbirth, which may explain something of the relief, joy, and sense of accomplishment seen in the letters that were sent out announcing the new arrival. Catherine de Medici wrote to her cousin, the Florentine grand duke Cosimo I: "My cousin . . . it pleased God to give my lord and me a second son newly born."[31]

Of all the means to show one's joy and appreciation at the birth of a child, the foremost seems to have come in the form of gifts, both to the chid and to the mother and father. In 1375 Francesco Datini had an illegitimate child. His foster mother wrote to him telling him that she gave "a thousand blessings" to the child. Margherita Datini and her circle of female friends (called a *brigata*) would bring gifts of water and linen for their friends' newborns and other gifts for the new mothers. Other Florentine women did the same thing. This activity maintained friendship and group solidarity among these female circles, these *brigate*. Fra Carnevale da Urbino's painting *The Visitation* (fifteenth century) shows a brigata of women trooping off to visit a new mother.[32]

Perhaps the most appropriate present for a new mother was a *desco da parto*. This was a small painted plate depicting weddings, births, or banquets that was a customary childbirth gift, usually given by women to other women. A desco da parto by Masaccio (1427) depicts a gift-giving session with trumpeters heralding the arrival of a number of men carrying gifts and women entering the room where the mother and child lie. One of the men is carrying a desco da parto. Although a desco da parto was the most appropriate gift, cloth and utensils, such as silver forks and spoons, were the most common gifts women gave each other to celebrate a birth. In May 1483, Lisa Guidetti received a cape and four pieces of damask cloth from a female friend for the birth of her son Giovanni Battista. In February 1489, when she delivered another son, Rinieri, four women, one of whom was a cousin, gave her gifts such as a dozen forks. One of the women also gave her marzipan candy.[33]

Sometimes present at the birth was another female professional, the wet nurse or *balia*, whose presence is often depicted in Renaissance paintings of birth. Wet nurses were the primary child care providers for many Florentine children during the first years of their life and sometimes commenced their activity from the moment of birth. Usually, however, families waited some time before sending the children off to the wet nurse. One ricordanze writer recorded that his daughter, Clemenza, was born on 20 August 1524 and that on 29 September 1524 she went off to the wet nurse. Paolo Sassetti emphatically stated that his newborn daughter, Lisabetta, remained at home for four days and then went off to the wet nurse.[34] Obviously, her mother nursed her, as did Clemenza's mother, despite most humanists' fears that colostrum was unhealthy for a child. Cristofano Guidini's wife consistently breastfed her children two weeks to two months before turning them over to a wet nurse. The humanist commentator on the family, Francesco da Barberino, even considered that the mother would temporarily breastfeed her own child before sending it out to the wet nurse. But at some point, most children of the merchant elite eventually went out to the suburbs or country for their stay with the wet nurse.[35]

Some modern historians have concluded that fathers usually decided the wet nursing arrangements and contracts by themselves, without any input from their wives. This conclusion may just reflect the bias of the ricordanze, since they are male records and the husband usually handed over the wet nurse's salary. My sense from reading the ricordanze is that Florentine parents usually made joint decisions. Moreover, we get hints from the ricordanze that both parents were involved in the choice of a wet nurse. On 12 March 1411, Cambio Petrucci and his wife invited a prospective wet nurse to their house for an inspection because both of them wanted to see her and evaluate the quality of her milk. Marco Parenti recorded that his wife arranged a wet-nursing contract with the wet nurse. The *balio* Piero Puro noted that he received children from both fathers and mothers. Tommaso Guidetti recorded that his wife made trips to the village where their son was at wet nurse, to pay the balia. In fact, his wife handled all the dealings with the wet nurse for this child. Alessandra Strozzi handled some of her children's wet-nursing payments, though in most of these cases, the wet nurse came to her.[36] Wet-nursing was very much women's business.

Because of the rigors of birth, most premodern mothers did not participate in the baptismal ceremony for their children, which followed within three days after the birth, sometimes just hours after the birth. And if the rigors of birth were not cause enough, their adherence to the Mosaic law of ritual female impurity after a birth would have kept most mothers from participating in the baptismal ceremony. Another woman (such as a servant, the wet nurse, a godmother, a relative, or a family friend) would carry the child to and from the baptistery. An idiom for becoming a godparent highlights the importance of touching during the baptismal ceremony. Giovanni Morelli wrote that at the baptism of his second son, "Telda, my mother, and Catellana, Morello's wife, held him at baptism (*tennelo a battesimo*)."[37]

Many of the godmothers whom Morelli listed for his children and his relatives' children had one thing in common. All had been present at the birth as midwives, guardadonne, or companions of the new mother. Women who aided in the birth of a child would have been obvious choices for this honor. Wet nurses, too, became godmothers. Like choosing a midwife or guardadonna as godmother, perhaps this represented one way to reward people who had aided the family. Moreover, since wet-nursing was a hazardous affair for the child, perhaps this was one way to ensure the safety of the child, by binding the nurse closer to the child and family through baptismal kinship. Sometimes the wet nurse for another child became a godmother to the new child, again perhaps as a gesture of reward.[38] In addition, since godparenthood was a way to solidify bonds of friendship, choosing godmothers from those women who had been present at the birth may have been the mother's way of maintaining her *brigate*.

Birth in premodern Florence, if nothing else, was an occasion for a significant demonstration of female solidarity. It was female-centered, female-oriented, and female-controlled. A newborn child was enveloped within many layers of women: First, obviously, the mother; second, the birth professionals (midwives and guardadonne) and attendants, such as female servants; third, the mother's friends and relatives, who brought gifts for the child and the mother and were the first to welcome the child and honor the mother publicly; fourth, the wet nurse, the primary child care provider for the newborn; fifth, the godmother, the newborn's spiritual protector. Women *were* and *made* the house in premodern Florence.

NOTES

1. During the latter half of the thirteenth century, Florentine businessmen began to keep secret records of their debits and credits. Over the course of time, these records began to include household expenses as well. Also over the course of time, these businessmen began to elaborate on the reasons for these business and household expenses in their secret account books. Moreover, these businessmen began to record other details about the family, such as their lineage and other particulars of family history: marriages, births, and deaths. These secret account books are the *ricordanze*, which represent, by the fourteenth century, the first European diaries. They are marvelous sources for historians to investigate the economic and social history of late medieval and Renaissance Florence.

2. Francesco Guicciardini, *Maxims and Reflections (Ricordi)*, trans. Mario Domandi, (New York, Harper & Row, 1965) 112; David Herlihy, "Santa Caterina and San Bernardino: Their Teachings on the Family," in *Atti del simpozio internazionale Cateriniana-Bernardiniano Siena, 17–20 Aprile 1980*, ed. Domenio Maffei and Paolo Nardi (Siena: Accademia Senese delgi Intronati, 1982), 923; Charles de la Roncière, "Tuscan Notables on the Eve of the Renaissance," in *Revelations of the Medieval World*, ed. Georges Duby and trans. Arthur Goldhammer, vol. 2 of *A History of Private Life*, ed. Philippe Ariès and Georges Duby (Cambridge, Mass.: Belknap, 1988), 169; Christiane Klapisch-Zuber, *Women, Family and Ritual in Renaissance Italy* (Chicago: Univ. of Chicago Press, 1985), 17, 117; Iris Origo, *The Merchant of Prato: Francesco di Marco Datini 1335–1410* (New York: Knopf, 1957), 168; David Herlihy, *The Family in Renaissance Italy* (St. Louis: Forum Press, 1974), 7; idem, "Deaths, Marriage, Births, and the Tuscan Economy," in *Population Patterns in the Past*, ed. R.D. Lee (New York: Academic Press, 1977), 147; Christiane Klapisch,

"Household and Family in Tuscany in 1427," in *Household and Family in Past Time*, ed. Peter Laslett and Richard Wall (Cambridge: Cambridge Univ. Press, 1972), 274; David Herlihy and Christiane Klapisch-Zuber, *Tuscans and Their Families: A Study of the Catasto of 1427* (New Haven: Yale Univ. Press, 1985), 241–45, 253, 287; David Herlihy, "Medieval Children," in *Essays on Medieval Civilization: The Walter Prescott Webb Memorial Lecture XII*, ed. Bede Karl Lackner and Kenneth Day Philip (Austin: Univ. of Texas Press, 1978), 124; Benvenuto Cellini, *Autobiography*, trans. George Bull (Baltimore: Penguin Books, 1956), 19.

3. Klapisch-Zuber, x; Leon Battista Alberti, *The Family in Renaissance Florence: I Libri della Famiglia*, trans. Renée Neu Watkins (Columbia, S.C.: Univ. of South Carolina Press, 1969), 115; Maria Teresa Sillano, ed., *Le ricordanze di Giovanni Chellini da San Miniato: medico, mercante, e umanista (1425–1457)* (Milan: F. Angeli, 1984), 187.

4. James Bruce Ross, "The Middle Class Child in Urban Italy, Fourteenth to Early Sixteenth Century," in *History of Childhood*, ed. Lloyd deMause (New York: Harper Row, 1975), 206; Margaret L. King, *Women of the Renaissance* (Chicago: Univ. of Chicago Press, 1991), 24–25; Giovanni di Pagolo Morelli, *Ricordi*, ed. Vittore Branca (Firenze, F. Le Monnier, 1969), 542; Alessandro Perossa, ed., *Giovanni Rucellai ed il suo Zibaldone* (London: Warburg Institute, 1960), 63–64.

5. King, 2.

6. Philip Gavitt, *Charity and Children in Renaissance Florence: The Ospedale degli Innocenti, 1410–1536* (Ann Arbor: Univ. of Michigan Press, 1990), 24, 33, 285; Herlihy and Klapisch-Zuber, 10; Niccolò Machiavelli, *Mandragola* (Prospect Heights, Ill.: Waveland Press, 1981), 35.

7. Origo, 25, 230; Alberti, 58.

8. Archivio di Stato, Florence (hereinafter, ASF), Acquisti e Doni, 20, fol. 76v.

9. Morelli, 141–42, 184–85; Origo, 166, 232.

10. ASF, Manoscritti, 77, fol. 22r.

11. Origo, 166, 168–89.

12. Alberti, 121.

13. Sillano, 185, 187; Klapisch-Zuber, 319; Origo, 204.

14. De la Roncière, 214; David Herlihy, "Tuscan Names, 1200–1530," *Renaissance Quarterly* 41 (1988): 577; Klapisch-Zuber, 318; Machiavelli, 28; Simone Baigellini, "Seven Merchants, One Dante—and an Angel," *Florenscape: The News Magazine of Florence,* 7 March 1987, 11.

15. Origo, 167.

16. Gene Brucker, *The Society of Renaissance Florence: A Documentary Study* (New York: Harper & Row, 1971), 267; Origo, 167.

17. Klapisch-Zuber, 317–20.

18. Machiavelli, 22, 25; Origo, 165–66; Ross, 206.

19. Judith C. Brown, *Immodest Acts: The Life of a Lesbian Nun in Renaissance Italy* (Oxford: Oxford Univ. Press, 1986), 21; de la Roncière, 217–18.

20. Rudolph M. Bell, *Holy Anorexia* (Chicago: Univ. of Chicago Press, 1985), 95, 98.

21. Nicholas Orme, *From Childhood to Chivalry* (London: Methuen, 1984), 8.

22. Biblioteca Nazionale Centrale di Firenze (hereinafter, BNF), Fondo Nazionale, 2, 2, 357, fol. 59r; ASF, Carte Strozziane, 5, 11, fols. 20v, 119v.

23. Iris Origo, "The Domestic Enemy: Eastern Slaves in Tuscany in the Fourteenth and Fifteenth Centuries," *Speculum* 30 (1955): 347; Peter Burke, *The Historical Anthropology of Early Modern Italy: Essays on Perception and Communication* (Cambridge: Cambridge Univ. Press, 1987), 208–9.

24. Morelli, 337; Judith Schneid Lewis, *In the Family Way: Childbearing in the British Aristocracy 1760–1860* (New Brunswick, N.J.: Rutgers Univ. Press, 1986), 163–4; BNF, Fondo Nazionale, 2, 2, 357, fol. 111r; ASF, Carte Strozziane, 5, 11, fol. 20v.

25. Bernardo Machiavelli, *Libro di Ricordi*, ed. Cesare Olschki (Firenze: F. Le Monnier, 1954), 75–6; ASF, CS, 4, 71, fols. 23v, 24r.

26. *Decameron*, X:4; Klapisch-Zuber, 175; Origo, *Merchant of Prato*, 339.

27. Burke, 211; Steven Ozment, *When Fathers Ruled: Family Life in Reformation Europe* (Cambridge, Mass.: Harvard Univ. Press, 1983), 108; Lewis, 193.

28. King, 4.

29. Lewis, 193.

30. Madelaine Jeay, "Sexuality and Family in Fifteenth-Century France," *Journal of Family History* 4 (1979): 337.

31. Herlihy and Klapisch-Zuber, 277; ASF, Carte Strozziane, 1, 10, fol. 243.

32. Origo, *Merchant of Prato*, 25, 166, 196.

33. Ibid., 252; de la Roncière, 248; Klapisch-Zuber, 238; ASF, Carte Strozziane, 4, 418, fols. 8v, 11v.

34. ASF, Acquisti e Doni, 21, fol. 6r; ASF, Carte Strozziane, 2, 4, fol. 24v.

35. Ross, 185, 187; Klapisch-Zuber, 144.

36. Klapisch-Zuber, 140–43; ASF, Carte Strozziane, 2, 10, fol. 10v; Elaine G. Rosenthal, "The Position of Women in Renaissance Florence: Neither Autonomy nor Subjection," in *Florence and Italy: Renaissance Studies in Honor of Nicolai Rubinstein*, ed. Peter Denley and Caroline Elam (London: Westfield College, Univ. of London, Committee for Medieval Studies, 1988), 376–77; ASF, Carte Strozziane, 4, 418, fols. 33r, 35r; ASF, Carte Strozziane, 5, 11, fols. 19v, 38v, 63v, 88v, 120v, 131v, 146v–147r, 148v, 157v.

37. Morelli, 361.

38. Morelli, 199, 337, 359, 380, 452; Klapisch-Zuber, 132–64.

SUFFERING AND SURVIVAL IN MEDIEVAL ENGLISH CHILDBIRTH[1]

Fiona Harris Stoertz

> The medieval Christians saw in childbirth the result of a carnal sin
> to be expiated in pain as defined in Genesis 3.16. Accordingly, the
> treatment given the child-bearing woman was vastly worse than the
> mere neglect among the primitive peoples. . . . During medieval times
> the mortality for both the child and the mother rose to a point never
> reached before. This rise of mortality was in part the consequence of
> indifference to the suffering of women. It was due also to the cultural
> backwardness of the civilization and the low value placed on life. . . .
> These were the "ages of faith," a period characterized as much by the
> filth of the people as by the fervor and asceticism of their religion;
> consequently nothing was done to overcome the enormous mortal-
> ity of the mother and of the child at birth. No greater crimes were
> ever committed in the name of civilization, religious faith, and smug
> ignorance than the sacrifice of the lives of countless mothers and chil-
> dren in the first fifteen centuries after Christ among civilized man-
> kind.[2]

The preceding quotation, extracted from a twentieth-century history of medicine, is an extreme statement of the widely held belief that the Middle Ages
had little or no concern for the sufferings of women in childbed.[3] It is unde-
niable that suffering was expected in medieval childbirth and that the mortality of mother and child was high. The author of *Hali Meidenhad*, a thirteenth-century homily, warning young girls away from marriage, described
in detail the torments and indignities of childbirth.

> Look what joy arises thereafter in the bearing of children, when the
> offspring in you awakens and grows. . . . Your rosy face shall become
> lean and green as grass. Your eyes shall become dusky and underneath

pale, and from the giddiness of your brain, your head aches. Within your belly, your swelling uterus bursts forth like a water bag. Your bowels hurt, pains are in your flanks, and always abundant in your loins, heaviness is in every limb. Your chest is burdened with your two breasts and the milk streams that trickle from you. All withers; your beauty is overthrown. Your mouth is bitter and everything you chew nauseous, and whatever your stomach disdainfully receives it, with dislike, throws it up again. . . . Ah wretch! The anxiety about the torment of labor deprives you of nightly sleep. When it then comes to it, there is the sorrowful anguish, the strong and stinking pains, the comfortless evil, the pain upon pain, the wandering lamentation.[4]

Among the reasons given to children for honoring their parents was the agony and danger that their mothers underwent in pregnancy and labor.[5] Cautious women, feeling the pangs of labor upon them, attended mass to ensure the safety of their immortal souls lest they should die in childbed. Church councils ordered midwives of the twelfth and thirteenth centuries to be prepared to baptize dying infants—even if they had to cut them from the womb of the dead mother to do so.[6]

Some authors, while recognizing the suffering and danger of women in childbirth, found positive implications in women's pain beyond the salvific benefits outlined in Paul's first letter to Timothy 2.15. Bartholomaeus Anglicus, a thirteenth-century encyclopedist, made the following suggestion:

Mothers have nausea and vomiting and are heavy and can not work. In labor, they are compelled to cry and are easily killed, especially young women with small and narrow members. The more woe and sorrow a woman has in childbirth, the more she loves the child when he is born.[7]

Nevertheless, Bartholomaeus did not believe that women should be made to suffer unnecessarily to promote maternal love. He later comments that a midwife's job is to help a woman give birth with less "woo and sorwe."[8]

Although suffering might be expected and even justified in theological or emotional terms, it is false to portray medieval women in childbirth as victims whose sufferings were meaningless to society, or as baby machines, easily replaced should they die in childbed. On the contrary, medieval people exhibited considerable concern for the pain and peril of women in childbirth and made serious efforts to lessen their physical and emotional suffering and ensure their survival, even at the expense of a child.[9]

Family, friends, and medical attendants offered emotional and practical aid for women's problems in the form of herbal remedies, charms, rituals, invocations of saints, and physical manipulation. Such remedies, often condemned by modern scholars as useless superstitions standing in the path of real medical advances, were intended to help women and, in fact, according to anthropological understandings of ritual and group behavior, probably did help women. It is anachronistic and unreasonable to condemn medieval people because they lacked the scientific advances in obstetrics and gynecology of the nineteenth and twentieth centuries. Scholars must look at the measures medieval people took to help women within the context of medieval society and medieval knowledge.

In this essay, I will examine the treatment of English women in childbirth from the Anglo-Saxon period to the late Middle Ages. I will argue that a concern for women's suffering and survival in childbirth is evidenced both by the many remedies proposed for obstetrical problems and by the role and identity of care givers who assisted at births. The most important sources for this study are saints' lives, miracle stories, and medical collections. The information in all these sources is to some extent atypical. Nevertheless, when examined together, they can help us to understand better the treatment of women in childbirth throughout the Middle Ages.

Saints' lives are accounts of the lives of medieval men and women who were recognized as possessing an extra measure of God's grace.[10] One of the marks of such sanctity was the holy person's ability to perform miracles both before and especially after his or her death; thus collections of miracles were appended to biographies of saints.[11] In the Anglo-Saxon period, such collections were small and few and far between, but beginning in the twelfth century, with the development of formal Papal canonization proceedings for which verified miracles were required, enormous collections, including the accounts of many witnesses, were compiled.[12]

Lives sometimes include accounts of the birth of the holy person, and many miracles involve childbirth. Although such information is often very detailed, and thus useful to a historian of childbirth, it must be approached with caution. The authors were usually monks who, in spite of the medical function of monasteries as infirmaries in the early Middle Ages, probably had no practical experience of birth. Their goal was illustration of the holiness of their subject rather than strict historical accuracy. Details of miracle stories may have been affected by their purpose of illustrating the power of the saint—thus witnesses and writers probably exaggerated the plight of some women to enhance the reputation of both the saint and themselves. Accounts of births often reflect biblical miracles or popular religious belief.

For example, holy flame, akin to Moses' burning bush, might accompany the birth of a saint.[13] Even if miracles were accurately reported and recorded, by their nature miracle stories dealt with unusual circumstances. People called upon the saints when things went wrong and medical aid was unsuccessful. Thus we do not receive a picture of a normal childbirth. Moreover, miracle stories are inherently biased toward my argument. The very act of invoking a saint in obstetrical and gynecological matters suggests concern for women's suffering and survival.

Medical works also show only positive attempts to help women. English medical texts, many of which contain suggestions for helping women in childbirth, survive from the ninth or tenth century onward in both Latin and vernacular forms, becoming increasingly plentiful toward the end of the Middle Ages.[14] Numerous remedies for a variety of obstetrical problems survive even from the Anglo-Saxon period, when medical texts were scarce.[15] Many more texts, including some devoted to female ailments, are available from the twelfth and thirteenth centuries, when many Latin adaptations and translations of classical sources were produced and compendia of medicine were written.[16] These texts, as well as new treatises, were widely transmitted in a remarkable explosion of vernacular translations in the fourteenth and fifteenth centuries.[17]

It has been claimed by historians that obstetrics and gynecology underwent a tremendous improvement in the twelfth and thirteenth centuries due to the influx of Greek medical knowledge in Arabic translations and the production of scholastic compendia of medicine by university-educated physicians.[18] This view should be accepted with caution, since the compilers of Anglo-Saxon medical works themselves borrowed heavily from classical sources.[19] In fact, most obstetrical advice changed very little. Many Old English herbal remedies and charms relating to women's problems continued to be recommended throughout the Middle Ages. Nevertheless, substantial texts devoted to women's health problems were adapted, translated, and written in the High and Late Middle Ages, appearing in England with compendia or on their own. Some included suggestions for problems ignored by early medieval texts (such as unnatural presentations, uterine prolapse, and tears of the peritoneum) in addition to many of the standard herbal or magical remedies.[20] In this respect, we do find a real improvement in the advice offered for women's medical care. Moreover, one can argue that the increase in production of these and other medical texts (including obstetrical advice) through the Middle Ages would have promoted some improvement in the level of knowledge about women's health care.

Unfortunately, although we know that compilers, translators, and copiers of medical texts generally considered recipes for female ailments worthy of inclusion, we have no way of knowing how widely such medical recipes were read and used or by whom.[21] Many medical manuscripts were stored in monasteries during the early Middle Ages. Some of these, as well as Arabic works and scholastic compendia, certainly circulated in universities in the High and Late Middle Ages. The popularity of vernacular texts in England throughout the Middle Ages suggests that less learned people may also have had access to written medical works, but the extent of the circulation of such works is unknown. At least one late medieval vernacular translation of a text devoted to female ailments claimed to be written exclusively for a female audience, but other versions of the same text appear to be directed toward a general or even masculine audience.[22] Whether they were used or not, the presence of remedies for female ailments in so many medical texts suggests considerable concern for female suffering.

A skeptic might argue that aids for women in childbirth were included in miracles and medical texts out of concern for children, not women. As I shall demonstrate, however, a careful consideration of the evidence reveals that, while medieval people were clearly interested in the production and survival of children, concern for the mother took first place.

Both Bartholomaeus Anglicus and the author of *Hali Meidenhad*, quoted above, suggested that women suffered greatly in pregnancy, especially during labor. Thus it is not surprising that a large number of medical recipes were concerned with hastening and easing the pain of birth.[23] Herbal remedies were consumed in potions or administered externally through baths, subfumigation (channeling the vapors of herbs into the woman's womb), or by sprigs of herbs tied to the body.[24]

Some medical texts contain only herbal remedies, but others are more varied. Among remedies for women's illnesses, it is in the realm of speeding and easing births that one finds the greatest number of nonherbal recommendations. Juxtaposed with herbal remedies, popular medical texts throughout the Middle Ages sometimes included prayers or incantations to be recited or written and tied to the body. Such charms combined Christian and pagan elements and often were written in a mixture of Latin and the vernacular.[25] One of the most popular, used throughout the Middle Ages to help women in childbirth, listed famous biblical births.

> For a womon þat travels on child: Bind þas writt to hir theghe + in + nomine + Patris + et Filii + et Spiritus Sancti + amen et per virtutem Dei sint medicina mea. Sancta + Maria + peperit + Christum + Sancta Anna + Peperit + Mariam + Sancta + Elizabeth + peperit + Johannem

+ Sancta Cecilia + Peperit + Reonigium [Remigium] + sator + arepo
+ tenet + opera + rotas + Christus + vincit + Christus + regnat +
Christus + imperat + Christus + te + vocat + mundas + te + gaudet +
lex + te + desiderat + Christus + dixit + Lazaro + veni foras + deus
ulcionum + dominus + deus ulcionum + libera famulam tuam +.N.+
dextra domini fecit virtutem + a + g + l + a + alpha + et o + Anna +
peperit + Mariam + Elizabet + precursorem + Maria + dominum +
nostrum + Jhesum + Christum + sine dolore et tristicia. O infans, sive
vivus sive mortuus, exi foras, quia Christus vocat te ad lucem + agios
+ agios + agios + Christus + vincit + Christus + regnat + Christus +
imperat + sanctus + sanctus + sanctus + dominus + deus + omnipotens
+ qui + es et qui eras + et qui venturus es, amen. Blrurcion + blrurun
+ blutanno + bluttiono + Jhesus + nazarenus + rex + judeorum + fili
+ dei + miserere + mei + etc.[26]

Other versions of this charm can be quite brief, but they usually contain the list of biblical names and a request for help in giving birth without excessive pain or danger.

High and later medieval treatises, especially those devoted to women's ailments, sometimes recommended physical manipulation and the application of unguents to ease the birth.[27] One obstetrical and gynecological text even included diagrams and detailed instructions for delivering both ordinary and unnatural presentations.[28] The same text recommended special girdles to promote a successful birth.[29] King Henry III's wife, Eleanor, when her time approached, is said to have sent for the girdle of the Virgin, which was kept at St. Peter's, Westminster.[30] The girdle of St. Gilbert enabled a noblewoman prone to miscarriages to produce two sons successfully.[31] Similarly, stones and crystals were thought to have special powers that could ensure a comfortable pregnancy and successful birth.[32]

Such measures can be related to the invocation of saints during difficult labor. This often involved certain ritual acts (such as measuring the woman with a thread, which would subsequently be used as the wick of a candle to be offered to the saint) and reciprocal promises, usually a visit to the saint's tomb with gifts.[33] Sometimes the use of a relic was all that was necessary.

Elinor, the wife of a certain knight . . . , was in danger three days and more, close to giving birth, but closer to death, so that about her life, nothing at all was hoped. For she was not yet of the age that she ought to become a mother. When her husband, feeling remorseful chiefly because of the danger she had suffered from unseasonable concep-tion, hung a relic of the martyr around her neck; in the blink of an eye, he saved two in one person, for the woman brought forth a boy.[34]

Often many methods might be tried to help a woman in childbirth. Will-iam of Norwich reportedly delivered a woman who had been in labor for fifteen days.[35] In this case, various medicines had been given to the suffer-ing woman without effect before she herself appealed to William.

Although many of my examples so far have exhibited considerable concern for the sufferings of women in childbirth, it must be admitted that a faster and easier birth would help both mother and child. Extended or delayed labor not only causes extra suffering for the mother, but can prove dangerous to both mother and child. According to an Anglo-Saxon expla-nation of the formation of the fetus, a child not born in the tenth month would become a "life destroyer" in the belly and the mother could not be expected to survive.[36] Guy de Chauliac, in the fourteenth century, was of the opinion that should the child not be brought out in due time, the woman would be endangered by the bones of the child exiting through her navel.[37]

Whatever the underlying theory, medieval people were interested in delivering not only live children but also dead ones, so that the lives of moth-ers would not be jeopardized. Recipes (for example, the charm quoted above) often promised to expel either a live or dead child, suggesting that the com-fort and survival of the mother was the focus of such remedies. In fact, over-all, I found more recipes promising to expel a dead fetus, than recipes of-fering to speed a live birth.[38] The expulsion of a dead fetus as well as the alleviation of female suffering, was also a concern in some miracle stories:

> The time for the woman to give birth had passed, however, and she was not able to give birth. Indeed she had conceived a son of whom she was not the future mother but the grave. For fifteen days, the fe-tus did not move in the woman's uterus. . . . She was despaired of. "What are we doing?" asked the father. . . . "We sit despairing and do not remember the martyr of Canterbury," and seizing a string with an invocation of his name [St. Thomas], he measured the dying, pledg-ing to the martyr a tribute of oblations, because she herself was not strong enough to make the vow. Shortly thereafter, she gave birth, but to a lifeless fetus so decocted that it resembled flesh cooking in a hot pot. And the woman escaped, although they believed her interior to have rotted.[39]

In this story, we see the influence of medical theories on popular belief. According to ancient and medieval theories of fetal development, the child was quite literally cooked in the womb during gestation.[40] Not surprisingly, overcooking was harmful or even fatal. The description of the unmoving fetus in the foregoing miracle story also resembles medical discussions about recognizing a dead fetus through its lack of motion, although such a diagnosis might be obvious to any mother.[41]

Concern for women is likewise illustrated by the large number of remedies for retention of the afterbirth.[42] The same herbal remedies that were used to promote birth or expel a dead fetus were often recommended to relieve a woman of the afterbirth. Retention of the afterbirth, like retention of a dead infant, was considered hazardous or even potentially fatal to the mother.[43]

It should be emphasized that there was generally no sense that a mother should ever be sacrificed to save a child. Medical treatises from many periods specifically mention abortifacients,[44] and of course, menstrual regulators and recipes to hasten births or expel a dead child could have been used for this purpose.[45] A treatise on women's health states that "when the woman is feeble and the child cannot come out, then it is better that the child be slain than the mother of the child also die."[46] If a fetus could not be aborted by herbal remedies or magical or religious rites, it would be removed in pieces.[47] We see this vividly illustrated in a miracle of Thomas of Canterbury concerning an unnatural presentation. Part of the arm of the child had come out and the attempts of the midwives to force it back had caused it to swell so that "help was absent for the woman unless the arm of the offspring was cut off."[48] Similarly, although midwives were encouraged to rescue live children from dead mothers so the babies could be baptized before they died, midwives were instructed to perform caesarian sections only on dead women.[49]

Nevertheless, although abortion certainly does seem to have been an available option, at least sometimes indicating concern for women, modern readers should not assume that all remedies designed to purge the womb or regulate the menses were intended to be abortifacients.[50] I have already demonstrated that the retention of a dead fetus or afterbirth was quite rightly considered dangerous. Similarly, since regular menstruation was considered necessary for women's health, inadequate or excessive bleeding could be indicative of a hazardous imbalance. In an age when many foods were only available seasonally, if at all, the diets of many women must have been nutritionally inadequate at times. Menstrual irregularities would have been a very real problem.[51] While some pregnant women might have tried to restore their menses by medical means (remedies were sometimes the same as those recommended to speed birth, expel a fetus or afterbirth, or even cause an abortion), medical authors pointed out quite correctly that the "flowers" must be restored before a woman could conceive.[52] Cures for excessive bleeding were recommended not only for excessive menstruation (which presumably would have hindered conception, besides incurring the obvious dangers of loss of blood), but also for women hemorrhaging after giving birth.[53] Suggestions for postpartum care beyond staunching excessive bleeding are mostly found in texts devoted to female ailments.[54] One popular text explained how to deal with the precipitation of the uterus and a torn peritoneum.[55]

Concern for women and desire and concern for children are not mutually exclusive. Many medical recipes taught the prevention of miscarriage and promotion of conception, issues important to women as well as men.[56] A handful of texts suggest ways to find out the gender of the fetus,[57] and at least two others, drawing on Pliny, explained how to conceive the gender of preference.[58] Miracle stories often described a saint giving a barren couple a child. In many cases, it was the woman who, in her desire for a child, took the initiative. For example:

> A man from Stamford had lived a long time with his wife without having children. It happened that Father Gilbert stopped at their house to spend the night. The discreet lady of the household put her trust in the holiness of the guest she had received, and prepared a place for him on her own couch so that through his merits she might be found worthy to bear a son, as the Shunammite did through Elisha. It turned out just as she believed. For when her husband came home to sleep, he before long fathered a son upon her, and they named him after Father Gilbert.[59]

Similarly, we learn from other stories that miscarriage was a serious problem for many women. One mother miscarried seven times and only produced a son on her eighth attempt through the intervention of St. Thomas of Cantilupe.[60]

Thus, it is clear that, while many medieval people were anxious to have children, they were nevertheless very much concerned with alleviating the suffering and ensuring the survival of women, even at the expense of children. This concern was also displayed by the attendance of care givers at births, inasmuch as the provision of care suggests concern and a desire to alleviate suffering.

We have little evidence as to who attended births in the Anglo-Saxon period. Female attendants are mentioned in the eighth-century miracles of St. Guthlac and St. Wilfrid. In both cases, other people (specifically men in St. Wilfrid's miracle) waited outside.[61] One assumes that at least some of the female attendants were members of the woman's family or community. Others may have been professional care givers, but we have no proof of this. Presumably, a birthing woman would be anxious to have experienced women nearby for support and advice. The appearance of midwives in the tenth-century Freising Christmas play suggests that such care givers were important in childbirth at this time.[62] Although we cannot be certain whether Anglo-Saxon men were ever present in the birthing room, at least some evinced considerable concern for their wives. Bede mentions a king who softened toward Christianity when a bishop told him that Christ made the queen's delivery safe and pain-free in answer to his prayers.[63]

We have more evidence about care givers from the High Middle Ages. Attendance at births does seem to have been primarily female, but there were notable exceptions to this rule. In the perilous circumstances recounted in miracle stories, the husband was often found at the scene of the birth. He displayed anxiety and grief for the experience of his wife and often played a central role in ritual behavior designed to relieve the woman's suffering, as is evidenced by the cases of the woman carrying a dead fetus and the too young mother (both quoted earlier).

Another male who might be present was the parish priest. Since childbirth was a potentially hazardous event in a woman's life, she might go to mass when she felt her pains begin. If her life was in danger, the priest might be summoned to administer last rites. In another miracle of St. Thomas of Canterbury, the priest seems to have witnessed much of the crisis and even offered a medical opinion.[64]

Other men occasionally fulfilled medical functions during childbirth. Matilda, wife of King Henry I, was attended in her first confinement in 1101 by two renowned Italian physicians, Faritus, abbot of Abbingdon, and his lay colleague Grimbald.[65]

Nevertheless, during childbirth, most medieval women were cared for by other women, either knowledgeable friends and family or professional midwives.[66] Depictions of birth scenes reveal almost exclusive female attendance.[67] Guy de Chauliac, although he provided copious obstetrical advice, insisted that births should be handled by women.[68] The introduction to a text devoted to women's ailments suggested one reason for the predominance of female attendants:

Because there are many women who have many diverse maladies and almost fatal sicknesses, and because they are also ashamed to reveal and tell their illnesses to any man . . . I will write of how to help women's private sicknesses, so that one woman may aid another in her illness and not divulge her secrets to such discourteous men.[69]

Thus some medieval women preferred to be tended by female care givers.

Joseph's predicament in the Coventry mystery cycle underlines the predominance of female care givers (especially midwives) during childbirth:

> It is not convenient to be a man
> When women go into labor.
> Therefore I wish I would see some midwife
> To help my wife that is so young.[70]

English midwives came under official regulation only in the very late Middle Ages; thus one cannot be sure what qualities, if any, separated the midwife from other experienced women.[71] Bartholomaeus Anglicus provided one description of the midwife in his encyclopedia:

> The midwife is a woman who has the skill to help a woman in labor, so that she will bear and bring forth her child with less woe and sorrow. And so the child should be born with less travail and woe, she anoints and applies balm to the mother's womb and helps her and comforts her in that way. Also she takes the child out of the womb and ties his cord four inches long.[72]

This is a very positive picture of the role of the midwife, emphasizing the comfort of both mother and child. Another text suggested that in the absence of a good midwife, women could suffer dangerous injuries, including a torn peritoneum.[73]

Miracle stories tend to support the idea of the importance of the midwife in the birth process. Midwives appear in several stories, sometimes several at a single birth, although their ability is always secondary to that of the saint.[74] Occasionally, one receives a more negative view. In one account, the meddling of the midwives caused the arm of a child to swell up so severely that delivery was impossible without dismemberment or the intervention of the saint.[75]

It is probable that the majority of care givers were family or friends. Most would not have been familiar with written medical lore, although some remedies might have been transmitted orally. Personal attendance often demonstrates love and support and, therefore, may have eased the sufferings of women in childbirth, regardless of the knowledge and experience of the care givers.

In the absence of family and friends, pregnant women were not left to give birth alone. The High and Late Middle Ages saw the rise of a new type of care giver, the hospital.[76] These institutions were very different from those we know today, since they served as refuges for the poor and insane as well as the physically ill. In the early Middle Ages, monasteries served as infirmaries. Hospitals were founded in England as early as the tenth century, but it was not until the High Middle Ages that widespread growth in the number of hospitals really began. Care in childbirth was often a function of these institutions. St. Bartholomew's in London, founded in 1123, cared for pregnant women until they were delivered.[77] We know from a 1363 reference that at St. Thomas' in Canterbury, lying-in women were taken care of until they were delivered, recovered, and churched. If they died in childbed, the children were brought up by the hospital.[78] In a petition and statute of 1414, aid to women in childbirth was mentioned as part of the established aim and scope of hospital charity.[79]

While the majority of women would have been cared for at home, surrounded by family and friends, hospitals provided a viable, if not wholly pleasant, alternative for the dispossessed. Their care for women in childbirth once again suggests concern for women's suffering in childbirth.

I believe that I have clearly demonstrated that medieval people displayed care and concern for women in childbirth. Yet one is left with the perhaps unanswerable question of whether medieval remedies truly helped women in childbirth. Many modern readers are apt to be somewhat skeptical of the value of "magical" stones, relics, girdles, and incantations.[80] Although we may recognize the efficacy of certain herbs taken in potions or baths, ritualized applications (such as the tying of a sprig of coriander to the thigh of a pregnant woman by a male or female virgin) or even subfumigation are far removed from most modern notions of medical treatment.[81] Even the efficacy of "practical" remedies such as turning a child in the case of an unnatural presentation or stitching tears in the peritoneum may seem dubious in the absence of modern antiseptics.

While any pronouncement on the effectiveness of medieval medicine must ultimately be speculative, I would argue that at least according to cultural and anthropological analyses of ritual and group behavior, medieval remedies were probably often beneficial.[82] Although such remedies may seem of little use to us, we must remember that they made sense within the cultural framework in which they were written. They were the logical result of knowledge and belief and would have been approached with hope and perhaps even confidence. Incantations, amulets, girdles, invocations, and rituals all had their place in the medieval birth experience. Girdles, amulets, and magic stones were a promise of safety in a hazardous experience. Worn against the flesh or held in the hand, they were a tangible reminder that one was not merely dependent on fate or one's own abilities. As such, they might reduce the emotional stress inherent in childbirth. Incantation, invocations, and rituals satisfied the human need for action in times of crisis. Their presence may have promoted group solidarity through shared belief, thus providing a positive atmosphere, in addition to soothing individual anxieties. Even if one did not wholly believe, the performance of a ritual, with its familiar themes, would tend to release tension. Herbal and practical remedies would have shared these functions, regardless of their individual properties. It has been understood through much of this century that women who feel less anxiety generally have an easier birth experience. Therefore, such remedies probably helped birthing women both physically and emotionally.

This conclusion should not be surprising. I have argued throughout this article that medieval people were anxious to help birthing women, and it seems unlikely that they would continue to prescribe entirely useless remedies for hundreds of years.

Pain in childbirth may have been perceived as the result of original sin, but it was neither neglected nor ignored in medieval England. Medieval people recognized feminine suffering and attempted to alleviate it through medical and religious remedies and personal and professional care. Although children were valued, the life of the mother was valued more, and care givers made every attempt to ensure her survival.

NOTES

1. A version of this paper was presented at the Twenty-seventh International Congress on Medieval Studies, Western Michigan University, Kalamazoo, Mich., May 1992. I wish to thank Richard Burton, Sharon Farmer, Philip Gavitt, Louis Haas, Lauren Helm Jared, Doug Lumsden, Deborah McBride, Christine McCann, Sharan Newman, and Jeffrey Russell, all of whom contributed useful suggestions. Any mistakes, of course, are strictly my own.

2. Howard W. Haggard, M.D., *Devils, Drugs, and Doctors: The Story of Healing from Medicine-Man to Doctor* (New York and London: Harper & Brothers, 1929), p. 4.

3. Haggard is admittedly rather dated, but he effectively and succinctly represents a negative view of medieval childbirth that is found in many other modern works. Two recent examples are E. Shorter, *A History of Women's Bodies* (New York: Basic Books, 1982), and Jenny Carter and Therese Duriez, *With Child: Birth through the Ages* (Edinburgh: Mainstream Publishers, 1986), see especially 16. Both of these works survey a broad time period and provide scant evidence and citations for their conclusions about medieval childbirth.

Whether through modesty or lack of interest, most surveys of medieval medicine have had little to say about obstetrics and gynecology, even though many medieval medical texts include a great deal of information about the subject. Wilfrid Bonser, *The Medical Background of Anglo-Saxon England: A Study in History, Psychology, and Folklore* (London: Wellcome Historical Medical Library, 1963), 264, currently the most comprehensive work on Anglo-Saxon medicine, justified this neglect with the assertion that women were overlooked due to Anglo-Saxon concerns about the production of male children. Actually, while there is only one extant Old English text including recipes (two) relating to the production of male children, many recipes attempted to alleviate feminine suffering.

Several medievalists recently have produced more balanced articles and chapters on medieval childbirth. However, the centrality of concern for women's suffering and survival in childbirth is implicit rather than explicit in their work. Monica Green, in her important article "Women's Medical Practice and Health Care in Medieval Europe," *Signs: Journal of Women in Culture and Society* 14 (1989): 434–73, hereinafter Green 1989, implies this notion most strongly. She is, however, concerned more with proving that both men and women participated in women's health care than with their motives for doing so. Shulamith Shahar includes an excellent chapter on childbirth in *Childhood in the Middle Ages* (London and New York: Routledge, 1990). Peter Biller, "Childbirth in the Middle Ages," *History Today* 36 (Aug. 1986): 42–49, provides an interesting, although brief, preliminary examination of the sources for medieval childbirth. Renate Blumenfeld-Kosinski, *Not of Women Born: Representations of Caesarean Birth in Medieval and Renaissance Culture* (Ithaca: Cornell Univ. Press, 1990), although focusing on Caesarian birth, supplies many sidelights on normal births. All of these authors discuss Europe in general. Marilyn Deegan, "Pregnancy and Childbirth in the Anglo-Saxon Medical Texts: A Preliminary Survey," in *Medicine in Early Medieval England: Four Papers*, ed. Marilyn Deegan and D.G. Scragg (Manchester: Centre for Anglo-Saxon Studies, Univ. of Manchester, 1989), 117–26, very briefly surveys obstetrical remedies in Anglo-Saxon sources.

4. *Hali Meidenhad: An Alliterative Homily of the Thirteenth Century*, ed. F.J. Furnivall and Oswald Cockayne, Early English Texts Society 18 (New York: Greenwood Press, 1922, repr. 1969), 48–51. loke we hwuch wunne ariseð þerafter i burðerne of bearne, hwen þat streon i þe awakeneð and waxeð . . . þi rudie neb schal leanen, and as gres grenen. Þin ehnen schulen doskin, and under þon wonnen; and of þi breines turnunge þin heaued ake fare. Inwið þi womb, swelin þe bitte, þhat beoreð forð as a water bulge: þine þarmes þralinge, and stiches i þi lonke, and in þi lendene far eche riue, Heuinesse in euch lime. Þine brestes burðen o þine twa pappes, and te milc strunden þat te of strikeð. Al is wið a welewunge, þi wlite ouer warpen. Þi muð is bitter, and walh al þat tu cheowest, and hwat mete se þi mahe hokerliche underfeð; þat is, wið unlust, warpeð hit eft ut . . . ah wrecche! Þe care again þi pinunge þrahen binimeð þe nihtes slepes. Hwen hit þerto cumeð, þat fare forhfule angoise, þat stronge and stikinde stiche, þat unroles uuel, þat pine upo pine, þat wondrende yeomerunge.

5. Shahar, 33.

6. For an excellent treatment of this subject and of caesarian birth in the Middle Ages in general see Blumenfeld-Kosinski.

7. Bartholomaeus Anglicus, *On the Properties of Things: John Trevisa's Translation of Bartholomaeus Anglicus De Proprietatibus Rerum*, ed. M.C. Seymour et al. (Oxford: Clarendon Press, 1975), 6.7. This version is a late fourteenth-century English translation of the original thirteenth-century Latin text. Þe modres haueþ wlatnesse and spewinges, and beþ heuy and mowen not wiþ trauaile. In trauaile of childe þey beþ compelled to crie, and ligtliche imperischid, and nameliche yonge wymmen with smale membres and streit. Þe more woo and sorwe a womman hath in trauaile of childe, þe more heo loueþ þat childe whenne he is ibore.

8. Bartholomaeus 6.10. See my discussion of midwives below for further details about Bartholomaeus' advice.

9. We must be careful not to exaggerate the negative aspects of childbirth. Both men and women in the Middle Ages frequently perceived birth to be a joyous event. A child's entrance into the world was often hailed with thanksgiving and gladness. Barren parents pleaded with the saints to give them children (see examples below). A fifteenth-century vernacular treatise described the contentment and happiness that a woman receives from the child within her. Beryl Rowland, *Medieval Woman's Guide to Health: The First English Gynecological Handbook* (Kent, Ohio: Kent State Univ. Press, 1981), 118–19.

10. Donald Weinstein and Rudolph Bell, *Saints and Society* (Chicago and London: Univ. of Chicago Press, 1982), is a useful study of saints' lives and what they reveal about society.

11. For discussions of miracles and miracle collections in the Middle Ages see R.C. Finucane, *Miracles and Pilgrims: Popular Beliefs in Medieval England* (London: J.M. Dent, 1977); Benedicta Ward, *Miracles and the Medieval Mind: Theory, Record, and Event* (London: Scholar Press, 1982); Jan Ryder, *Miracles and Mentality: The Medieval Experience*, Ph.D. dissertation, Department of History, University of California, Santa Barbara (1993); Jonathan Sumption, *Pilgrimage: An Image of Mediaeval Religion* (London: Faber and Faber, 1975); Pierre-Andre Sigal, *L'homme et le miracle dans la France medievale (XIe–XIIe siecle)* (Paris: Cerf, 1985).

12. Ryder convincingly argues that a more critical attitude toward miracles was developing in the twelfth century even before the papal canonization movement began. For institutional changes (but little discussion of miracles) see also E.W. Kemp, *Canonization and Authority in the Western Church* (New York: AMS Press, 1980).

13. Eddius Stephanus, *The Life of Bishop Wilfrid*, ed. Bertram Colgrave (Cambridge: Cambridge Univ. Press, 1927), 4–5.

14. Talbot (C.H. Talbot, *Medicine in Medieval England,* London: Oldbourne, 1967) provides an overview of medieval English medicine, although he has little to say about obstetrics and gynecology. Due to the breadth of this essay, I have read only published medical texts. Unless otherwise stated, details concerning texts, including dates, are based on the opinions of the editors of the texts. Tremendous numbers of manuscripts remain unpublished. Monica Green surveys "Obstetrical and Gynecological Texts in Middle English," in *Studies in the Age of Chaucer* 14 (Norman, Okla.: Univ. of Oklahoma, 1992): 53–88, hereinafter Green 1992. For a more general, although incomplete, survey see Rossell Hope Robbins, "Medical Manuscripts in Middle English," *Speculum* 45 (1970): 393–45.

15. Most extant Anglo-Saxon medical texts were collected by Oswald Cockayne in his three-volume *Leechdoms, Wortcunning and Starcraft of Early England* (rev. ed. London: Holland Press, 1961); an earlier edition appears in *Rolls Series* 35 (London, 1864–1866). Cockayne provides editions of the four major surviving Anglo-Saxon medical works—the *Laeceboc* or *Leechbook of Bald* (unfortunately, a portion of this ninth- or tenth-century work, including forty-one recipes for obstetrical and gynecological problems, has been lost; the missing portions are outlined in the table of contents), the *Lacnunga* (tenth or eleventh century, possibly later), the *Herbarium Apulei* or *Old English Herbarium* (tenth century or earlier Old English translation of fifth-or sixth-century Latin compilation), and the *Medicina de quadrupedibus* (usually compiled with the *Herbarium*)—as well as a number of minor or fragmentary works, including charms. Cockayne provides a facing modern English translation, but tends to render obstetrical and gynecological material in Greek or Latin. The *Lacnunga* has been reedited by J.J.G. Grattan and Charles Singer, *Anglo-Saxon Magic and Medicine* (London: Oxford Univ. Press, 1952). The *Herbarium* has been reedited by Hubert Jan De Vriend, *The Old English Herbarium and Medicina de Quadrupedibus*, Early English Text Society 286 (London, New York, and Toronto: Oxford Univ. Press, 1984), hereinafter de Vriend. This edition has facing Old English and Latin versions. Charms, including some omitted by Cockayne, have been edited by Felix Grendon, "Anglo-Saxon Charms," in the *Journal of American Folklore* 22

(1909): 105–237; G. Storms, *Anglo-Saxon Magic* (The Hague: M. Nijhoff, 1948); and Elliott Van Kirk Dobbie, *The Anglo-Saxon Minor Poems* (New York: Columbia Univ. Press, 1942), 116–28.

Deegan provides a summary of Anglo-Saxon medical advice for pregnancy and childbirth. K.L. Jolly, "Anglo-Saxon Charms in the Context of Popular Religion," Ph.D. dissertation, Department of History, University of California, Santa Barbara (1987), provides a thoughtful analysis of medical charms as serious attempts at healing, especially chapter 4.

16. Unfortunately, modern editors have neglected medieval Latin medical compendia, apart from vernacular editions (see note 17 below on Middle English texts). Sir Percival Horton-Smith Hartley and Harold Richard Aldridge, *Johannes de Mirfeld of St. Bartholomew's Smithfield: His Life and Works* (Cambridge: Cambridge Univ. Press, 1936), hereinafter Mirfeld, have edited portions of Mirfeld's late fourteenth-century Latin compendium. Nancy G. Siraisi, *Medieval and Early Renaissance Medicine: An Introduction to Knowledge and Practice* (Chicago and London: Univ. of Chicago Press, 1990), provides a good discussion of scholastic medicine, although she has little to say about obstetrics. Tony Hunt reproduces a wide variety of nonscholastic English medical works in Latin, Anglo-Norman, and Middle English, mostly from the thirteenth century but some from the twelfth and fourteenth centuries, in *Popular Medicine in Thirteenth-Century England* (Cambridge: D.S. Brewer, 1990).

17. I will refer to the following Middle English works: Beryl Rowland, *Medieval Woman's Guide to Health: The First English Gynecological Handbook* (Kent, Ohio: Kent State Univ. Press, 1981), is a fifteenth-century English adaptation of the obstetrical and gynecological portions of Rober Baron's High medieval compendium (Green 1992, 73–3, convincingly demonstrates that this is not an English Trotula as Rowland claims). Green 1992, 84–87, includes an abbreviated fourteenth-century translation of a Latin adaptation (probably thirteenth-century) of Muscio's second-century *Gynaecia*. Robert von Fleischhacker, *Lanfrank's Science of Cirurgie*, Early English Text Society 102 (Berlin, New York, and Philadelphia: K. Paul, Trench, Trubner & Co., 1894), hereinafter Lanfrank, is a translation of Lanfrank of Milan's treatise on surgery. Margaret S. Ogden, *The Cyrurgie of Guy de Chauliac*, Early English Text Society 265 (London, New York, and Toronto: Oxford Univ. Press, 1971), hereinafter Chauliac, is a fifteenth-century translation of Guy de Chauliac's fourteenth-century compendium. Gosta Frisk, *A Middle English Translation of Macer Floridus de Viribus Herbarum* (Upsala: Lundequist, 1949), hereinafter Macer, is a late fourteenth-century translation of an influential herbal written between the ninth and twelfth centuries. Pol Grymonprez, *Here men may se the vertues off herbes: A Middle English Herbal*, Scripta 3 (Brussels: Scripta, 1981), is a fifteenth-century herbal drawing heavily upon Macer's herbal and the twelfth-century herbal of Matthaeus Platearius. Patrick Fordyn, *The Experimentes of Cophon, the Leche of Salerne: Middle English Recipes*, Scripta 10 (Brussels: Scripta, 1983), is a fifteenth-century translation of Cophon's eleventh-century work (largely herbal). Warren R. Dawson, *A Leechbook or Collection of Medical Recipes of the Fifteenth Century* (London: Macmillan, 1934), contains mostly herbal remedies. George Henslow, *Medical Works of the Fourteenth Century* (repr. New York: B. Franklin, 1972, originally published 1899), contains extracts from four fourteenth-century manuscripts. F. Holthausen, "Medicinische gedichte aus einer Stockhomer handschrift," in *Anglia* 34 (1911): 163–93, hereinafter Holthausen, is a fifteenth-century treatise closely related to the one edited by Garrett. M.S. Ogden, *The Liber de diversis medicinis*, Early English Text Society 207 (Oxford: Oxford Univ. Press, 1938, rev. repr. 1969), is a fifteenth-century collection.

For discussion of Middle English translations, see Green 1992; Robbins; and Faye Marie Getz, "Charity, Translation, and the Language of Medical Learning in Medieval England," *Bulletin of the History of Medicine* 64 (1990): 1–17.

18. For example, Peter Biller, "Childbirth in the Middle Ages" *History Today* 36 (Aug. 1986), 42–49. However, John Benton, "Trotula, Women's Problems and the

Professionalization of Medicine in the Middle Ages" *Bulletin of the History of Medicine* 59 (1985): 30–53, argues that academic medicine may actually have been more harmful, since it was farther removed from its practical roots. Since much of Anglo-Saxon medicine was borrowed, too, this is a dubious claim.

19. Edward J. Kealey, *Medieval Medicus* (Baltimore and London: Johns Hopkins Univ. Press, 1981), 4.

20. For examples of such texts, see Rowland and Green, 1992, 84–87. See Green 1992 for a review of obstetrical and gynecological texts. Other types of "specialist" texts were produced during the same period.

21. Various authors have argued that compilers and translators did not slavishly copy classical documents but, instead, used them selectively and even adapted them according to local custom and ingredient availability. Luke Demaitre, "Scholasticism in Compendia of Practical Medicine, 1250–1450," in *Science, Medicine, and the University, 1200–1550: Essays in Honor of Pearl Kibre* (Saint Louis: Saint Louis Univ. Library, 1976), 89–90. Linda E. Voigts, "Anglo-Saxon Plant Remedies and the Anglo-Saxons," *Isis* 70 (1979), 250–68. Green 1992 discusses the changes made in obstetrical texts throughout her work. An excellent example of scribes adapting a manuscript to suit specific needs is Faye Marie Getz's *Healing and Society in Medieval England: A Middle English Translation of the Pharmaceutical Writings of Gilbertus Anglicus* (Madison, Wisc.: Univ. of Wisconsin Press, 1991). Getz suggests that the manuscript she edited belonged to a male monastery because the copiest deliberately removed all the sections dealing with women, children, travel, and the use of animals in medical preparations. These exclusions are unique among the dozen or more other English versions.

22. For this address, see Rowland, 58–59. Green 1989, 463–64, points out that other versions of this text employ neutral or masculine addresses. Benton argues throughout his article that the feminine address was written by men pretending to be women in an attempt to seize control of obstetrics and gynecology, but Green 1989, 461–62, convincingly refutes this view, pointing out that the same address also says that women may be reluctant to be treated by men.

23. *Herbarium*, 82.2 (De Vriend, 82.1), 104.2, 143.3; *Lacnunga* 169b (Cockayne ed. 103–4); *Laeceboc*, 2.60 (text lost); Dobbie, 123–24; Grendon, 159, 206–9; Henslow, 32–33; Rowland, 122–23, 136–39, 164–65; Ogden, 56–57; Dawson, 256; Chauliac, 530; Hunt, 90, 92, 98–99, 133, 232, 233, 257, 258, 303, 302–3, 367 (note 22); Grymonprez, 51, 125; Macer, 73, 95, 132, 154; Holthausen, 314; Garrett, 171; Green 1992, 87–88.

24. For example, coriander in *Herbarium*, 104.2, and Rowland, 68–69.

25. For analyses of such charms see Jolly, chap. 4, and the introductions of Grendon and Grattan and Singer.

26. Hunt, 98–99. This is longer and contains more gibberish than most versions. Similar recipes include Henslow, 32–33; Grendon, 159; Hunt, 90, 92, 98–99, 133, 233, 278, 302–3, 367 note 22; Ogden, 56–57. Mirfeld (6.2.3), in the late fourteenth century, includes a similar prayer, but expresses skepticism about its effectiveness (cited but not reproduced on page 44 of the published edition of Mirfeld).

27. Rowland throughout, but see especially 122–35; Chauliac, 530; Green 1992, 87; Hunt, 258; Bartholomaeus, 6.10.

28. Rowland, 122–35. The same author offered help for swollen legs during pregnancy, 152–53.

29. Rowland, 138–39.

30. Rowland, 32.

31. St. Gilbert (see note 59) (late twelfth century), 115.

32. Thomas Forbes, "Chalcedony and Childbirth" in his *The Midwife and the Witch* (New Haven and London: Yale Univ. Press, 1966), examines the use of stones and other aids throughout. For example, see Rowland, 138–39.

33. For example, see James Craigie Robertson, *Materials for the History of*

Thomas Becket, Archbishop of Canterbury, Roll Series 67 (London: Kraus Reprint, 1876, repr. 1965), vol. 2, 196, hereinafter Thomas of Canterbury.

34. Thomas of Canterbury, vol. 1, 469–70. Periclitabatur dies tres et eo amplius Alienor, Willelmi cujusdam militis uxor, de vico Oxenefordia nati, vicina partui, sed vicinior morti, ut de vita ejus nihil omnino speraretur. Nam nondum erat ejus aetatis ut mater fieri deberet. Unde vir ei compatiens, praecipue quod intempestivae conceptionis pericula pateretur, collo ejus reliquias martyris appendit, et in ictu oculi duos in uno homine conservavit; nam puerpera puerum edidit.

35. Thomas of Monmouth, *The Life and Miracles of William of Norwich* (Cambridge: Cambridge Univ. Press, 1896), 78–79 (mid-twelfth century).

36. Cockayne, vol. 3, 146–47: "Feorhadle."

37. Chauliac, 530.

38. *Laeceboc,* 2.60 (lost), 3.37; *Herbarium,* 63.2 (De Vriend, 63.1), 94.7 (De Vriend, 94.6); *Medicina de Quadrupedibus,* 4.4, 4.5; Henslow, 33; Rowland, 68–71, 74–75, 120–23, 134–39, 142–43, 154–57; Ogden, 57; Dawson, 256, 257, 258, 259; Chauliac, 530; Hunt, 98–99, 133, 199–200, 367 (note 22); Grymonprez, 31, 47, 53, 71, 83, 103, 111; Getz, 301–2 (notes 150-12, 151-16); Macer, 83, 87, 95, 96, 97–98, 111, 121, 140, 144, 149, 156, 165, 169, 175.

39. Thomas of Canterbury, vol. 2, 196. Mulieri autem impletum est tempus pariendi, et parere non potuit; filium quidem conceperat, cujus non mater esset futura sed sepulchrum. Diebus quindecim se foetus in utero materno non moverat; jacebat funus in funere, mortuum in moriente, ante subtractum quam visum, ante sepultum quam natum. Computruisse putabatur vivens ex mortuo; obstupuit, desperata est. "Quid agimus" inquit paterfamilias . . . "desperantes sedemus, et martyris Cantuariensis non reminiscimus"; et arrepto filo, cum invocatione nominis ejus morentem commentitur, spondens martyri munus oblationis, quod illa vovere non valebat. Mille passus nemo post votum confecisset antequam peperit; sed foetum exanimem itaque decoctum ut carnis in olla ferventi decoctae instar videretur habere. Et evasi mulier quam interius computruisse credebant.

40. For various ancient and medieval theories of generation, see Joan Cadden, *Meanings of Sex Difference in the Middle Ages* (Cambridge: Cambridge Univ. Press, 1993).

41. For example, Rowland, 134–37; Chauliac, 530.

42. *Laeceboc,* 2.60 (lost), 3.37; *Herbarium,* 82.3 (De Vriend, 82.2), 143.2; *Medicina de quadrupedibus,* 1.8 (De Vriend, 2.4); Rowland, 96–97, 134–39, 144–47; Dawson, 258; Chauliac, 531; Hunt, 230, 258; Grymonprez, 31, 57, 83, 87; Macer, 67, 95, 134–35, 154; Holt, 309; Garrett, 166; Green 1992, 87–88.

43. For example, Macer, 135.

44. *Herbarium,* 165.5 (De Vriend, 165.4); Dawson, 321; Macer, 87, 96, 134, 139, 142; Rowland, 74–75, 96–97, 134–35, 156–57.

45. John Riddle, *Contraception and Abortion from the Ancient World to the Renaissance* (Cambridge, Mass: Harvard Univ. Press, 1992), provides the most thorough treatment of the subject.

46. Rowland, 96–97. "For whan the woman is feble & þe chyld may nogt comyn out, than it is better that þe chylde be slayne than the moder of þe child also dye."

47. Chauliac, 530–31, recommends that midwives use hands and hooks.

48. Thomas of Canterbury, vol. 1, 227–28. "quod puerperae deerat auxilium nisi partui praecideretur brachium."

49. Blumenfeld-Kosinski emphasizes this point throughout her book. Chauliac, 531, repeats this stricture.

50. Riddle makes this assumption throughout his book.

51. For discussions of menstruation in the Middle Ages see Charles T. Wood, "The Doctors' Dilemma: Sin, Salvation, and the Menstrual Cycle in Medieval Thought" *Speculum* 56 (1981): 710–27; Darrel W. Amundsen and Carol Jean Diers, "The Age of Menarch in Medieval Europe" *Human Biology* 45 (1973): 363–69; Vern

Bullough and Cameron Campbell, "Female Longevity and Diet in the Middle Ages" *Speculum* 55 (1980): 317–325; J.B. Post, "Ages at Menarche and Menopause: Some Mediaeval Authorities" *Population Studies* 25 (1971): 83–87.

52. Dawson, 325, and Fordyn, 63, make this claim. Recipes to restore menses include *Laeceboc*, 3.38; *Herbarium*, 152.1, 165.2 (De Vriend, 165.1), 165.5 (De Vriend, 165.4), 173.2; *Medicina de quadrupedibus*, 1.7 (De Vriend, 2.3), 2.4 (De Vriend, 3.4); Rowland, 96–97, 110–13, 134–35, 146–47, 152–57; Dawson, 239–40, 245, 252, 258–60; Grymonprez, 31, 57; Macer, 57, 61, 65, 73, 77, 83, 89, 95, 97–98, 101, 111, 114, 116, 126, 134, 138, 149, 151, 158, 161, 169, 182, 183, 184, 194; Green 1992, 85–86.

53. *Laeceboc*, 2.60 (lost); 3.37, 3.38; *Herbarium*, 60.2. 89.2, 128, 173.2 (De Vriend, 173.1), 175.3 (De Vriend, 175.2), 178.6; *Medicina de quadrupedibus* 1.6 (De Vriend, 2.2), 2.4 (De Vriend, 3.4); Rowland, chaps. 2 and 13; Ogden, 57; Dawson, 317, 318, 319, 320, 323, 324; Fordyn, 66–67; Hunt, 134, 235, 238; Macer, 147, 172; Green 1992, 1992, 85–86.

54. *Medicina de quadrupedibus*, 4.6, deals with pain after childbirth, as does Rowland, 108–9, and 118–21; Green 1992, 88, discusses care after birth.

55. Rowland, 98–105, 164–67.

56. *Laeceboc*, 2.60 (lost); 3.37; *Medicina de quadrupedibus*, 2.17 (De Vriend, 3.17), 4.14 (De Vriend, 5.14); *Lacnunga*, 169b (Dobbie, 123–4, Grendon, 206–9, Cockayne, vol. 3, 103); Rowland, chap. 12, 168–69; Ogden, 56–57; Dawson, 325, 523; Fordyn, 62–63; Hunt, 238, 245; Grymonprez, 31; Macer, 128; Garrett, 164, 170–71; Holthausen, 314.

57. *Laeceboc*, 2.6 (lost); Cockayne, vol. 3, 144–45; Ogden, 56; Hunt, 134.

58. *Medicina quadrupedibus*, 4.12 and 4.13, explains how to get a male. Rowland, 168–69, explains how to get a male or female.

59. Raymonde Foreville and Gillian Ker, *Book of St. Gilbert* (Oxford: Oxford Univ. Press, 1987): 112–15. This miracle was compiled as part of Gilbert's canonization proceedings in the very early thirteenth century. The translation is that supplied by the editors, not my own. [Vir quidam de Stanfordia cum uxore sua diu uixerat absque liberis. Diuertit forte ad domum eorum pater Gilbertus hospitandi gratia. Hospita cauta, de sanctitate suscepti hospitis confisa, locum ei parat in proprio grabato, ut meritis eius tanquam altera Sunamitis suscipere filium mereretur per Helyseum. Quod factum est ut credidit mulier. Nam dormiendi ueniens domum maritus eius mox genuit ex ea filium et uocauerunt eum nomine huius patris Gileberti.] An amusing finale to this story is that Gilbert, hearing of the miracle, sends the boy a cow to provide for his upkeep as if he were the father.

60. "Miracula S. Thomae de Cantilupe Episc." *Acta Sanctorum*, Oct. 2, 1643, Tomus primum, 666–67, (part 4, chap. 3, no. 46).

61. Felix, "Life of St. Guthlac" in *Anglo-Saxon Saints and Heroes*, ed. Clinton Albertson (Bronx, N.Y.: Fordham Univ. Press, 1967), 172–73; Eddius Stephanus, *The Life of Bishop Wilfrid*, ed. Bertram Colgrave (Cambridge: Cambridge Univ. Press, 1927), 4–5.

62. *English Nativity Plays*, ed. Samuel B. Hemingway (New York: Russell and Russell, 1964), xi.

63. Bede, *A History of the English Church and People*, trans. Leo Sherley Price (New York: Dorset Press, rev. ed. 1968), 2.9.

64. Thomas of Canterbury, vol. 1, 227–28.

65. Stanley Rubin, *Medieval English Medicine* (London: David Charles, 1974): 182. When Henry I subsequently supported Faritus as a candidate to become Archbishop of Canterbury in 1109, several bishops argued against the appointment, suggesting that it was improper for a man renowned for his treatment of women's disorders to be granted such a lofty office.

66. Green 1989, 434–73, convincingly demonstrates that both men and women filled a variety of professional roles in women's health. Women and men present at a

birth could be physicians, surgeons, barber-surgeons, apothecaries, or other types of healers. Midwives, however, were undeniably the most common professionals present at births. With the growth of universities and the professionalization of medicine, women healers were officially marginalized. Male medical practitioners joined in guilds and attempted to define qualifications and conditions. In 1421 a petition formally excluding women from medicine was put before Parliament. Nevertheless, Green demonstrates that women continued to fill a variety of professional roles. Midwifery only came under restrictive legislation in the late Middle Ages, since there was little competition from other groups.

67. Blumenfeld-Kosinski's work and D. Alexandre-Bidon and M. Closson, *L'Enfant a l'ombre des cathedrales* (Lyons: Presses Universitaires de Lyon, 1985), provide many illustrations of birth scenes.

68. Chauliac, 530.

69. Rowland, 58–59. For as moche as ther ben manye women that hauen many diuers maladies and sekenesses nygy to þe deth and thei also ben shamefull to schewen and to tellen her greuaunces unto eny wyght . . . I wyl wright of women prevy sekenes the helpyng, and that oon woman may helpe another in her sykenesse & nought diskuren her previtees to such vncurteys men.

70. "Coventry Nativity," *English Nativity Plays*, ed. Samuel B. Hemingway (New York, 1964), scene 4, ll. 133–36 (late fourteenth century). It is not conuenyent a man to be/ther women gon in travalynge,/ wherefore sum mydwyff ffayn wold I se/ my wyff to helpe that is so yenge. See also "Chester Nativity," scene 7, ll. 472–79.

71. Thomas G. Benedek, "The Changing Relationship between Midwives and Physicians during the Renaissance," *Bulletin of the History of Medicine* 5 (1977): 551. Early regulation in the fifteenth and sixteenth centuries was primarily concerned with moral behavior, not levels of skill. Midwives became a popular target for accusations of sorcery during the Renaissance because of their association with incantations and magical devices. On this subject, see also Rowland, 31–32.

72. Bartholomaeus 6.0. A midwif is a womman þat hath craft to helpe a womman þat trauaileþ of childe, þat sche bere and bring forthe here childe with þe lasse woo and sorwe. And for þe childe schulde be ibore with þe lass trauaile and woo sche annoyntiþ and bawmeþ þe modir womb, and helpiþ and comfortiþ here in þat wise. Also sche fongiþ þe childe out of þe womb, and knettiþ his nauel foure ynche long.

73. Rowland, 164–65.

74. Of course, it is possible that any woman assisting at a birth was referred to as a midwife by those recording the miracles.

75. Thomas of Canterbury, vol. 1, 227–28.

76. For a discussion of medieval hospitals see Rotha Mary Clay, *The Medieval Hospitals of England* (London: Methuen, 1909); Margaret Wade Labarge, "Women as Healers and Nurses" in *A Small Sound of the Trumpet: Women in Medieval Life* (Boston: Beacon Press, 1986), 182–94; and C.H. Talbot, "Hospitals" in *Medicine in Medieval England* (London: Old Bourne, 1967), 170–85.

77. Rubin, 186.

78. Clay, 8.

79. Ibid.

80. In fact, the use of invocations of saints, incantations, and magical objects fell into disrepute at the end of the Middle Ages, especially after the English Reformation. See Rowland's introduction (especially 31–32) for examples of English measures against these remedies.

81. Riddle discusses modern analyses of the possible efficacy of herbal remedies throughout his book.

82. My discussion of the beneficial effects of ritual within appropriate cultural frameworks is inspired by my reading of a number of cultural historians, anthropologists, and sociologists. Most important here were Bronislaw Malinowski (dated, but still very useful), Natalie Zemon Davis, Lynn Hunt, and Victor Turner.

THE CARE OF ORPHANS IN THE BYZANTINE EMPIRE

Timothy S. Miller

According to Hegel, to understand freedom one must also comprehend slavery, to perceive the good one must have seen evil, and to know oneself, one must come to the knowledge of the other. It is, therefore, not out of place in a study of the medieval family to turn our attention to orphans, to those who had lost their families and had to face the world without the support of their fathers and mothers. This study will examine how Byzantine society—the medieval Greek world centered on the great metropolis of Constantinople—provided material assistance, protection, and education for its orphans and even for refugee children of its barbarian neighbors.

The society of the Byzantine Empire, like that of the medieval West, accepted the moral imperatives of the Old and New Testaments as binding commands. Thus, the imperial government and the Orthodox church endeavored to shape Byzantine institutions and mores according to the guidelines of Holy Scripture.[1] This was especially true with respect to the Christian obligation to aid the unfortunate. At the Last Judgment, Christ would reward those who fed the hungry, sheltered the homeless, and visited the sick (Matt. 25:31–46). Recent studies have shown that, motivated by this Gospel command to help those in need, medieval Greek Christians supported an array of philanthropic institutions: hospitals for the sick, shelters for the homeless, rest homes for the aged and chronically ill.[2] The Byzantine church and government developed these specialized charitable institutions during the fourth, fifth, and sixth centuries to assist the thousands of poor who congregated in the large cities of the eastern Mediterranean such as Antioch, Alexandria, and Constantinople.[3]

Because both the Jewish and the early Christian tradition stressed that of all the needy, God especially loved the orphans, one would expect that the Byzantines (or East Roman) empire would have taken special care to address their needs.[4] Careful study of Byzantine philanthropic institutions has, in fact, revealed that the oldest and most prestigious charitable facility in Constantinople was the Orphanotropheion, or orphanage, established some time in the mid-fourth century to shelter and educate the orphan children of the Eastern capital.[5]

As large as the Orphanotropheion of Constantinople became, it was never designed to care for all the orphans and abandoned children of the capital, nor to shelter and nourish the orphans of the far-flung provinces of the empire. Rather than supporting a large number of institutions for orphans, the Byzantine government and church evolved a complex system to provide for these children, a system that included four methods of care. First, the government developed the Roman law concept of guardianship in an effort to find for orphans conscientious adults—usually from among the children's nearest relatives—to protect, support, and educate them. Second, the church required its bishops to provide for orphans. Third, monasteries also played a role in nurturing abandoned children. Finally, the church and imperial government together supported the Orphanotropheion in Constantinople, which offered shelter, sustenance, and a superior education to Greek orphans and to many children from barbarian lands.[6]

Most Byzantine orphans never entered any philanthropic institution, whether the Orphanotropheion of the capital or the smaller episcopal and monastic schools. Instead, their relatives accepted these children into their homes and cared for them until the orphans reached adulthood. East Roman society had inherited this practice from all three earlier cultures that had shaped it: the classical Greek world, the ancient Roman state, and the Hebrew tradition. With regard to family obligations concerning orphans, however, the Byzantine state was most influenced by Roman practice, because the family obligation to care for children who had lost their parents was, in fact, an important part of the Roman legal system—the law of guardianship (*tutela*). As the legitimate successor of the empire of Augustus and Hadrian, the Byzantine state accepted *in toto* the Roman legal traditions, and thus the Roman rules, regarding guardianship.[7]

Classical Roman law—the legal system of the Empire as it had developed by the third century A.D.—distinguished three categories of guardians. The oldest category was the *tutela legitima*, the guardianship obligation based on agnatic (male) relationships.[8] According to the rules of the tutela legitima, the closest male relative through the father's line became the child's guardian. If a child's paternal grandfather was still living when the father died, that grandfather assumed the role of protecting, nurturing, and educating the minor.[9] If the father died and there were no living ascendants (grandfather or great-grandfather), an adult brother was to accept guardianship; if no brother, then a paternal uncle; and if no paternal uncle, then a cousin on the father's side. According to classical Roman law, women could not function as guardians; in fact, an adult, unmarried woman needed her own guardian to represent her in any legal action. Thus, a child whose father had died but whose mother was still living was classed as an orphan and required a male guardian.[10]

The second category of guardianship was the *tutela testamentaria*. As early as the XII Tables (450 B.C.), Roman law recognized the right of the testator—only a male who had no living father or grandfather—to appoint a guardian in his will.[11] The testator did not need to follow the order of the tutela legitima; he could choose anyone he wished from among his close friends or relatives. The testator presumably chose the person whom he most trusted to protect his children. By the third century A.D., Roman law also allowed mothers or other relatives to establish guardians for their heirs by testament, but such appointments required the confirmation of a magistrate.

The third category of guardianship was the magisterial *tutela*. In those cases in which the father died before he wrote a will, and no agnate relatives could be found either because such relatives did not exist or all those living claimed excuses (Roman law recognized specific excuses from serving as a guardian), Roman law empowered specific magistrates to appoint guardians. If the child had a living mother, the law required that she seek a magisterial guardian. It is important to remember that women, even mothers, could not serve as guardians.[12]

During the fourth century, the early Byzantine emperors began to alter the rules of guardianship. In 314, only two years after Constantine's victory at the Milvian Bridge, this first Christian emperor issued a law that placed a lien on all property of the guardian until such time as the guardian successfully concluded his duties, i.e., finished his term as guardian and demonstrated in an official accounting that he had honestly represented the interests of his ward. This lien (*hypotheca*) was to have undisputed claim on the guardian's property over the claims of any previous creditors of the guardian.[13]

Constantine clearly intended that this hypotheca would provide a surer method of protecting orphans from devious guardians who used their office not to assist the children but to despoil their estates. Perhaps Constantine instituted the hypotheca in response to the Christian command to protect orphans. According to Saint James, protecting orphans and widows was a sign of a pure and spotless Christian faith (1:26). On the other hand, classical Roman law had been moving in the direction of providing orphans greater security against unscrupulous guardians, and it is possible that the emperor was simply completing a process of protecting orphaned children that had begun as late as the later Republic.[14]

Constantine continued to legislate additional protection for orphaned children. In 316 he required that a guardian bear any financial loss caused by delays in fulfilling terms of subsequent testaments (wills other than that of the child's father);[15] in 326 he forbade a guardian to sell any of his ward's property;[16] finally, in 333 he insisted that the guardian had to compensate the orphan for losses in managing land leased from the imperial estates.[17]

Perhaps the greatest Byzantine innovation in the Roman law of guardianship came at the end of the fourth century (390). The emperor Theodosius decided that, in cases in which a father had not instituted a guardian by testament for his child and no male relative on the father's side could be found, the mother could serve as the legal guardian. Theodosius, however, required that the mother first promise not to remarry.[18] It is possible that in issuing this law, Theodosius was motivated by a desire to aid children and their widowed mothers who were being oppressed by extrafamilial guardians. Only a few years earlier, a widow named Julietta had appealed to the famous bishop of Caesarea, Basil, to assist her against the oppression of an unjust guardian.[19] Cases such as Julietta's might well have influenced Theodosius' legislation.

More than a century later, the emperor Justinian expanded the role of women in serving as guardians. He decided that not only mothers but also grandmothers were to precede all other male relatives, whether on the father's side or the mother's side. Only guardians expressly appointed by the deceased father in a proper testament now blocked the surviving mother or, if she too were dead, the grandmother.[20] Moreover, Justinian gave to mothers special legal privileges in exercising the guardianship of their children.[21]

Did these changes in the Roman law of guardianship actually guarantee orphans better care? That the early Byzantine emperors issued so many new regulations to control the behavior of guardians suggests that, in fact, adult guardians regularly despoiled the property of their wards. Justinian's Novel 72, issued in 538, frankly admits that the emperor had to hear many cases involving dishonest guardians.[22]

Given the fragmentary nature of Byzantine sources, it is impossible to know how many orphans were conscientiously nurtured, educated, and protected by their guardians and how many were neglected, abused, and despoiled. Although the paucity of evidence precludes any statistical study, it is nevertheless helpful to examine a few specific cases regarding family care of orphans to see how well in practice the Byzantine-Roman system of guardianship functioned.[23]

In 533 the emperor Justinian adjudicated the case of Martha, the daughter of the deceased senator Sergios. Martha's mother, Auxentia, assumed the duties of guardianship over Martha and took the oath not to remarry. Auxentia, however, soon broke her oath and remarried. Before this second marriage, however, she appointed a man named Peter to serve as Martha's guardian. Subsequently, Auxentia had two male children by her second husband. In the interest of these boys, she began concocting a scheme against her daughter Martha. Auxentia removed Peter from the guardianship and then forced Martha to sign an agreement renouncing any claim to a subsequent audit of the guardianship. Not yet thirteen, Martha was too young to understand that her mother was planning to seize her inheritance, but after a few years had passed, Martha sought the return of her father's estate. Fortunately, she persisted in her demands and, eventually, received her inheritance by command of the emperor Justinian himself. Had her family not been prominent, one wonders if she would have been able to appeal her case to the imperial court. Martha's case shows, first, the danger second marriages posed for children who had lost one parent and, second, that the legal safeguards against the problems caused by second marriages were not always effective.[24]

From sixth-century Alexandria comes a story concerning a wealthy pagan girl both of whose parents had died. For some reason, she received no guardian. She subsequently lost all her property primarily because of her extravagant generosity. Eventually, she became so impoverished that she was forced to become a prostitute. Shortly before she died, however, she was miraculously baptized because God was pleased with her philanthropic deeds.[25] Found in the seventh-century *Pratum Spirituale* of John Moschos, this tale might well be apocryphal, an edifying story to illustrate how charity can save even a pagan prostitute.[26] But the extraneous details—that a wealthy, non-Christian girl might end up in sixth-century Egypt without a guardian and that female orphans might be forced into prostitution—no doubt seemed plausible to Moschos' readers. Two other tales found in Byzantine hagiography (one also from sixth-century Egypt and another from eleventh-century Asia Minor) describe orphan girls whom poverty drove to prostitution.[27]

In several of his orations, the renowned Byzantine monastic leader Theodore Stoudites recounted the experiences of his mother and her two siblings, who had lost both their parents on the same day. A severe epidemic in Constantinople during the reign of Constantine V (743–65) had left these three children—two girls (including Theodore's mother) and a boy named Plato—orphans at very young ages. One of the children's uncles assumed the guardianship of Plato and provided him with an excellent education. Theodore, however, observed that it was rare for orphans to acquire such wisdom as Plato had obtained because they lacked the special care parents provided.[28] Theodore did not describe how the two girls were cared for but, in another speech, he does state that his mother had never learned to read because she had been an orphan.[29] Theodore's account therefore indicates that his mother's guardian(s) had failed to provide adequately for her education while Plato's uncle had been unusually attentive in training the boy.

According to his *vita*, the tenth-century Bithynian saint Paul the Younger lost both his father and mother. Deprived of parental protection, Paul fell into desperate poverty. His fellow villagers paid him a very low wage to tend their pigs. Paul had an elder brother, Basil, who should have functioned as Paul's guardian, but Basil had left the family earlier to join a monastery. Eventually, Basil was able to rescue Paul from his mean station and bring him to the monastery. The villagers, however, had initially tried to prevent Basil from taking Paul by accusing Basil's messenger of trying to sell Paul into slavery. It is inconceivable that the villagers were legitimately interested in the young boy's welfare, and it is more likely that they did not want to lose an inexpensive swineherd.[30] This story raises the possibility that rural communities were not above exploiting the plight of orphans to find cheap workers for unpleasant community tasks.

From the early fourteenth century comes one final example. The famous historian, humanist, and theologian Nikephoros Gregoras had lost both his parents before he reached the age of 10. His uncle John, Metropolitan of Herakleia in Pontos, became the boy's guardian and, according to Gregoras, provided him with an excellent education. He introduced young Gregoras to both the Greek classics and the spiritual riches of Christianity. John stressed that Gregoras should contemplate the natural world as a gate to understanding spiritual truths. By both word and example, John provided Gregoras with the training that enabled him to become one of the leading Byzantine intellectuals of the fourteenth century.[31]

From the nine individual cases mentioned above, only two orphans had favorable experiences: Plato in the eighth century and Nikephoros Gregoras in the fourteenth.[32] Although it is assuredly more likely that unsuccessful rather than successful cases found their way into the written sources, especially into court records, one cannot escape the conclusion that the system of guardianship did not meet the needs of all orphans, a conclusion that seems especially true regarding female children. Moreover, in cases of abandoned children and victims of war and invasion, the Roman law system of guardianship could play no role. Byzantine society, like that of the medieval West, expected the church to accept those orphans whom the system of guardianship was unable to assist.

Many early Christian documents stressed the significance of aid to orphans, a class of persons these same documents almost always linked with widows. *The Shepherd of Hermes* (early second-century Rome) recommended that Christians aid orphans and widows with what believers saved through fasting;[33] Saint Justin (mid-second-century Rome) described how individual Christians gave their alms to the bishop, who provided some sort of organized aid to the orphans.[34] By the mid fourth century, the Church of Alexandria maintained both food and shelter (*oikoi*) for orphans and widows.[35] Finally, *The Constitutions of the Apostles* from late fourth-century Syria encouraged Christians without children to adopt orphans and suggested that bishops maintain a school to train such children in useful crafts.[36]

The first detailed description of how an East Roman bishop organized orphan care comes from Caesarea in Cappadocia. By the time he became bishop of that city (371), Basil the Great had established several charitable institutions; a hospital for the sick and a hospice for travellers, both located at the city gates, are specifically mentioned in the sources.[37] In addition, he organized a boarding school for which he accepted both orphans and children with living parents. Basil incorporated this school within the monastic community that he had also established at the gates of Caesarea. His rules for this school provide a detailed view of institutional church care for orphans.[38]

Basil accepted both boys and girls at his school, but, of course, he required that the boys and girls be kept separate. Surprisingly, however, he placed more importance on the necessity of keeping younger children divided from the older ones. Basil thus established two completely separate divisions with different daily routines: an upper and a lower school. He required that the more mature and patient among the older students be set over groups of the younger children, to assist them and discipline them. Regarding academics, Basil emphasized the study of scripture over Greek myths and recommended a series of contests to encourage students to study with greater diligence, because he appreciated how much young children and adolescents loved competition. Basil also allowed those students who displayed a particular talent in a craft to leave the confines of the school during the day to receive training in that particular vocation from qualified teachers.

Basil's school was clearly designed as part of a monastic community. At the end of their studies the students were to choose whether they wished to join the monastery. Basil emphasized that his students had to make this choice free of any compulsion. Basil, however, subordinated his monastic community to episcopal authority. Thus, his school represented not only an expression of monastic *philanthropia* but also a highly developed exercise of the bishop's obligation to care for orphans.[39]

How many bishops heeded the advice of the *Constitutions of the Apostles* and followed Basil's example by maintaining a school for orphans? Sometime before the mid fifth century, the bishops of Constantinople had begun to support the Orphanotropheion, which included a school (see p. 129). Outside of the capital, however, there are no references to episcopal orphanages for many centuries after Basil's death. Finally, from tenth-century Greece comes evidence of an orphan school founded by Bishop Peter of Argos, who himself had lost his parents at an early age.[40]

As soon as Peter became bishop of Argos, he initiated a wide-scale philanthropic program to aid persons displaced by the frequent pirate raids launched from Arab-controlled Crete. To help the young orphans among these victims, Peter established a school that provided the children with training in whatever crafts they wished to pursue. If the children needed to leave Argos for necessary learning experiences, Peter offered the means for their travel. If they needed specific tools, he also paid for those.

All the information regarding Peter's school appears in the vita written by his successor as bishop of Argos.[41] The author did not describe any training in grammar or literature for the orphans. At the beginning of the vita, however, the author revealed that, as a child, he himself had been rescued by Peter and trained at the school.[42] Apparently, he had received an education in letters and literature sufficient for joining the Argos clergy and rising to the episcopal office.

The most fascinating references to an episcopal orphan school come from the pen of John Apokaukos, Metropolitan of Naupaktos in central Greece (1200–32).[43] In one of his letters, Apokaukos stated that God had blessed him with the privilege of "taking in many orphans."[44] Apokaukos provided these orphans with the basic grammar curriculum and with musical training so that they could sing the Psalter and, he hoped, join the clergy of his church. The bishop also allowed some of the orphans to leave his school for advanced training in accounting and calligraphy.[45] Apokaukos' letters reveal that conditions at his orphan school were not always ideal. Two of the students developed such a hatred of the bishop that they fled from his care.[46] One reason for the boys' flight might have been Apokaukos' harsh discipline. In another letter the bishop recommended that a troublesome orphan be beaten with a rod, flogged with whips, and harshly criticized to correct his lax character.[47] This boy's fellow students had nicknamed him "the thief." Despite Apokaukos' attempt to disguise this name as a reference to the boy's pranks, it seems clear that "the thief" had won renown for stealing.[48]

Basil of Caesarea not only provided a model of organized episcopal care for orphans, he also inspired Byzantine monasteries to assume some responsibility for nurturing orphans. This monastic tradition continued throughout the entire Byzantine era, even after many Byzantine monasteries had become completely independent of their bishops.[49]

Some of these monasteries, such as the seventh-century Syrian community of Skopelos or the thirteenth-century monastery of Saint Michael in Bithynia, simply provided food for orphans at the gates, but others accepted more responsibility for their nurture.[50] A sixth-century monastery near Antioch located wet nurses for abandoned babies. It is impossible to determine whether this monastery later received the children back into its care, but other Byzantine ascetic communities certainly did.[51] The eleventh-century *typikon* or rule of the famous monastery of Saint John on Patmos clearly stated that the monks nurtured children from infancy.[52] A twelfth-century monastery for women in Constantinople always maintained two homeless girls within the community.[53] The famous imperial monastery of the Pantokrator (twelfth century) supported twelve orphans to serve as candle lighters in the community's public church.[54] The Pantokrator typikon does not mention any school, but it is possible that some arrangements for orphan care were, in fact, standard procedures at monasteries and did not require a chapter in the typikon.

According to Anna Komnena, daughter of the emperor Alexios (1081–1118), many monasteries of Constantinople accepted orphans and assumed responsibility for educating them. After one of his campaigns in Asia Minor, Alexios brought back many war orphans to the capital. He assigned some of these to their relatives—a reference to those children for whom Alexios managed to find guardians. Others whom Anna described as pious the emperor assigned to monasteries, and he expressly required that these ascetic communities educate the children and train them in sacred letters. According to Anna's account, the emperor Alexios handed over a third group of Anatolian orphans to the great Orphanotropheion of Constantinople.[55] It is appropriate now to explore briefly this most renowned of Byzantine philanthropic foundations: first, to examine who were the orphans residing at the Orphanotropheion, and second, to discuss the course of study they pursued there.

According to tradition, the Orphanotropheion was the oldest Christian philanthropic institution in Constantinople. A priest named Zotikos founded it, most probably in the reign of the emperor Constantius (337–

61).[56] No information exists, however, concerning the orphans themselves until the mid-fifth century. In 472 Emperor Leo I granted to the *orphanotrophos* (director of the orphanage) the right to serve as guardian for the children in his institution. Although the orphanotrophos had to accept the children's property before the magistrate of the census, he was exempt from the customary audit at the close of guardianship. Leo's law reveals clearly that at least some of the children at the Orphanotropheion possessed property; not all of them were homeless waifs from the streets of Constantinople.[57]

The tenth-century *Book of Ceremonies* presents the first evidence that the orphanage also accepted children from outside the empire. On the Wednesday of Easter Week the orphanotrophos customarily introduced to the emperor twelve newly baptized persons: six adults and six orphans.[58] It seems likely that the orphanotrophos had charge of these newly initiated Christians because they had received religious training at the orphanage. From an eleventh-century letter of Michael Psellos comes evidence that the orphanotrophos worked regularly with Bulgarians and Scythians (various peoples from north of the Black Sea).[59]

In her *History* Anna Komnena offered the most detailed information regarding foreign children at the Orphanotropheion. She described Latin orphans from the west and Scythians from the north together with native Byzantines, all listening attentively to the orphanage teachers.[60] The monk Cyril Phileotis—a contemporary of Anna and of her father, Alexios—praised the Orphanotropheion for its services in catechizing the many war orphans from Turkish Anatolia, children who had been born Christian but had begun to absorb the beliefs of Islam.[61]

Cyril's observations help explain Emperor Alexios' triage of war orphans on his return from Asia Minor. The first group had relatives in Constantinople and, therefore, family guardians. The second group, whom Anna described as pious, were orphans with a firm foundation of Christian faith, children ready for the monastic schools. The third group, the children who were semi-Islamicized, needed the catechism lessons of the Orphanotropheion.

The doctrines of the Christian faith clearly formed an essential element in the curriculum at the Orphanotropheion. From Anna Komnena's description of the orphanage, however, it is possible to extract additional evidence concerning the educational program for children at the Orphanotropheion. Anna mentioned two distinct programs at the school: a primary course in grammar and a more advanced study of classical Greek literature called the *enkyklios paideia*.[62] Although there are no earlier descriptions of this two-tiered educational program at the orphanage, it was undoubtedly the system used for centuries. It corresponded to the traditional pattern of education described in many Byzantine sources. Moreover, it adhered to the structure recommended by Basil the Great for his orphan school.[63]

Anna also mentioned that some orphan students were busy solving grammatical problems. Were these children perhaps engaged in some sort of contest such as Basil had suggested? Other students were working with *schede*, short compositions on various themes from Greek literature that were written primarily to illustrate points of grammar, syntax, or meter.[64] Working with these schede became a major focus of the study program at the orphanage. Two twelfth-century teachers at the Orphanotropheion, Theodore Prodromos and Stephen Skylitzes, became famous as skilled composers of these didactic exercises.[65]

Early in its history, the Orphanotropheion also won renown for its training in singing. During the patriarchate of Gennadios (458–71), the people of Constantinople enjoyed visiting the Orphanotropheion to hear the children sing. Timokletos, brother of the orphanotrophos, wrote songs especially for the orphan chorus.[66] Through the centuries, this musical tradition remained strong. Andrew of Crete, orphanotrophos at the end of the seventh century, gained fame throughout the Orthodox Christian world as a composer of hymns.[67] In the ninth century, people identified a particular mode of antiphonal singing as the orphans' style.[68] In the reign of Leo VI (886–912) the orphans customarily performed before the emperor and high church officials on the Feast of the Epiphany (6 January).[69] On the Feast of the Purification (2 February) the orphan choir stood on benches to the right of the great door of Hagia Sophia and greeted the emperor with prayers and traditional acclamations. According to the tenth-century *Book of Ceremonies,* the orphans sang at several other imperial celebrations during the year.[70]

Theodore Prodromos, the most famous literary figure of twelfth-century Constantinople, spent his entire professional life as an instructor at the Orphanotropheion. While teaching grammar and the *enkyklios paideia,* he composed many famous schede to aid his students.[71] He also seems to have taken part in musical instruction because, at the request of the orphanotrophos, he wrote a lengthy commentary on a collection of Byzantine *kanones,* a particular form of liturgical hymn developed during the seventh century. Prodromos dedicated this commentary to Constantine, the orphanotrophos who had encouraged him to prepare it.[72] Subsequently, this commentary became the standard Byzantine reference work on these kanones.[73]

For institutional care, as for legal guardianship, it is impossible to arrive at any statistical conclusions about the effectiveness of Byzantine orphan schools in preparing their wards to be happy, well-adjusted adults. There are, nevertheless, a few concrete examples that ought to be noted. First, the tenth-century author of Peter of Argos' vita qualifies as a successful graduate of a Byzantine orphanage. As a result of what he learned in Peter's school, he was able to succeed his benefactor as bishop of Argos.[74] Second, the twelfth-century *typika* reveal two superiors who had been raised in monastic schools from an early age. Athanasios, superior of the Mamas Monastery in Constantinople, had been nurtured from infancy and educated at the Monastery of the Savior Philanthropos, also in the capital. Athanasios' words imply that he was a true orphan, not a child dedicated to the monastery (those called "oblates" in the West).[75] Similarly, a monk named Blasios became superior of the Monastery of Saint Philip in Sicily. According to the typikon, Blasios had come as an infant to the same monastery.[76] Together with Peter's hagiographer, these two superiors represent successful graduates of orphan schools.

A fourth example—this time, a young man who had lived at the Orphanotropheion—demonstrates that sometimes institutional care was less successful. Although Byzantine sources frequently mention the Orphanotropheion, they rarely describe the institution or its children in any detail. A valuable exception is a little-known poem by Constantine Stilbes, a man who taught at the orphanage at the end of the twelfth century.[77] Stilbes composed this poem to commemorate the premature death of an orphan-student of his.[78] Stilbes hailed this young man as one of the brilliant lights among his former students. Despite his academic success, the young man died long before his time, in the city of Patras, far from any friends or relatives. Moreover, he died in a philanthropic institution under the care of monks or confraternity members. This former student probably came from Constantinople. Why did he not remain in his home city? Why did he have no job, no friends, and no connections save his former teacher? Stilbes' poem omits too much to answer these questions, but it seems that this orphan failed to find a place in Byzantine society and thus died, in Stilbes' words, "a stranger in a strange land."

How common were cases such as Stilbes' student? How common were women such as the mother of Theodore Stoudites, a woman orphaned at a young age, apparently neglected by her guardian, and never taught to read or write? The scarcity of sources prevents any attempt to answer such questions. This brief essay has demonstrated, however, that Byzantine society made efforts to assist its orphans. On the one hand, it recognized the desirability of leaving children within the existing family structure, if this were possible, and, on the other hand, the necessity of institutional care in specific cases. The Byzantine system was, in fact, remarkably similar to that adopted by modern states during the past 100 years.

NOTES

1. For a summary of the Christian foundations of Byzantine society see Herbert Hunger, *Reich der neuen Mitte: Der christliche Geist der byzantinischen Kultur* (Graz, Vienna, Cologne: Styria, 1965); with regard to the subject of Byzantine law, of key importance to this present study, see especially 143–63 ("Christliche Einfluss auf die Gesetzgebung").

2. Demetrios Constantelos, *Byzantine Philanthropy and Social Welfare*, 2nd ed. (New Rochelle, N.Y.: Caratzas, 1991); Robert Volk, *Gesundheitswesen und Wohltätigkeit im Spiegel der byzantinischen Klostertypika*, Miscellanea byzantina monacensia, 28 (Munich: Institut für Byzantinistik, neugriechische Philologie, und byzantinische Kunstgeschichte der Universität Münchens, 1983); Timothy S. Miller, *The Birth of the Hospital in the Byzantine Empire*, Henry E. Sigerist Supplements to the Bulletin of the History of Medicine, 10 (Baltimore and London: Johns Hopkins Univ. Press, 1985).

3. Miller, *Hospital*, 68–88.

4. For the Jewish tradition see Marcus Cohn, "Jüdisches Waisenrecht," *Zeitschrift für Rechtswissenschaft einschliesslich der ethnologischen Rechtsforschung*, 37 (1919–20), 417–45. This article examines the Byzantine Christian tradition.

5. For the date of the orphanage, see Timothy S. Miller, "The Orphanotropheion of Constantinople," in *Through the Eye of the Needle: Judeo-Christian Roots of Social Welfare*, ed. Emily Hanawalt and Carter Lindberg (Kirksville, Mo.: Thomas Jefferson Press, 1993), 84–88. See also "Zoticos de Constantinople, nourcier des pauvres et serviteur des lépreux," ed. Michel Aubineau, *Analecta Bollandiana* 93 (1975): 95–99.

6. No thorough study has been completed on the Orphanotropheion. See my short article (Miller, "*Orphanotropheion*," 81–101) for an overview of this institution's history; see also Raymond Janin, *La géographie ecclésiastique de l'empire byzantine. première partie: La siège de Constantinople et la patriarcat oecuménique, III. Les églises et les monastères*, 2nd ed. (Paris: Institut Français d'études byzantines, 1969), 567–69. For the history of the Orphanotropheion school see Sophia Mergiali-Falangas, "L'école Saint-Paul de l'orphelinat à Constantinople: bref aperçu sur son statut et son histoire," *Revue des Études Byzantines* 49 (1991): 237–46.

7. Dieter Simon, "Die Epochen der byzantinischen Rechtsgeschichte," *Ius Commune* 15 (1988): 73–106.

8. For the most complete summary of the classical Roman law of guardianship, see Max Käser, *Das Römische Privatrecht. Vol. I: Das altrömische, das vorklassische, und klassische Recht, Handbuch der Altertumswissenschaft*, 10.3.3, pt. 1, 2nd ed. (Munich: Beck, 1971), 352–72. See also the English translation of a more compact textbook by Max Käser, *Roman Private Law*, trans. Rolf Dannenbring (Pretoria: Univ. of South Africa, 1980), chap. 62, 316–28; this is an English translation with minor revisions of the original German text (Max Käser, *Römisches Recht*, 10th ed. [1977]), which summarizes Käser's *Das Römische Privatrecht* (above) and his *Das Römische Zivilprozessrecht* (1966).

9. Strictly speaking, the grandfather or great-grandfather did not function as a guardian. According to the Roman-law rule of *patria potestas*, the oldest living male within a family was the only person the law recognized. Thus, even when the child's father was alive, the paternal grandfather, if he were still living, would have borne all legal responsibility both for the child and for that child's father. As long as the grandfather or the great-grandfather lived, the child's father had no legal standing. Legally,

therefore, nothing changed when the child's father died, if that father had a surviving ascendant (father, grandfather, or great-grandfather). Technically, the law of guardianship applied only when a child was left *sui iuris* (i.e., as an independent legal person, subject to no living male's *patria potestas*). See Käser, *Roman Private Law*, chap. 60 (*patria potestas*).

10. For the rules of guardianship for women (*tutela mulieris*), see Käser, *Das Römische Privatrecht*, 367–69; Käser, *Roman Private Law*, 324–25.

11. For the XII Tables, see Käser, *Das Römische Privatrecht*, 88-89.

12. Ibid., 311–13.

13. Codex Theodosianus (*CodTheo*) 3.30.1, *Theodosiani libri XVI cum constitutionibus Sirmondianis*, ed. Theodor Mommsen and Paul Meyer, 2 vols. (Berlin: Weidmann, 1905). For the *hypotheca*, see Käser, *Das Römische Privatrecht*, 463–69; and Käser, *Roman Private Law*, 156–57.

14. Käser, *Das Römische Privatrecht*, 352–54.

15. *CodTheo* 3.30.2.

16. *CodTheo* 3.30.3.

17. *CodTheo* 3.30.5.

18. *CodTheo* 3.17.4.

19. Saint Basil, *eps.* 107–9, *Letters*, ed. Roy J. Defferrari, Loeb Classical Library (London: Heinemann, 1930), vol. 2, 202–8.

20. *Novellae* (*JustNov*) 118.5, *Corpus juris civilis, III: Novellae*, ed. Rudolf Schoell and Wilhelm Kroll (Berlin: Weidmann, 1928).

21. *JustNov* 94.

22. *JustNov* 72, praef.

23. *JustNov* 155.

24. The problems of second marriages were well understood by Church leaders. See John Chrysostom, *Vidua eligatur*, chaps. 5–6, *Patrologia ¢ursus ¢ompletus. Series Graeca*. Ed. J.P. Migne, Paris, 1857–1886 (hereinafter PG), 51: 325–27.

25. *Ioannis Moschi Pratum Spirituale*, chap. 207, PG, 87.3: 3097–3100.

26. *The Oxford Dictionary of Byzantium* (New York and Oxford: Oxford Univ. Press, 1991), vol. 1, 1415.

27. *Apothegmata Patrum*, PG, 65: 218–20; *De Sancto Lazaro monacho in Monte Galesio, Acta Sanctorum*, Novembris, vol. 3 (Brussels: Société des Bollandistes, 1910), 529.

28. *Laudatio Sancti Platonis Hegumeni*, PG, 99: 804–8.

29. *Laudatio funebris in matrem*, PG, 99: 885.

30. *Vita Sancti Pauli Iunioris in Monte Latro*, ed. H. Delehaye, *Analecta Bollandiana* 11 (1892): 20–26.

31. "La vie de Jean, Métropolite d'Héraclée du Pont," ed. V. Laurent, *Archeion Pontou* 6 (1934): 53–61. For a brief biography of Nikephoras Gregoras, see *Oxford Dictionary of Byzantium*, vol. 1, 874–75.

32. Nine cases, including the two orphan girls who ended up as prostitutes (see note 27).

33. *Der Hirt des Hermes*, ed. Molly Whittaker, Griechische-Christliche Schriftsteller, 48 (Berlin: Akademie Verlag, 1967), 56.7 (parable 5.3).

34. *Justini apologia prima*, 67.6–8, *Saint Justin: Apologies*, ed. André Wartelle (Paris: Études Augustiniennes, 1987), 192.

35. *Socratis scholastici ecclesiastica historia*, 2.28, ed. Robert Hussey (Oxford, 1853), vol. 1, 270–71.

36. *Les Constitutions Apostoliques*, 4.1–2, ed. Marcel Metzger, Sources Chrétiennes, 329 (Paris: Éditions du Cerf, 1986), 170–73.

37. Miller, *Hospital*, 85–88.

38. The rules for Basil's school are contained in Interrogatio XV, in *Basilii Magni regulae fusius tractatae*, PG, 31: 952–56.

39. Miller, *Hospital*, 118–22; Gilbert Dagron, "Les moines et la ville: Le

monachisme à Constantinople jusqu'au concile de Chalcédoine (451)," *Traveaux et Mémoires*, 4 (1970), 229–76.

40. *Vita et conversatio Sancti Petri episcopi Argivorum*, in *Patrum nova bibliotheca*, ed. Angelo Mai (Rome, 1888), vol. 9, pt. 3, 1–8.

41. Ibid., 17.

42. Ibid., 1.

43. *Oxford Dictionary of Byzantium*, vol. 1, 135.

44. *Ep.* 27, "Unedierte Schriftstücke aus der Kanzlei des Joannes Apokaukos," ed. N.A. Bees, *Byzantinische-Neugriechische Jahrbücher* 21 (1971–72): 85–86.

45. *Epp.* 100 and 101, ibid., 150–52.

46. *Ep.* 27, ibid., 85–86.

47. *Ep.* 101, ibid., 152.

48. *Ep.* 100, ibid., 150–51.

49. Miller, *Hospital*, 120–40. Regarding independent churches and monasteries, see John P. Thomas, *Private Religious Foundations in the Byzantine Empire* (Washington, D.C.: Dumbarton Oaks, 1987).

50. For the Monastery of Skopelos, see *Joannis Moschi pratum spirituale*, PG, 87.3: 2941; for the Monastery of the Archangel Michael, see Aleksei Dmitrievskij, *Opisanie liturgiceskih rukopisej hranjascihsja v bibliotekah pravoslavnago vostoka, I: Typika* (Kiev, 1895), 783–85; see commentary on this *typikon*, in Volk, *Gesundheitswesen*, (see Note 2), 236.

51. *La vie ancienne de S. Syméon Stylite le jeune (521–94)*, ed. Paul Van den Van, Subsidia Hagiographica, 32 (Brussels: Société des Bollandistes, 1962), vol. 1, 146–47. This case has been studied by John Boswell, *The Kindness of Strangers: The Abandonment of Children in Western Europe from Late Antiquity to the Renaissance* (New York: Pantheon, 1988), 195; Boswell implied that women were being kept within the monastery. I can find no justification for Boswell's conjecture in the Greek text.

52. Franz Miklosich and Joseph Müller, *Acta et diplomata graeca medii aevi*, 6 vols. (Vienna, 1860–90), vol. 6, 83. A Byzantine *typikon* was both the rule of the monastery and the foundation charter of that institution. For the first time a complete collection of these important documents will soon be available. See *Byzantine Monastic Foundation Documents: A Complete Translation of the Surviving Founders' Typika and Testaments*, ed. John P. Thomas, Angela C. Hero, et al. (Washington, D.C.: Dumbarton Oaks, forthcoming).

53. "Le typikon de la Théotokos Kécharitôménè," ed. Paul Gautier, *Revue des Études Byzantines* 43 (1985): 41.

54. "Le typikon du Christ Sauveur Pantocrator," ed. Paul Gautier, *Revue des Études Byzantines* 32 (1974): 75–79.

55. Anna Comnène, *Alexiade* 15.7, ed. Bernard Leib (Paris: "Les Belles Lettres," 1945), vol. 3, 213–18, esp. 214 regarding the three methods of providing care for the orphans of Asia Minor.

56. Miller, "*Orphanotropheion*," 84–88.

57. *Codex Justinianus* 1.3.31(32), *Corpus juris civilis, II: Codex Justinianus*, ed. Paul Krüger (Berlin: Weidmann, 1929).

58. *Le livre de Cérémonies* 1.21(12), ed. Albert Vogt (Paris: "Les Belles Lettres," 1935), vol. 1, 82.

59. *Ep.* 240, *Michaelis Pselli scripta minora. II: Epistulae*, ed. Eduard Kurtz and Franz Drexl (Milan: "Vita e Pensiero," 1941), 290–91.

60. Anna Comnène, *Alexiade* 15.7.9, p. 218.

61. *La vie de saint Cyrille le Philéote, moine byzantin*, ed. Étienne Sargologos, Subsidia Hagiographica, 39 (Brussels: Société des Bollandistes, 1964), 225–31.

62. Anna Comnène, *Alexiade* 15.7.3 and 9, pp. 214 and 218.

63. *Basilii Magni regulae fusius tractatae*, PG, 31: 952–53.

64. Anna Comnène, *Alexiade* 15.7.9, p. 218. Regarding *schede*, see Giuseppe Schirò, "La schedografia a bisanzio nei secoli XI-XII a la scuola dei ss. XL martiri," *Bolletino della Badia greca di Grottaferrata*, n.s. 3 (1949): 11–29.

65. Regarding Prodromos, see *ep.* 1 of Michael Italikos, *Michel Italikos: Lettres et discours*, ed. Paul Gautier, Archives de l'Orient Chrétien, 14 (Paris: Institut français d'études byzantines, 1972) 61; and "Monodie de Nicétas Eugénianos sur Théodore Prodromos," ed. Louis Petit, *Vizantiiskij Vremennik* 9 (1902): 461–62. Regarding Stephen Skylitzes, see "Monodie de Théodore Prodrome sur Étienne Skylitzes métropolitain de Trébizonde," ed. Louis Petit, *Bulletin de l'institut archéologique russe à Constantinople* 8 (1903): 7.

66. *The Syriac Chronicle known as that of Zachariah of Mitylene* 4.11, trans. F.J. Hamilton and E.W. Brooke (London, 1899), 79–80.

67. Miller, "*Orphanotropheion*," 88–89.

68. *Vita Sancti Antonii*, in *Pravoslavnij Palestinskij Sbornik* 19, no. 3 (1907): 211–12.

69. *Kleterologion of Philotheos (Le Traité de Philothée)*, ed. Nicholas Oikonomides, in *Les listes de préséance byzantines des IXe et Xe siècles* (Paris: Éditions du centre national de la recherche scientifique, 1972), 185–86.

70. *Le livre de Cérémonies* 1.36(27); 39(30), vol. 1, 139–40 and 153.

71. "Monodie de Eugénianos sur Prodrome," 461–62.

72. *Theodori Prodromi commentarios in carmina sacra melodorum Cosmae Hierosolymitani et Joannis Damasceni*, ed. Henricus M. Stevenson (Rome, 1888), 1–2. See also Giovanni Mercati, "*Orphanotrophos*," in *Opere minori, raccolte in occasione della settantesimo natalizio*, Studi e Testi 78 (1937): vol. 3, 331.

73. Wolfram Hörandner, *Theodor Prodromos: Historische Gedichte*, Wiener Byzantinische Studien, 11 (Vienna: Österreichische Akademie der Wissenschaften, 1974), 44.

74. *Vita Sancti Petri Argivorum*, 1 and 17.

75. "Typikon tes en Kōnstantinopolei monēs tou agiou megalomartyros Mamantos," ed. Sophronios Eustratiades, *Hellenika* 1 (1928): 258–59.

76. *Le Pergamene greche esistanti nel grande archivio di Palermo*, ed. and trans. Giuseppe Spata (Palermo, 1861), 200–1.

77. Stilbes alludes to his twelve-year career at the orphanage in his inaugural speech as *didaskalos* (teacher) of the Apostle (Paul); see *Constantino Stilbes: La Prolusione del Maestro dell' Apostolo*, ed. Lia Raffaella Cresci, Letteratura e civiltà bizantina, 2 (Messina: Edizioni Dr. A. Sfameni, 1987), 48.

78. The oldest copy of this poem appears in *Vaticanus graecus* 672, fols. 290–290ʳ. A critical edition of the poem, collated from ten manuscripts, exists in typescript, prepared by J. Diethart, *Der Rhetor und Didaskalos Konstantin Stilbes*, Univ. of Vienna doctoral dissertation (Wien: Universitäts Bibliothek, 1971), 88–90.

Infant Death in Late Medieval Florence

The Smothering Hypothesis Reconsidered[1]

Philip Gavitt

> *The current quest for the child in history is missing the point by not considering boys and girls separately.*
>
> *—Richard Wall*

The tendency to conflate abandonment and infanticide has as one of its most powerful expressions the figure of the smothering wet nurse. Infanticide committed by parents, the argument runs, became supplanted by infanticide committed by institutions and, specifically, by those institutional mother-substitutes, wet nurses. These wet nurses had a financial interest in infanticide, as one historian of Renaissance Italy noted, because "the supply [of babies] from the parish wardens was unlimited."[2] The malfeasance of wet nurses was a staple of contemporary writing as well, and fifteenth-century parents were so convinced that babies sent to a wet nurse were vulnerable to accidental or deliberate smothering that Tuscans invented the *arcuccio*, a bassinet with an arched rib so that it would be impossible for a nurse to roll over in bed and accidentally smother a child.[3] As Barbara Kellum's work on England has suggested, early medieval penitentials recognized the problem of overlaying and prescribed relatively lenient penalties.[4] In the late Middle Ages also, theologians and bishops even warned parents not to bring their small infants into bed with them, and doing so made parents (or wet nurses) automatically culpable.[5]

Taking such sources at face value, a surprising number of historians have worked the smothering parent and the smothering wet nurse into larger arguments concerning the lack of an affective dimension within the premodern family, suggesting that high infant mortality was at the root of a seriously depraved indifference to infant human life. Emily Coleman's study of the ninth-century polyptychs of Saint Germain-des-Pres, for example, noted serious discrepancies in gender ratios on manses: the smaller the land area, the fewer the females. Coleman concluded from this that early medieval parents practiced widespread female infanticide to confront the economic necessity of limiting population growth.[6] John Boswell—in his more recent study, *The Kindness of Strangers*—has pointed out that such conclusions assume that there was no movement of labor from one manse to another, and he suggests convincingly that to some extent larger landholders absorbed the excess female population of the smaller ones.[7] Boswell also dismisses the argument that evidence from Icelandic sagas proves the practice of infanticide, arguing instead that children left exposed were meant to be found.[8] Although Carol Clover argues cogently and persuasively that the sagas describe intentional infanticide, it is still salutary to heed Boswell's cautions concerning the nature of literary source material.[9] Barbara Kellum's study of England was able to find considerable evidence of the accidental death of older children, but in her own words:

> Estimating from the number of times overlaying and infanticide appear in the penitential context alone, it would only seem likely that similar cases would be mentioned in the contemporary coroners' and judicial records. Instead, they are conspicuously absent. Not one case of what now could technically be termed infanticide—the killing of a child under a year old—is reported in the Coroner's Rolls (A.D. 1265–1413) published by the Selden Society.[10]

When infanticide did occur, as it did in eighty-seven cases from early modern Nürnberg, it involved the violent deaths of young children rather than the smothering of infants.[11] Indeed, all discussions of infanticide by smothering have been taken from court and other judicial records, not the records of charitable or other kinds of municipal institutions.

Late medieval Tuscan sources, however, offer the unique advantage of allowing at least partial study of infant and child death, not only through the *ricordanze* of wealthy families but also through books of the dead used by grain officials to calculate the amount of grain they needed to import to feed the population of fourteenth- and fifteenth-century Florence.[12] Foundling hospital records, even if they do not always give the exact cause of death, do at least allow certain patterns to emerge. Using records from the foundling hospital of the Innocenti in late medieval Florence, I will both cover the wide variety of causes of death among late medieval Florentine infants and argue, from both epidemiological and "eyewitness" evidence, that most attributions of suffocation can be shown conclusively to have been cases of sudden infant death. This is not a new hypothesis: Todd Savitt's study of children entrusted to slaves (who were subsequently accused of smothering) in nineteenth-century Virginia revealed patterns of infant death similar to those associated with sudden infant death syndrome (SIDS) in King County, Washington State, a century later.[13] For late nineteenth-century England, Elizabeth Hansen has argued that

> the predominantly urban and lower-class distribution of SIDS, as well as the similarity of its symptoms to infant disorders caused by malnutrition, point to the possibility that the infant mortality figures reflected a large number of infant deaths not due to infanticide but to SIDS.[14]

But to date, historians, except for Hansen, have not drawn out the implications of Savitt's findings for the smothering hypothesis in general, largely because evidence of the beliefs of contemporaries seems to offer such a formidable consensus and because direct accounts are so rare. Moreover, anthropologists, biologists, and physicians have incorporated much of the secondary historical literature on infanticide into studies of infanticide among humans and animals, surrounding these historical studies with an unmerited aura of scientific credibility.[15] Although, indeed, infant death was much higher within orphanages and other children's institutions than outside them, both the types of symptoms and the patterns of mortality suggest plague, malnutrition, and outright starvation as more direct causes of infant death than smothering. In the anthropological literature as well, starvation or nutritional disadvantage were traditional methods of infanticide, especially female infanticide.[16] Smothering, accidental or purposeful, is rarely the method of infanticide in the twentieth-century cultures that have been observed.

The data for this study were gathered in 1991 from the hospital of Santa Maria degli Innocenti in Florence, which was designed in 1419 by the architect Filippo Brunelleschi. Brunelleschi worked on the construction project until 1427, although the hospital did not finally open its doors until 1445. Between 1445 and 1485, however, this charitable institution kept detailed records of the 6,470 children admitted, approximately 90 percent of whom were infants, and of the wet nurses (both in-house and in the countryside) who served them.[17] Perhaps in a flush of administrative enthusiasm, the hospital's scribe and treasurer, Lapo di Ser Piero Pacini, recorded the causes of death of some fifty-one children admitted between April 1445 and August 1451.[18] After that date scribes recorded cause of death only rarely, so that by the late 1450s, only when hospital officials suspected malfeasance or neglect did they record a cause of death at all. Although both admissions and mortality rates more than doubled over the period 1445 to 1485, scribes recorded the causes of fifty infant and child deaths in the first five years of the period, but of only seven in the last five years of the period. It would seem that in the 1460s, death rates became so high that hospital officials were desensitized to its causes, or too overwhelmed to write them down. The unfortunate result for the historian is that the higher the mortality rate was at the Innocenti, the more unreliable are the data as diagnostic tools, so that further study from the Innocenti records, at least for the late fifteenth and sixteenth centuries, is not a feasible method of determining causes of death.

The 163 children for whom we have a cause of death represent about 4 percent of the nearly 4,000 children we know died during this forty-year period. The distribution by gender of this 4 percent, however, reflects the distribution by gender among the larger group: about 57 percent of deaths were among female infants and children, a percentage that roughly reflects their percentage in admissions statistics as well. Of the 163 children of both sexes whose cause of death is known, 34 percent died from plague, which affected males and females equally (see table 1). Hunger or malnutrition accounted for another 17 percent, slightly higher among female than among male children. Intestinal diseases claimed 12 percent of the hospital's share of deaths, at a rate considerably higher for females (16.3 percent) than for males. Another 8 percent died from either "febre" or "mal maestro," seizures caused by high fever (the distribution by gender is virtually equal), and 5 percent from smallpox, which hit females especially hard. Accusations that the wet nurse suffocated the child account for about 6 percent of listed causes of death, with the balance heavily weighted toward males.

Two obvious problems occur with the use of these figures. First, once we break down our 163 cases into diagnoses, the sample is too small to draw any firm conclusions about epidemiology and gender. Even without breaking down the figures by gender, we can only describe this as a very rough sketch of causes of infant and child mortality over those forty years. Second, as Ann Carmichael has astutely noted in her book *Plague and the Poor in Renaissance Florence*, the task of reconstructing a twentieth-century medical diagnosis from such picturesque expressions as "mal maestro" runs a real risk of distorting the experience of the past.[19] To take a more modern example as an illustration, when archaeologists over the course of the next millennium dig up millions of bottles that once contained Italian mineral water, they are likely to infer from the labels that in the middle years of the twentieth century there was a virulent epidemic of "mal di fegato." This problem is compounded not only by the lack of any premodern category that describes what we know as SIDS, but also by the way the term "sudden in-

TABLE 1

Causes of Infant and Child Death, Hospital of Santa Maria degli Innocenti, Florence: 1445–1485

	Male	Female	Total
Accidents	3	3	6
Intestinal diseases	4	15	19
Plague	24	32	56
Malnutrition/starvation	11	17	28
Fever/convulsions	6	7	13
"Suffocation"	7	3	10
"Found dead"	3	3	6
Neglect	1		1
"Evil befell him/her"	7	2	9
Respiratory diseases (not counting plague)	1		1
Rubella (German measles)	1	1	2
Smallpox	2	7	9
"God pardon the wet nurse"	1	2	3
Total	71	92	163

Source: Archivo dell'Ospedale degli Innocenti (Florence), Balie e Bambini A–L (XVI, 1–12), 1445–1485.

fant death syndrome" in modern medical terminology eludes precise definition.[20] Its diagnosis can only be made by autopsy, from which it is often impossible to tell deliberate from adventitious suffocation.

In a context more specifically premodern, Carmichael has argued convincingly that diagnoses of "mignatti" or "bachi" (worms) probably refer to intestinal symptoms involving diarrhea.[21] This is certainly the case with breast-fed infants, who after all would not have been capable of ingesting foods containing parasites. Carmichael's study of the Florentine books of the dead notes that the vast majority of cases occurred between twelve and twenty-four months of age, when parents would have been weaning their children and when these diarrheal symptoms began to occur as a result of switching from breast milk to solid foods. The organization of table 1 therefore follows Carmichael and includes "bachi," "mignatti," and "mal di pondi" under intestinal diseases that closely resemble dysentery.[22] Carmichael also argues that communal and hospital officials, especially in years of plague epidemics, overdiagnosed plague as a cause of death, effectively lumping any symptoms they did not understand under the category of "morbo."[23] Unfortunately, there is no way to test this at the Innocenti; suffice it to say that the vast concentration of deaths attributed to plague does occur in the plague years of 1449 and 1457.

It is Carmichael's discussion of infant death that is the least convincing, however. In her survey of Florentine books of the dead of the early fifteenth century, she notes that, among thirteen attributions of infant death to wet-nurse suffocation, eight victims were male. Nonetheless, despite raising the possibility that these cases might involve SIDS, and noting that the gender ratios involved reflect the epidemiology of SIDS, she curiously dismisses the conclusion that these deaths are due to SIDS.[24]

But what is the epidemiology of SIDS?[25] Sudden infant death syndrome, or "crib death," is still one of the more elusive causes of infant death, although it is the leading cause of death among children less than one year old.[26] Researchers have noticed a predominance of males among the victims of SIDS, although, because samples involved in research are so small, the significance of this predominance is unclear. The highest ratio mentioned of male to female victims is 60:40, with most studies forming a consensus of around 55:45.[27] It is thus difficult to establish, even now, whether the male predominance in SIDS simply reflects the lesser resilience of male infants in the face of disease in general, or whether it reflects this specific syndrome. The consensus of studies, again, is that a pattern of male predominance does not by itself indicate a pattern of sudden infant death.[28] Much more indicative is the age of the victims. The death of an infant under one month of age or of a child over twelve months of age is usually sufficient to rule out SIDS, and 85 percent to 90 percent of cases involve children between one and five months of age, with the incidence of SIDS peaking at two–three months of age.[29]

Its incidence ranges from 0.36 to 3 infant deaths per 1,000 live births in modern populations to 4.2 per 1,000 live births among populations in economic and social circumstances comparable to those of the pre-industrial era.[30] Certain infants can now be identified as at-risk infants: those with sleep apnea and low-birth-weight, premature infants. The highest-risk group are babies born to young mothers who space pregnancies very closely together.[31] This is, of course, especially pertinent to the demography of fifteenth-century Florence, where the average age of marriage for females was in the middle to late teens, and where families consciously pursued a strategy of maximizing fertility and minimizing the amount of time between pregnancies by packing off a nursing infant to a rural wet nurse as soon as possible.[32] In many cases, SIDS presents no prior or identifying symptoms beyond sudden and otherwise unexplained death. In other cases, it may follow a mild respiratory infection or a low-grade fever.[33] Closely related to this set of symptoms is the seasonality of deaths: 54 percent to 62 percent of SIDS deaths occur between October and March, which the late nineteenth-century Scottish police surgeon Templeman attributed to the tendency of poorer families to huddle together for warmth during the winter.[34] More recent research, however, notes this seasonal pattern even in Hawaii, suggesting that prevalence of respiratory diseases, not climate, constitutes the link between winter and sudden infant death.[35] In most cases, the dead infant will have blood-tinged mucus below the nostrils or around the mouth.[36]

As perilous as any sort of epidemiological conclusions might be, it is worth venturing a closer look at the Innocenti data from 1445 to 1485, especially since only a study of two or more centuries' worth of data (or a study of several different cities) would provide a sufficient sample for generalization. Of the ten infants whose wet nurses were accused of smothering, seven were male and three were female (see table 2). If we extend the study to include those who were found dead next to the wet nurse, ten were male and six female, which still shows an exaggerated pattern of male infant mortality due to alleged suffocation (table 2). When one refers to table 1, it is clear that, although males represented 43.6 percent of total deaths, they represented 62.5 percent of deaths by alleged suffocation. This is not, however, the only cause of death in which deaths are disproportionate by gender. Female children were even more disproportionately represented among deaths by intestinal disease: 78.9 percent of children dying from intestinal disease were female, while females represented only 56.4 percent of total deaths. The importance of this will be discussed below.

Of the fourteen cases of alleged suffocation or sudden unexplained death for which the age of the infant can be determined, only four fall outside the range of the highest incidence of SIDS and only two would be disqualified altogether. Moreover, because of the lack of specificity of the Innocenti records, some of the infants I have described as "newborn" may well be as old as a week or two, which might theoretically allow us to include them as well. Even without them, however, the data show a remarkable correlation by age to the victims of SIDS, with a distinct peak between two and three months of age. Excluding the two infants less than a month old, three infants died during their second month of life, five during their third month, two during their fourth or fifth month, and two beyond their sixth month (table 2).

Patterns of the seasonality of death among the Innocenti children make the case with somewhat less conviction. Only 40 percent (six out of fifteen), instead of the expected 54–60 percent, died between October and March, while another 40 percent died during the summer months. This may reflect the small size of the sample, but since so many of the deaths occur in

July, August, or September, the deaths may reflect correlations to respiratory infections connected to outbreaks of pneumonic plague, at its most deadly in the late summer and early autumn months.[37]

Were it possible to make this case on the basis of epidemiology alone, one could simply add this to a growing number of studies such as that of Todd Savitt's for nineteenth-century Virginia.[38] But Christiane Klapisch-Zuber's discussion of smothering in her article "Blood Parents and Milk Parents: Wet-Nursing in Florence 1300–1450" also raises some interesting points of circumstantial evidence.[39] Of eight cases of alleged suffocation mentioned in seven fifteenth- and sixteenth-century diaries, five involve infant boys and three involve infant girls. Excluding the case of Biagio Buonaccorsi, whose infants, a boy and a girl, were allegedly suffocated before they were a month old, we are still left with four boys and two girls.[40] If deliberate or accidental smothering was somehow connected to infamous Mediterranean misogyny, why does this pattern of either equal or predominantly male mortality continue to prevail?

TABLE 2

"Suffocation" Deaths: 1445–1485

Sex	Approximate Age at Admission	Approximate Age at Death	Month and Year of Death
F	newborn	10m, 14d	June 1453
M	newborn	2m, 24d	July 1453
F	?	?	August 1456
F	newborn	3–5m	between 19 July and 18 Aug. 1462
M	newborn	1m, 23d	May 1471
M	newborn	2m, 13d	January 1472
M	newborn	1m	February 1474
F	newborn	26d	October 1475
M	newborn	7m, 4d	October 1475
M	newborn	2m, 11d	September 1477
M	newborn	1m, 7d	October 1478
M	newborn	3m, 16d	August 1480
M	newborn	2m, 23d	November 1480
M	?	?	?
F	newborn	over 20d	after 6 July 1483
F	newborn	2m, 16d	April 1483

Source: Archivio dell'Ospedale degli Innocenti (AOIF), Balie e Bambini A–L (XVI, 1–12), 1445–1485.

Even more curious is Klapisch-Zuber's discussion of the *arcuccio*, mentioned as early as 1403 in the *ricordanze* that she studied. Out of twenty-five families, thirteen included a cradle with an infant's trousseau, and ten of those cradles had arched ribs that surely—whether or not they were intended to prevent smothering—would have prevented smothering. In Klapisch-Zuber's words, however:

> In any event, the frame evidently did not prevent all accidents, and in at least two of the cases of suffocation studied here the child's trousseau included a cradle with a frame. Thus, either the nurse took the baby in with her at night, removing him from the protective frame, or the frame was insufficient protection against the couple's heavy sleep.[41]

Although the first possibility might well be admitted, the second possibility presupposes not only the heaviness of sleep but the heaviness of the couple as well, who indeed would have to defy both architectural principle and Tuscan craftsmanship to make themselves lethal. Surely the more plausible hypothesis is that these two infants died of SIDS rather than of deliberate suffocation.

Richard Trexler's study of infanticide, on which Klapisch-Zuber relied for her discussion of foundling-hospital wet nurses, also proceeds from mistaken assumptions about the economics of wet-nursing. Although in theory the supply of infants from hospital officials was unlimited, in practice, as Professor Takahashi has observed, almost all the wet nurses the hospital of the Innocenti employed worked for the institution only once, often to pay off a family debt.[42] Moreover, his study of infanticide prosecutions in the diocese of Fiesole in the first three decades of the sixteenth century fails to establish any pattern whatsoever by gender. In a society in which male infants were especially valued, what possible economic interest would a wet nurse have had in their suffocation?

Yet my conviction that such deaths were crib deaths rests not even on the circumstantial case presented above. It rests instead on a documentary description of several cases of alleged suffocation, and of one crucial case in particular. On 3 September 1480, a certain Mona Lazera from La Castellina, near Florence, left her newborn son, wrapped in rags, on the baptismal font at the hospital of the Innocenti. She was not an especially reticent parent; she remained long enough to tell the scribe that she had given birth that morning. Hospital officials immediately baptized him with the names Giano and Francesco.

Although Giano Francesco was fed by an in-house wet nurse, not until the end of September, when he was nearly a month old, did the hospital place him with a rural wet nurse. Mona Antonia di Piero Feretti contracted to take Giano for thirteen months and to be paid 50 soldi a month until he was weaned, and then 25 soldi per month. She took him back to her home parish of San Piero a Quintole a Girone, a rural location in the fifteenth century but close enough that it is now a suburban neighborhood of Florence. The hospital supplied her with nine cloth pieces, plus three woolens and three sets of swaddling bands.

Nothing was heard from the wet nurse until nearly two months later. In the words of the scribe:

> She brought him back dead on November 26, 1480. Our women say that they think the baby was suffocated because the wet nurse says there was blood coming out of his mouth. And she brought back four fewer pieces of cloth than we gave her.[43]

What is important here is not merely the wet nurse's identification of a common symptom of sudden infant death, but rather the criterion that the women of the hospital used to make the judgment that the wet nurse had suffocated the child. At least implied is the notion that the hospital's women made this judgment in all cases of suspected suffocation, and that, therefore, these cases represent crib death rather than malfeasance on the part of wet nurses. In addition to all the other evidence cited above, this case strongly suggests that the figures of the smothering wet nurse and the smothering parent are characters in medieval penitential literature who had few equivalents in actual practice. This is not to suggest that infanticide was nonexistent or even rare in premodern society, but rather to argue that accidental suffocation by overlaying is no more satisfactory an explanation of sudden infant death than evil spirits or demonic magic.[44]

Moreover, even if these were cases of suffocation, they appear so infrequently in the records that premodern views of wet nurses should be attributed to misogyny rather than experience.[45] Undoubtedly, infanticide occurred in the past as it occasionally does today, and undoubtedly it occasionally took the form of deliberate smothering. The most recent research on crib death, moreover, suggests that concerted attention to preventive health care can have dramatic results. In Australia and New Zealand, for example, physicians are suggesting that the traditional practice of placing infants on their stomach to avoid choking or crib death is misguided, and that young infants should be placed on their backs, a recommendation that grew out of the experience of Hong Kong's low rate of sudden infant death.[46] Among several populations where this solution has been implemented, substantial reductions in the incidence of crib death have been reported. Recent American studies suggest that as many as one-quarter of deaths attributed to SIDS actually involve accidental suffocation of infants on soft pillows, beanbags, and certain types of foam mattresses, while other studies suggest that from 2 percent to 10 percent of cases in which SIDS seems to be implicated are deliberate infanticides.[47]

I would be especially reluctant to argue that, by virtue of the foregoing evidence, early modern foundling hospitals were either benign or advanced in their approach to infant care. Indeed, now that we have eliminated deliberate suffocation as the cause for most unexplained infant deaths, the burden of explaining why infant mortality within institutions was so much higher than in society at large remains. Estimates of infant mortality in the nineteenth century, for example, placed infant mortality at about 40 percent outside institutions and at 75–80 percent within them.[48] In the fifteenth century, infant mortality may have been as low as 20 percent outside institutions, but usually 40 percent to 50 percent inside them.[49]

Certainly, in the fifteenth century plague years account for elevated mortality both inside and outside of foundling homes. Institutions such as the Innocenti, which often had more than one infant in a bed, would have been especially vulnerable to any type of epidemic outbreak. Moreover, René Spitz's work on a Connecticut foundling home in the 1930s—where, despite massive inoculations against measles, he had to cancel his study because twenty-three of the eighty-eight infants died from a measles outbreak—noted that mortality from measles outside the institution was less than 0.5 percent. Since the institution itself maintained the strictest standards of hygiene, Spitz suggested (as have others since) that the lack of touch and affection in the institutional environment severely depressed infants' immune systems.[50]

But looking back at causes of death at the Innocenti, it is immediately clear that, among diseases, only plague took a truly devastating toll of children, and that the two other leading causes of death, intestinal diseases and malnutrition, had a direct link to wet nurses. Children were much more vulnerable to dehydration, malnutrition, and outright starvation than they were to rubella or smallpox. These cases of malnutrition did not involve older children, whose diet in the hospital, if monotonous, was both adequate and nutritious.[51] Instead, almost every death attributable to malnutrition was connected with children in the countryside at wet nurse. Most of these were listed as death from hunger (*fame*), but on those occasions in which scribes were more inquisitive, they wrote that these malnourished children were fed "latte prengno" (pregnant milk) or "latte cattivo" (also so-called pregnant milk). In other cases, scribes would write, "The child was not given milk" or the wet nurse "did not have milk."

On still other occasions, a neighbor would report that the wet nurse had substituted soggy bread for milk or, more inventively, would use goat's or cow's milk.[52] Although mastitis might account for a small fraction of these cases, clearly the issue involved in cessation of the flow of milk was the wet nurse's pregnancy. Moreover, the tendency of wet nurses to become pregnant a few months after taking on a child from the foundling hospital is also connected to intestinal diseases among their charges. As Carmichael has pointed out, weaning was associated with intestinal symptoms that fifteenth-century Tuscans thought were worms, and one might well speculate that the symptoms would be more acute for those infants prematurely weaned.[53] This might suggest that not only the urban wealthy but also the rural poor sought to maximize fertility by closely spacing births, the rural poor hoping at the same time to collect payments from the hospital for services they were no longer able to perform.

Such an explanation does not, however, adequately account for the predominance of female deaths from intestinal diseases, symptomatic of hunger and malnutrition. In this respect, the association that Trexler noted between being a female infant and dying at wet nurse is wrongly paired with clerical concern about smothering but rightly focused on the issue of the differential treatment of male and female infants.[54] Lauris McKee has suggested a crucial relationship in envionmentally stressed, pre-industrial societies between a cultural preference for males, arising from their greater biological vulnerability, and female mortality, pursued as a deliberate strategy to compensate for the greater likelihood of female survival.[55] In these societies, reducing the survival rate of female infants and children can take several forms, including reduced access to breast milk, less food, greater exposure to heat and cold, and early weaning, which has been practiced by several male-preference societies in the twentieth century and was counseled in the late Middle Ages by the Paduan physician Savonarola.[56]

Whatever the cause of the increased likelihood of girls dying from intestinal diseases, it is clear that these diseases account for greater death rates among female children in general:

As malnutrition develops because of the poor weaning diet, acute diarrheal disease becomes increasingly likely to lead to death. At the same time, diarrheal disease reduces appetite, increases metabolic loss of nitrogen, and leads to further dietary restriction, all of which hastens the lowering of resistance to infection.[57]

Citing another study of South Asia from the mid-1960s, Barbara Miller notes:

> Of the major causes of death of infants in the Khanna study area reported by Gordon, Singh, and Wyon (1965), infantile diarrheal diseases were much more widespread among infant girls. The greater presence of the disease was paralleled by higher death rates for girls.[58]

Although the anthropological literature finds excess female mortality due to weaning diarrhea beginning not in the first but the second year of life, both the Innocenti data and the data cited by Carmichael suggest that in late medieval Florence diarrheal disease was a significant contributor to *infant* mortality as well.[59] Finally, Mildred Dickeman has noted a strong association between societies (among which she includes late medieval Florence) in which dowry-hypergamy plays a large role in marriage alliance and excess female mortality in childhood.[60]

The anthropological literature suggests two relevant conclusions. First, in a society such as that of late medieval Florence, dominated by male preference, causes of death in which males outnumber females are more likely to be biological than infanticidal, and certainly "suffocation" falls under the latter rubric. Second, since females have a greater likelihood of biological survival, cultural preference is to be suspected in causes of death that are predominantly among female children. Thus, if Tuscan fathers rightly feared the malfeasance of wet nurses, the danger was not deliberate or accidental suffocation but the cultural preconceptions that made female infants more likely to starve to death.

NOTES

1. This is an expanded version of a paper read at the International Conference on Medieval Studies, Kalamazoo, Mich., May 1992. Among the many helpful commentators at that conference, I wish especially to thank Joan Cadden and Louis Haas.

2. R. Trexler, "Infanticide in Florence: New Sources and First Results," *History of Childhood Quarterly* 1 (1973): 113n.

3. A staple of humanist and merchant treatises on the family was the figure of the coarse wet nurse who transmitted her own rough qualities through the milk she fed infants. For this reason, moralists strongly encouraged maternal breastfeeding, an exhortation honored more in the breach. See, for example, Matteo Palmieri, *Della vita civile* (Bologna: N. Zanichelli, 1944), 11. On the *arcuccio*, see Trexler, "Infanticide," 108. See also C. Klapisch-Zuber, "Blood Parents and Milk Parents: Wet-Nursing in

Florence, 1300–1530," in *Women, Family, and Ritual in Renaissance Italy* (Chicago: Univ. of Chicago Press, 1985), 149.

4. B. Kellum, "Infanticide in England in the Later Middle Ages," *History of Childhood Quarterly* 1 (1973–74): 369–71.

5. Trexler, "Infanticide in Florence," 103, 113n–114n.

6. E. Coleman, "L'infanticide dans le Haut Moyen Age," *Annales: Economies, Sociétiés, Civilisations* 29 (1974): 334: "L'avortement et l'infanticide n'ont pas pour but d'éliminer les enfants mais de contrôler leur nombre."

7. J. Boswell, *The Kindness of Strangers: The Abandonment of Children in Western Europe from Late Antiquity to the Renaissance* (New York: Pantheon, 1988), 264.

8. J. Boswell, "*Expositio* and *Oblatio:* The Abandonment of Children in the Ancient and Mediaeval Family," *American Historical Review* 89 (1984): 10–33.

9. Carol Clover, "The Politics of Scarcity: Notes on the Sex Ratio in Early Scandinavia," *Scandinavian Studies* 60 (1988): 155–56; J. Boswell, *The Kindness of Strangers*, 6–8. For Boswell's response, see *The Kindness of Strangers*, 288–89, 53n.

10. B. Kellum, "Infanticide in England," 371. Since infanticide was a crime under the jurisdiction of the ecclesiastical courts, perhaps this absence from civil records is not so surprising.

11. W.L. Langer, "Infanticide: A Historical Survey," *History of Childhood Quarterly* 1 (1974): 356.

12. Klapisch-Zuber, "Blood Parents and Milk Parents," *passim.* Ann Carmichael, *Plague and the Poor in Renaissance Florence* (New York: Cambridge Univ. Press, 1986), 28–30.

13. T.L. Savitt, "Smothering and Overlaying of Virginia Slave-Children: A Suggested Explanation," *Bulletin of the History of Medicine* 49 (1975): 400–4.

14. E. deG. R. Hansen, "'Overlaying' in 19th-Century England: Infant Mortality or Infanticide?" *Human Ecology* 7 (1979): 335.

15. S.C.M. Scrimshaw, for example, in "Infanticide in Human Populations: Societal and Individual Concerns," in G. Hausfater and S. Hrdy (eds.), *Infanticide: Comparative and Evolutionary Perspectives* (New York: Aldine Pub. Co., 1984), 443, writes that "it is clear from the literature that this [accidental smothering] was often a covert form of infanticide." Scrimshaw then cites Langer, "Infanticide: A Historical Survey," and Edward Shorter, *The Making of the Modern Family* (New York: Basic Books, 1975). But Langer's article has no supporting scholarly apparatus for his discussion of "accidental" smothering (although there is brief reference to R. Trexler's findings concerning episcopal absolutions to "suffocating" parents—see R. Trexler, "Infanticide in Florence," 109ff.), and there is no discussion of this issue whatsoever in Shorter.

16. For an ample bibliography, see G. Hausfater and S. Hrdy (eds.), *Infanticide: Comparative and Evolutionary Perspectives*, 521–88. Within this volume, the following articles on human infanticide, even with their historical limitations, are quite useful: M. Dickeman, "Concepts and Classifications in the Study of Human Infanticide," 427–37; S.C.M. Scrimshaw, "Infanticide in Human Populations: Societal and Individual Concerns," 439–62; S.R. Johansson, "Deferred Infanticide: Excess Female Mortality during Childhood," 463–85; M. Daly and M. Wilson, "A Sociobiological Analysis of Human Infanticide," 487–502; P. Bugos and L. McCarthy, "Ayoreo Infanticide: A Case Study," 503–20.

17. For more detailed information on the infants of the Innocenti from 1445 to 1485, see P. Gavitt, *Charity and Children in Renaissance Florence* (Ann Arbor, Mich., 1990), 209–28, and idem: "Perche non avea chi la ghovernasse: Cultural values, family resources, and abandonment in the Florence of Lorenzo de' Medici, 1467–85," in J. Henderson and R. Wall (eds.), *Poor Women and Children in the European Past* (London: Routledge, 1994), 65–93. See also T. Takahashi, "I bambini e i genitori-<<espositori>> dello Spedale di Santa Maria degli Innocenti di Firenze nel XV secolo,"

Annuario dell'Instituto Giapponese di Cultura 25 (1991–1992): 35–75.

18. Archivio dell'Ospedale degli Innocenti (hereinafter AOIF) A–B (XVI, 1– 2).

19. A. Carmichael, *Plague and the Poor*, 59.

20. Leigh Dayton, "Cot Death Studies Hampered by Imprecise Terms," *New Scientist* 133 (29 Feb. 1992): 15. At issue is whether to adopt a narrow definition of SIDS (confirmed by autopsy) or a broader definition that would include death unattributable to other causes involving any infant from one month to one year old. See also C.B. Nam, L.W. Eberstein, and L.C. Deeb, "Sudden Infant Death Syndrome as a Socially Determined Cause of Death," *Social Biology* 30 (1989): 7, in which the authors argue, "Given the widespread absence of other morbid conditions on the death certificate for SIDS cases, it seems reasonable to conclude that perhaps many physicians assign infant death to the SIDS category when diagnosis is uncertain or in order to mercifully conclude a medical investigation, especially if the possibility exists of maternal or familial neglect of an infant."

21. Carmichael, *Plague and the Poor*, 41–46.

22. Ibid., 46–49. D. Herlihy and C. Klapisch-Zuber, *Tuscans and their Families: A Study of the Florentine Catasto of 1427* (New Haven and London, 1985), 279, point out that "in some poverty-stricken areas of Central America, 'worms' are listed as a cause of children's deaths, when, according to nutritionists, the basic cause is malnutrition."

23. Carmichael, *Plague and the Poor*, 14–15.

24. Ibid., 51–52.

25. A useful summary of the literature up to 1982 can be found in M.P. Johnson and K. Hufbauer, "Sudden Infant Death Syndrome as a Medical Research Problem since 1945," *Social Problems* 30 (1982): 65–81. On the epidemiology of SIDS, see Bernard Knight, *Sudden Death in Infancy* (London: Faber & Faber, 1983), 15–42.

26. Knight, *Sudden Death in Infancy*, 20.

27. The 60:40 ratio comes from A.B. Bergman, "Sudden Infant Death Syndrome in King's County, Washington," in A.B. Bergman et al. (eds.), *Sudden Infant Death Syndrome: Proceedings of the 2nd International Conference on the Cause of Sudden Death in Infants* (Seattle, 1970), 49. The 55:45 ratio comes from L. Adelson and E.R. Kinney, "Sudden and Unexpected Death in Infancy and Childhood," *Pediatrics* 17 (1956): 681.

28. S.L. Morrison, J.A. Heady, and J.N. Morris, "Social and Biological Factors in Infant Mortality," *Archives of Disease in Childhood* 34 (1959): 113.

29. J. Werne and I. Garrow, "Sudden Deaths of Infants Allegedly Due to Mechanical Suffocation," *American Journal of Public Health* 37 (1947): 678–79.

30. W. Guntheroth, *Crib Death: The Sudden Infant Death Syndrome*, 2nd rev. ed. (Mt. Kisco, N.Y.: Futura Pub. Co., 1989), 78–82. The lowest rate of 0.36 per 1,000 is reported from Hong Kong, where infants are routinely placed on their backs. The highest rate, reported among nonwhite populations in Philadelphia and in Kings County, New York, may be a reflection of a reporting bias in which infant deaths from low-income populations are more often labeled SIDS without benefit of autopsy and other investigation. See M. Bass, R.E. Kravath, and L. Glass, "Death Scene Investigation in Sudden Infant Death," *New England Journal of Medicine* 315 (1986): 100–4, and Nam, Eberstein, and Deeb, "Sudden Infant Death Syndrome as a Socially Determined Cause of Death," 7.

31. Morrison, Heady, and Morris, "Social and Biological Factors," 105, fig. 4a.

32. See Herlihy and Klapisch-Zuber, *Tuscans and their Families*, 80, 204–11, on age at marriage in Florence. On the use of wet nurses to maximize fertility and minimize the time between pregnancies, see V. Fildes, *Breasts, Bottles and Babies: A History of Infant Feeding* (Edinburgh, 1986), 98–133.

33. Adelson and Kinney, "Sudden and Unexpected Death" 665–70.

34. "Seasonality in Sudden Infant Death Syndrome," *Journal of the Ameri-*

can Medical Association 265 (1991): 708; and discussion, 266 (1991): 361–62. C. Templeman, "Two Hundred and Fifty-Eight Cases of Suffocation of Infants," *Edinburgh Medical Journal* 38 (1892): 322–29.

35. T.A. Burch, *Sudden Infant Deaths in Hawaii* (Honolulu: Hawaii State Dept. of Health, 1979); and D.S.Y. Seto, *SIDS: The Epidemiology of Sudden Infant Death Syndrome in Hawaii* (Honolulu, 1984).

36. Templeman, "Two Hundred Fifty-Eight Cases," 324. A particularly graphic photograph of this phenomenon can be found in Adelson and Kinney, "Sudden and Unexpected Death in Infants," 671, fig. 14.

37. On seasonality of fatal disease in Renaissance Florence, see Herlihy and Klapisch-Zuber, *Tuscans and their Families*, 275–77.

38. Savitt, "Smothering and Overlaying of Virginia Slave-Children," 400–4.

39. C. Klapisch-Zuber, "Blood Parents and Milk Parents: Wet-Nursing in Florence, 1300–1530," in *Women, Family and Ritual in Renaissance Italy*, 132–64.

40. Ibid., 146–53.

41. Ibid., 149.

42. T. Takahashi, "Il baliatico nella Toscana del XV secolo attraverso i registri dello Spedale degli Innocenti di Firenze," *Shigaku-zasshi* 101 (1992): 78.

43. AOIF, Balie e Bambini K (XVI, 10), fol. 63r, 3 September 1480: "rechòllo morto adì 26 di novembre 1480 disono le donne nostre che credavano fusse stato afoghato per che dice gli usciva sanghue per la boccha. E rechò meno 4 pezze line."

44. In parts of Latin America popular culture continues to associate sudden infant death with supernatural forces. See, for example, H. Fabrega and H. Nutini, "Witchcraft-Explained Childhood Tragedies in Tlaxaca, and their Medical Sequelae," *Social Science and Medicine* 36 (1993): 793–805.

45. Hansen, "'Overlaying' in 19th-Century England," 347, comes to a similar conclusion: "I think that the attribution of infant deaths among the poor to more or less willful 'overlaying' may have been an expression of social distance by middle- and upper-income people from working-class people."

46. A brief summary of these studies can be found in "Looking Up: Cot Deaths," *The Economist* 323 (9 May 1992): 108–9.

47. M. Bass, "Asphyxial Crib Death," *New England Journal of Medicine* 296 (1977): 555–56. This article was one of the first to raise concerns about the proper spacing of crib slats to prevent accidental strangulation. B. Thach and J. Kemp have argued that carbon dioxide trapped between the baby's mouth and the mattress (or beanbag chair) might account for infant death, a contention disputed by Guntheroth. For a brief summary of views see, "Looking Up: Cot Deaths," *The Economist* 323 (9 May 1992): 109. See also M. Bass, R.E. Dravath, and L. Glass, "Death Scene Investigation in Sudden Infant Death," *New England Journal of Medicine* 315 (1986): 100–4, who argue that at least five cases attributed by the medical examiner in Kings County, N.Y., to SIDS were due to "overlying." The estimate that 2 percent to 10 percent of cot deaths are infanticide comes from J.L. Emery, "Infanticide, Filicide, and Cot Death," *Archives of Disease in Childhood* 60 (1985): 506.

48. A. Chaumoux, "L'enfance abandonées a Reims à la fin du XVIIIᵉ siècle," *Annales de Démographie Historique* (1973): 263–301; J.-P. Bardet, "Enfants abandonées et assistés à Rouen," in *Sur la population française au XVIIIᵉ et au XIXᵉ siècles: Hommage à Marcel Reinhard* (Paris: Societe de Demographie historique, 1973), 19–47.

49. For estimates of infant mortality in the fifteenth century, see Klapisch-Zuber, "Blood Parents and Milk Parents," 151. Klapisch-Zuber argues that the infant mortality rate of 17 percent among the families whose *ricordanze* she studied represents the low end of the premodern experience, with the Ospedale degli Innocenti's 50 percent at the high end, though by the end of the century this would increase to 75 percent.

50. R. Spitz, "Hospitalism: An Inquiry into the Genesis of Psychiatric Condi-

tions in Early Childhood," *The Psychoanalytic Study of the Child* 1 (1945): 53–59.

51. Gavitt, *Charity and Children,* 307–9.

52. For an example, see AOIF, Balie e Bambini G (XVI, 7), fol. 98r, 19 February 1467 [=1468 modern]; fol 398r, 26 January 1471 [=1472 modern].

53. Carmichael, *Plague and the Poor,* 41–45, 150n.

54. Trexler, "Infanticide," 109ff.

55. L. McKee, "Sex Differentials in Survivorship and the Customary Treatment of Infants and Children," *Medical Anthropology* 8 (1984): 91–108. I am deeply grateful to Professor Joan Cadden for this reference. See also M. Daly and M. Wilson, "A Sociobiological Analysis of Human Infanticide," in Hausfater and Hrdy (eds.), *Infanticide: Comparative and Evolutionary Perspectives,* 487–502.

56. McKee, "Sex Differentials," 97, citing L. DeMaitre, "The Idea of Childhood and Child Care in Medical Writings of the Middle Ages," *The Journal of Psychology* 4 (1939): 462–90. Although the physician Savonarola counseled early weaning of girls, there is no evidence from the records of the Ospedale degli Innocenti that this counsel was put into practice. Infants of both sexes were returned after weaning at eighteen to twenty-four months of age (although it is not inconceivable that wet nurses themselves weaned girls earlier). On early weaning in the ninth-century polyptych of St. Victor, cf. S. Blaffer-Hrdy and E. Coleman "Why Human Secondary Sex Ratios Are Conservative: A Distant Reply from Ninth Century France," paper read at the Wenner-Gren Symposium on Infanticide in Animals and Man, Cornell University, Ithaca, N.Y., 16–20 August, 1982.

The anthropological literature on the preferential feeding of males and other practices that worked to the disadvantage of females is rich indeed. To cite only a few: B. Miller, *The Endangered Sex: Neglect of Female Children in Rural North India* (Ithaca and London: Cornell Univ. Press, 1981), esp. 83–106; M. Dickeman, "Demographic Consequences of Infanticide in Man," *Annual Review of Ecology and Systematics* 6 (1975): 107–37; idem, "Female Infanticide, Reproductive Strategies, and Social Stratification: A Preliminary Model," in N. Chagnon and W. Irons (eds.) *Evolutionary Biology and Human Social Behavior: An Anthropological Perspective* (North Scituate, Mass.: Duxbury Press, 1979), 321–67; idem, "Infanticide and Hypergamy: A Neglected Relationship," paper presented at the American Anthropological Association Meetings, 1976.

57. N.S. Scrimshaw, C.E. Taylor, and J.E. Gordon, *Interactions of Nutrition and Infection* (Geneva: World Health Organization, 1968), 253.

58. B. Miller, *The Endangered Sex,* 88, citing J.E. Gordon, S. Singh, and J.B. Wyon, "Causes of Death at Different Ages by Sex and by Season in a Rural Population of Punjab, 1957–59," *Indian Journal of Medical Research* (1965): 906–17.

59. Carmichael, *Plague and the Poor,* 41–46.

60. M. Dickeman, "Infanticide and Hypergamy: A Neglected Relationship," paper read at the 1976 meetings in San Francisco of the American Anthropological Association, cited in Miller, *The Endangered Sex,* 43. A. Molho, in his recent monograph *Marriage Alliance in Late Medieval Florence* (Cambridge, Mass.: Harvard Univ. Press, 1994), 217, 297, is at pains to describe late medieval Florentine marriage arrangements as homogamous, rather than hypergamous or hypogamous.

III. Family Ties

"THE APPALLING DANGERS OF FAMILY LIFE"

INCEST IN MEDIEVAL LITERATURE[1]

Elizabeth Archibald

Incest is a subject of intense social concern in late twentieth-century society: although it seems that the incidence of incest is high, until recently there has been little explicit writing about it, factual or fictional. The Middle Ages offers an apparently opposite situation: we know little about the actual incidence of incest, but there is a remarkable amount of fictional writing (including romance, hagiography, and exempla) that focuses on it. In many fields of medieval studies, there is an increasing emphasis on interdisciplinary work and, in particular, on reading literary texts as material for historical studies. The rise of the women's movement has produced a great deal of impressive work on the lives, roles, and experiences of women in medieval society, and on the representation of women in medieval literature. Incest can be seen as a point of intersection for many of these concerns: gender roles in the family and in society; theological, legal, and social attitudes toward sex and marriage; the influence of the Church on lay society; the relationship between literature and everyday life. I am interested here in nuclear-family incest, but it should be noted that for medieval theologians and canon lawyers, incest meant an extraordinarily wide range of relationships, extending far beyond the biblical taboos: for several hundred years before the Fourth Lateran Council of 1215 relaxed the rules somewhat, marriage was forbidden between those related by consanguinity or by affinity to the seventh degree, and also between godparents and godchildren and their immediate families.[2]

The Middle Ages inherited from the classical world a number of incest stories. Oedipus is the most famous, of course, known to medieval readers through Seneca's tragedy, the opening of Statius' *Thebaid*, and countless references and allusions. Ovid is also an important source: his *Heroides* includes letters from Phaedra (who unsuccessfully propositioned her chaste stepson Hippolytus, with the result that they both died) and Canace (who fell in love with her brother, became pregnant by him, and was forced by her furious father to kill herself). The *Metamorphoses* includes Myrrha (who fell in love with her father and managed to sleep with him unrecognized before being turned into a myrrh tree) and Byblis (whose love for her brother was not consummated before she was turned into a fountain). The classical incest myths tend to end badly, with the death or metamorphosis of the incestuous protagonist, and often catastrophe throughout a whole family: there can be no place in society for anyone who has committed or contemplated incest. A late classical "romance" that remained popular throughout the Middle Ages, the *Historia Apollonii Regis Tyri*, foregrounds incest as a form of domestic tyranny.[3] King Antiochus, who lives incestuously with his own daughter and beheads all her suitors, is finally killed by a thunderbolt while in bed with his daughter. The hero Apollonius, who discovered their guilty secret and was persecuted by Antiochus, is later tested by a confrontation with his own unrecognized daughter, but displays no incestuous desire; their meeting brings about the happy ending in which Apollonius is restored to royal status and reunited with his long-lost wife and daughter, and they are revenged on all their enemies. Classical history and pseudohistory offered, among other incestuous characters, Semiramis, (the legendary queen who took as a lover—or perhaps even as a husband—her own son Ninus and was later murdered by him) and the Roman emperors Caligula and Nero, widely believed to have slept with their sisters. Charges of incest were often used in attacks on an unpopular ruler or an unpopular group (such as the early Christians).

Although medieval writers did retell these classical stories, they developed some striking variations on them, heavily colored by the major new factor and influence in medieval culture: Christianity. In a Christian world in which sex was closely linked to original sin, carnality was a prime example of mankind's weakness, and divine grace was always available to the genuinely contrite, incest was clearly an appealing topic for cautionary tales and propaganda. It could also be worked into romance, the narrative genre so popular from the twelfth century on, which made much of the quest for identity, family separation and reunion, and recognition scenes, as well as love and marriage. There is a remarkable amount of literature about incest from the Middle Ages; it can be found in many different genres, and not all of it was written by clerics. Some incest stories end in tragedy, some end in contrition and penance; in some the incest is deliberate, in others it is unwitting; sometimes incestuous lust is consummated, sometimes it is merely a threat that acts as a catalyst for the adventures of the protagonist. It is difficult to decide how to categorize and discuss these texts: by relationship (mother-son, father-daughter, or sibling), by outcome (incest consummated or not, comic or tragic ending), or by genre (exemplary or entertaining). I am going to attempt here to divide them by genre, to show how widespread this theme was in all kinds of medieval narratives.[4]

Perhaps the most predictable use of the incest theme in medieval literature is in hagiography and exemplary literature, to emphasize the value of contrition and penance.[5] In saints' lives the protagonist is usually male, whereas in *exempla* the protagonist is very often female, and the apportioning of blame also seems to vary somewhat according to both gender and genre. Incest appears in saints' lives from the late eleventh century on. The most striking and influential of these stories is the legend of Pope Gregorius (not attached to any of the historical popes of that name, though the name obviously had significant resonances), which resembles the Oedipus legend but has some startling additions and changes. My synopsis here is based on the German version by Hartmann von Aue, written about 1200; there were earlier French versions, as well as many later translations and adaptations in both Latin and the vernacular.[6]

> The orphaned son and daughter of a nobleman sleep together, tempted by the Devil. When the daughter becomes pregnant, the son goes on a pilgrimage to the Holy Land, where he dies, and the newborn baby is exposed at sea, with tokens and a letter. He is found by fishermen and raised by an abbot; when he discovers that he is a foundling born of incest, he determines to find his parents. He is knighted and sets out: his first adventure is to rescue and marry a besieged duchess, who turns out to be his mother. Both are horrified by their sin and do rigorous penance for many years. Gregorius is chained to a rock in a lonely lake, where he is found seventeen years later by envoys from Rome seeking the new pope, directed by a vision. Gregorius becomes a famous pope. His mother comes to him to seek absolution—he identifies himself and absolves her, and they live piously ever after.

The duplication of the incest seems to be a new medieval twist, unprecedented in classical mythology. It is clearly intended to make the sin of both Gregorius and his mother overwhelmingly shocking: he is the child of incest who repeats his parents' crime by marrying his own mother; she is incestuous twice over: once knowingly, once unknowingly. In medieval theology intention was crucial to sin, but their ignorance cannot entirely cancel out the horror and unnaturalness of their union—they are both represented as feeling extremely guilty. The sins of the parents are visited not only on the innocent child but also a second time on the surviving parent. But rather than mutilate or kill themselves, as they might well have done, like Oedipus and Jocasta, the protagonists rely on their Christian faith in the possibility of God's grace; and their faith is rewarded in the most unexpected way. At the end of the story they not only are reunited physically but are also spiritually united as "children of eternal God" rather than as mother and son or husband and wife—though we might notice that it is Gregorius who acquires worldly recognition and power as pope. This is usually the case in mother-son incest stories: it is the rehabilitated man who is publicly recognized, rather than the woman.

There are many romance elements in this story: until the first recognition scene, it appears to be a typical chivalric adventure.[7] But Hartmann explicitly says in both prologue and epilogue that the story is an *exemplum* of the power of contrition and the availability of grace. It is striking that he, a secular writer, seems to have been the first to introduce the story in Germany (his source was a French version); his poem was soon translated into Latin for ecclesiastical use by Arnold of Lübeck, at the request of his abbot.[8] This is an unusual reversal of the usual pattern whereby didactic tales produced in Latin for ecclesiastical use gained wider secular popularity when translated into the vernacular.

Among other saints' lives focusing on unwitting mother-son incest and clearly influenced by the Gregorius story or its analogues is the legend of St. Albanus.[9] In some versions this, too, is an extended narrative, with named protagonists and locations, and it also ends with recognition for the spiritual achievements of the male protagonist:

> Albanus, the product of deliberate father-daughter incest, is exposed; later he unwittingly marries his mother. When this is discovered, all three do penance separately for seven years. When they meet again, father and daughter lapse into their old sin; Albanus catches them in the act and kills them. He does penance for seven more years and then becomes a hermit. When he is murdered by robbers, his corpse effects miraculous cures.

Here, as in the story of Gregorius, mother-son incest seems to be the worst possible crime, the discovery of which changes the course of the protagonist's life and propels him toward sanctity. With such legends in circulation, it is no wonder that in the late sixteenth century Beatrice Cenci's tyrannical father is reported to have argued, when trying to seduce her, that all children born of incest became saints![10]

But it should be noted that at the same time that these optimistic stories of incest leading to contrition and sanctity were being developed, a much darker story of exposure, incest, and parricide was also growing in popularity: the legend of Judas[11]:

> In Jerusalem, Judas' future mother dreams that she will bear a child who will be the downfall of her race. When Judas is born, his anxious parents expose him at sea. He is found by a childless queen who pretends that he is hers but who later has a son of her own. Judas bullies his foster brother; when the queen reveals how she found him, Judas kills his foster brother and flees to Jerusalem, where he takes service with Pilate. He is sent to steal apples from the orchard of his natural father, whom he kills in the ensuing brawl. Pilate rewards Judas with the land and widow of his victim. Soon they discover their true relationship and are horrified. Judas seeks absolution from Jesus. After betraying him, Judas commits suicide.

The parricide and incest in Judas' story were presumably added to blacken further the reputation of an acknowledged villain, the logic being that the man who could betray Christ was clearly capable of the worst imaginable sins. The orchard and the apples suggest an echo of the Fall of Man in the Garden of Eden; the Fall and original sin are also invoked in the moralizations of several incest stories in the *Gesta Romanorum* (the Gregorius story and "De Amore Inordinato," chap. 13, discussed below).

Judas' story can also be read as a cautionary tale, a warning against dying unrepentant and unconfessed. This is the theme of many of the brief exempla that were so popular in the later Middle Ages, and incest occurs frequently in such tales. However, the central figure is usually a woman, not a man, and to the sin of incest there is often added that of infanticide, and sometimes other murders too.[12] In these exempla it is clear that women are perceived as particularly weak and subject to lust, and to subsequent acts of violence. The heroine—or the villainess—confesses and is absolved only just in time: she usually dies straight afterward.

The exemplum "De Amore Inordinato" ("About Irregular Love," *Gesta Romanorum*, chap. 13) is interesting as a female version of the Gregorius story, perhaps even more horrifying since the incest is deliberate in both cases:

> An emperor seduces his beautiful daughter and dies soon after their son is born. She is so attached to this son that she sleeps in his bed until he is eighteen. The Devil induces the son to have intercourse with

his mother; when she becomes pregnant, he travels far away. The mother kills her newborn baby, but drops of its blood make four ineradicable marks on her hand, so that she has to keep it covered with a glove. She is too ashamed to confess, but the Virgin appears to her confessor and tells him that the glove contains evidence of the lady's secret sin. He persuades her to remove it, and finds letters forming a Latin inscription relating to her sin. The lady confesses, is absolved, and dies a few days later.

There are several striking differences here from the Gregorius pattern. The first is that the lady has no name—nor do most other incestuous mothers in the exempla. The second is that she does not undergo long and impressive penance: her death follows immediately on her repentance, showing how narrowly she has escaped damnation. Nor does she become a saint: it is enough that she dies saved. It is also striking that the focus here is on the mother's sin and subsequent contrition and absolution, to the virtual exclusion of the son, who makes her pregnant and then disappears from the story. His sin appears to be negligible: his mother created the opportunity, and the Devil tempted him.[13] I do not know any tale about a son deliberately initiating an affair with his mother—except one in which the cynical protagonist is testing his mother, who has not recognized him, to see if it is true that women are inordinately lustful.[14] He sleeps in her bed but does not make love to her; when she discovers his identity in the morning, she drops dead and he takes a vow of silence for the rest of his life.

On the other hand, in stories of father-daughter incest it is always the father who takes the initiative and is duly punished (or, less usually, repents); the daughter is completely innocent. An exception that proves this rule, and also shows the misogynistic view of woman's capacity for sin and violence, is a story that exists as a tantalizing fragment of a late medieval morality play, *Dux Moraud*, and also as an exemplum[15]:

> A father seduces his daughter, and they have a long affair. When the mother catches them *in flagrante*, the daughter cuts her throat and buries her. In due course she bears two children, whom she kills at birth. When her father gets old, he confesses to a priest, so the daughter kills him too. She goes far away and becomes a prostitute. Eventually St. Augustine converts her; she confesses and dies immediately. (In one version, the townspeople do not want her buried in the local churchyard, but from the mouth of her corpse roses appear with a Latin warning to her detractors that they, too, will come to judgement.)

This bizarre story is very suggestive about medieval ecclesiastical attitudes toward women and toward incest. Here, it is the primary sin that underlies all the later transgressions: parricide and matricide, infanticide, prostitution. The story of the repentant prostitute was also popular in the Middle Ages, but how much more effective it is when the prostitute has also committed the same terrible crimes as Judas and Albanus: parricide, matricide, and incest! This is an extreme view of woman's carnality and lust and potential for violence—a cautionary tale indeed.

In other kinds of narrative, however, incest is not always treated in such an explicitly moralizing way. From the twelfth century on, incestuous-father stories appear in all the western European vernaculars (for instance, the thirteenth-century *La Manekine* and the fourteenth-century Middle English *Emaré*).[16] Some of these incestuous-father narratives are included by critics in the somewhat elastic category of romance, though the standard definitions of romance are usually predicated on a male hero ("the knight-hero rides forth to seek adventure or to accomplish an established task"); it is not clear what happens when a victimized and passive woman is the protagonist.[17] The tone of incestuous-father narratives varies considerably: some include a good deal of explicit religious material. They can all be described as adventure stories, but the definition of romance has to be stretched considerably to include them, in my view.

In these stories, incest is the catalyst that causes the heroine to leave home and wander unprotected in a hostile world. She marries, but is falsely accused of producing a monstrous child (the Calumniated Wife/Accused Queen theme), and is again exiled from her new home. At the end of the story she is reunited with her husband, now convinced of her innocence, and sometimes also with her repentant father (though in some versions he dies early on). It is made very clear that the initial incest proposition appalls the heroine (and all right-minded readers/listeners); but few of these stories return to the problem of incest at the end. It seems to be largely a plot mechanism—though a very serious one. The happy ending is distinctly secular: the marginalized heroine is restored to her status as wife (and often queen), and her husband is reunited not only with his wife but also with his heir (for their child is always a boy).

If the rite of passage for a knight is winning his spurs (and his lady, too) by proving his prowess, the comparable rite for a lady is being married. Incestuous-father stories show what happens when this ritual transition from the father's protection to the husband's is perverted by the father's incestuous desires. The heroine quite rightly refuses to marry her father, but then she becomes socially marginalized (this is often represented by her flight or exile and, in some cases, by years spent drifting at sea in a rudderless boat); although she does marry, she is vulnerable to the plotting of a jealous mother-in-law or steward and to the lust of unscrupulous men, and she and her little child must suffer for many years before they can be reintegrated into the family and restored to their proper status in society. Throughout her ordeal the heroine is supported by her faith in God, and sometimes she is preserved from disaster by miracles; but she usually remains a secular heroine, not a saint (the Irish Dympna and the Italian Oliva are exceptions).[18]

Whether or not these stories can be called romances, they were certainly very popular in the Middle Ages—disturbingly so, we might think.[19] Sometimes they were inserted into longer narratives, when a previously respectable character suddenly becomes an incestuous father. This happens in *Yde et Olive*, a continuation of *Huon de Bordeaux*, and in *Lion de Bourges*. In the latter, the unhappy story of Joieuse is a minor episode intertwined with many chivalric adventures, and once she has been reunited with her husband and repentant father in the usual way, the men go off to battle once more.[20] Elsewhere, the same plot is used as an explanation of the historical enmity between France and England (a French princess runs away from an incestuous father and marries an English king).[21]

Incest is unlikely to be a central theme in a romance with a male protagonist. Characters who commit incest knowingly are usually villains; those who sin unawares need to repent and retreat from the secular world; and chivalric heroes are unlikely to be unwilling victims like the heroines of the incestuous-father stories.[22] Heroes can only safely be associated with incest when they commit it unknowingly—and preferably, when they do not actually consummate the forbidden relationship. This titillating theme of near-miss incest with no evil consequences seems to have become more popular in the later Middle Ages. In the Middle English romances *Sir Degaré* and *Sir Eglamour*, the newborn child of a clandestine affair is separated from both parents. In the middle of the work he wins his unrecognized mother's hand in a tournament and actually marries her in church but, before they go to bed, a token effects a recognition scene and disaster is averted.[23] The author of *Sir Degaré* remarks that one should be careful about marrying a stranger in case she or he turns out to be a relation (l.l. 613–20)—but these are romances, not cautionary tales, and the main function of this incest episode is to initiate the son's reunion with his parents. Finding his mother is only the first step; he must try his strength against his unrecognized father before the couple can be reunited and a happy ending achieved for all the protagonists. Amazingly, the story of Gregorius was also rewritten in this sanitized form with a secular happy ending, in a sixteenth-century Spanish version: Gregorius discovers the truth in time to avoid consummating his marriage to his mother, the scandal is hushed up, and he marries a respectable widow.[24]

There is a significant exception to the rule that romance heroes cannot be associated with consummated incest: King Arthur, doyen of chivalric heroes. From the early thirteenth century, if not before, some writers included in his legend his unwitting incest with his unrecognized half-sister Morgause of Orkney, on whom he begets the fatal Mordred, destined to destroy his father and the kingdom.[25] Merlin reveals to Arthur the enormity of his sin and its inevitable consequence, and it is on the basis of Merlin's information that Arthur sends for all children born about May Day and dispatches them to sea in the hope of killing his nemesis. In the *Suite du Merlin*, Mordred is not in fact among them, and though the boat is shipwrecked, the babies are all saved; in Malory's bleaker version, Mordred is on the boat and he alone of all the babies survives to fulfill his destiny. This episode in the Arthurian legend raises puzzling questions. Why was such a damaging incident (sibling incest followed by a Herod-like Massacre of the Innocents) introduced into the legend of one of the greatest literary heroes of medieval Europe, the worthy whose court was the apex of chivalry? There is no hint of divine grace and no expectation of it: we seem to have returned to a fatalistic story of the classical type. Like Oedipus, Mordred is fated to kill his father: Merlin prophesies this, and eventually the prophecy is fulfilled, with the extra twist that Mordred is also killed by his father. As there is no question of Arthur's contrition or penance in most of the texts, the incest episode can only be viewed as didactic in a negative sense, not so much a cautionary tale as an explanatory one, to account for the fall of Camelot and the Round Table, though this point is not made explicitly in most texts that include Arthur's incest.[26] In most versions, from Geoffrey of Monmouth on, Mordred appears at the end of the story as Arthur's nephew, the treacherous usurper who brings Arthur's reign to an end. If this was not enough, one would have thought that the limitations revealed by the later addition of the Grail quest, and the affair of Lancelot and Guinevere, might have offered sufficient explanation. Did the Cistercian-influenced writers who composed the moralizing Vulgate Cycle feel the need to find a fatal flaw in Arthur, and does incest stand here for original sin, even though Arthur was unaware of his partner's identity (except that she was a married woman)?[27] If so, why did they not develop the incest theme more clearly and forcefully?

Another major hero associated with incest is Charlemagne, and it has been suggested that his legend may have been responsible for the addition of incest to Arthur's story, since in some accounts Charlemagne was sup-

posed to have fathered Roland on his own sister.[28] There are very significant differences in the two stories: Charlemagne is reluctant to confess his
sin but does so eventually after the intervention of an angel, so the story is
propaganda for the church; Roland is not a villain, and his death is a public and private tragedy for the emperor but does not cause the end of his
reign. But nevertheless it is striking that the two greatest literary heroes of
the age should both be accused of the "fashionable" sin of incest. Clandestine conception is a feature of many heroes' birth stories, as Otto Rank has
shown.[29] Arthur and Mordred offer an interesting contrast to Lancelot and
Galahad: how ironic that the great king, himself the product of a clandestine and deceitful affair, should slip unintentionally (though lustfully) and
produce his own bane, whereas Lancelot's slip, equally unintentional and
in fact caused by magic, produces the perfect Galahad.

I think we see very clearly in the Arthurian legend the influence of
the hagiographic incest stories that had become so popular in the eleventh
and twelfth centuries. We can see the Arthur and Mordred story as a sort
of inside-out version of Gregorius: the deliberate sibling incest at the beginning of Gregorius is replaced by Arthur's unwitting incest with his sister; the
subsequent mother-son incest in Gregorius is hinted at in Mordred's pursuit
of Guinevere, his stepmother. The rigors of penance in Gregorius, which lead
to grace and eventual happiness (in a spiritual sense) are replaced by fatalistic stoicism in the form of silence at court about Mordred's parentage and
destiny, and this leads to simultaneous parricide and filicide, and the end of
Camelot. If Arthur can be seen in the Gregorius role as the good sinner,
Mordred is surely a kind of Judas, doomed to destroy his race, surviving his
cruel exposure, trying to marry his stepmother (in some versions, he succeeds), and managing to kill his father and wreck the Arthurian world.

There is no single answer to the question of why incest stories became
so popular in western Europe from the twelfth century on. It is true, of
course, that we have much less literature from the early period and have very
little knowledge of oral vernacular traditions. It may be that similar stories
circulated orally in the preceding centuries and were not written down until the so-called twelfth-century Renaissance. But although incest features
very rarely in earlier saints' lives (and in such adventure narratives as do
survive, I think it more likely that there was indeed a new interest in the eleventh and twelfth centuries, which had nothing to do with the actual incidence of incest in medieval society), I am sure that incest has always been
an all too frequent occurrence, as much in the twelfth century as in the twentieth. I have argued elsewhere that incest stories may have become popular
as a result of various aspects of church activity and anxiety at this time: the

rise of contritionism, which emphasized individual soul-searching and guilty conscience, and also the hot debate about marriage which occupied the canonists: whom one could or could not marry, and what happened to those who broke the Church's rules, and to their children.[30] Duby has argued that the Church constructed its remarkably complex rules about exogamy in order to exert control over the aristocracy; Goody has suggested, more cynically, that the Church stood to gain financially from making marriage difficult, since more legacies would be left to the Church by the unmarried.[31]

The effect of all these rules on laymen is debatable: we know of a number of historical characters who used or ignored the consanguinity rules to their own advantage, divorcing barren wives on the pretence that they had just discovered they were related within the prohibited degrees, buying papal permission to marry close relatives, or openly living with forbidden consorts.[32] In both *Emaré* and *La Manekine*, the incestuous father obtains papal permission to marry his daughter; this is, no doubt, a comment on the laxity with which the Church's rules were enforced, at least for the great and the good. Clearly the rules were not taken seriously by all. Boccaccio tells several stories of young men who exploit their privileged positions as godfathers to seduce the mothers of their godchildren.[33] At the beginning of Book VIII of Gower's *Confessio Amantis*, the narrator, Confessor, explains that though marriages frequently took place between close relations in the early history of the world, such unions have now been forbidden by the Pope; nevertheless he acknowledges that many people ignore the consanguinity rules, and urges Amans to confess if he has ever sinned in this way:

> Bot thogh that holy cherche it bidde,
> So to restreigne Mariage,
> Ther ben yit upon loves Rage
> Ful manye of suche nou aday
> That taken wher thei take may
> . . . .
> Mi Sone, thou schalt understonde,
> That such delit is forto blame.
> Forthi if thou hast be the same
> To love in eny such manere,
> Tell forth therof and schrif the hiere.[34]

Amans is shocked and denies any such sin, but Confessor goes on to describe (briefly) the sins of Caligula, Ammon, and Lot and then, at much greater length, tells the story of Apollonius of Tyre.

Although the Church's complex system of prohibitions was aimed largely at unions with second and third cousins and relations through marriage or spiritual kinship, there is little reflection of these rules in contemporary fiction: nuclear-family incest was much more sensational and dramatic.[35] There is little formal evidence of cases of nuclear family incest that were brought to court, but I see no reason to doubt that this kind of incest occurred as frequently then as now, though documentary proof is hard to find (the questions about incest in confessors' manuals, like Confessor's speech quoted on the previous page, seem to support this view).[36] What the texts I have discussed do suggest is that nuclear-family incest, though shocking, was considered a perfectly acceptable literary subject in the later Middle Ages, both plausible and morally valuable, and that mother-son incest was the most heinous of the various possible forms of incest (for male protagonists, it is always mother-son incest that triggers the retreat from the world and the penance that leads to sanctity).[37] Ecclesiastical and lay authors would have endorsed Shelley's comment, "Incest is like many other *incorrect* things a very poetical circumstance."[38] Medieval writers also acknowledged that stories of incest were very shocking but morally valuable: a twelfth-century French chronicler remarked that though nothing could be more horrible than the story of Apollonius of Tyre, it contained useful material for Christians, like gold in a dungheap.[39]

NOTES

1. The phrase "the appalling dangers of family life" is taken from chapter 3 of Aldous Huxley's *Brave New World*.

2. See A. Esmein, *Le Mariage en droit canonique*, 2nd ed., rev. R. Genestal (Paris: Librairie du Recueil Sirey, 1929); J. Fleury, *Recherches historiques sur les empêchements de parenté dans le mariage canonique* (Paris: Recueil Sirey, 1933); J. Gaudemet, *Le mariage en occident: les moeurs et le droit* (Paris: Cerf, 1987); and James A. Brundage, *Law, Sex, and Society in Medieval Europe* (Chicago: Univ. of Chicago Press, 1987). For possible explanations of these draconian rules, see G. Duby, *Medieval Marriage*, trans., E. Forster (Baltimore: Johns Hopkins Univ. Press, 1978); *The Knight, the Priest, and the Lady*, trans., Barbara Bray (New York: Pantheon, 1983); now *Love and Marriage in the Middle Ages*, trans., Jane Dunnett (Chicago: Univ. of Chicago Press, 1994); Jack Goody, *The Development of the Family and Marriage in Europe* (Cambridge: Cambridge Univ. Press, 1983); and David Herlihy, "Making Sense of Incest: Women and the Marriage Rules of the Early Middle Ages," in *Law, Custom, and the Social Fabric in Medieval Europe: Essays in Honor of Bruce Lyon*, ed. B. Bachrach and D. Nicholas (Kalamazoo, Mich.: Medieval Institute Publications, Western Mich. Univ., 1990), 1–16.

3. The standard edition is that of G.A.A. Kortekaas, *Medievalia Groningana* 3 (Groningen, 1984); see also Elizabeth Archibald, *Apollonius of Tyre: Medieval and Renaissance Themes and Variations* (Cambridge: D.S. Brewer, 1991), which includes a text and translation.

4. This is necessarily a superficial overview: there are a great many incest stories in medieval literature, and they do not all fall into neat generic categories, as will

be seen below. For more detailed discussion and bibliography, see my forthcoming study of the incest theme in the Middle Ages. The only existing survey is that of Otto Rank, *The Incest Theme in Legend and Literature*, trans. Gregory C. Richter (Baltimore: Johns Hopkins Univ. Press, 1992); this important text, first published in 1912, covers mythology and literature from the ancient world to the twentieth century, so the discussions are brief (and the bibliography is, of course, out of date).

5. In the twelfth and thirteenth centuries, the Church was encouraging a sense of personal responsibility and interior guilt, through the contritionist movement and through the requirement for annual confession (instituted by the Fourth Lateran Council in 1215). On stories that emphasize this, see Erhard Dorn, *Der Sündige Heilige in der Legende des Mittelalters,* Medium Aevum: Philologische Studien 10 (Munich: W. Fink, 1967); and Jean-Charles Payen, *Le Motif du repentir dans littérature française médiévale. Des origines à 1230* (Geneva: Droz, 1967). See also Elizabeth Archibald, "Incest in Medieval Literature and Society," *Forum for Modern Language Studies* 25 (1989): 1–15.

6. Hartmann von Aue, *Gregorius,* ed. Hermann Paul, 13th ed., rev. Burghart Wachinger (Tübingen: M. Niemeyer Verlag, 1984); *La Vie du Pape Grégoire: 8 versions françaises médiévales de la légende du Bon Pécheur,* ed. H.B. Sol (Amsterdam: Rodopi, 1977). See also Lowell Edmonds, "Oedipus in the Middle Ages," *Antike und Abendland* 22 (1976): 147–55.

7. There are many medieval stories of fosterlings, foundlings, or Bel Inconnu figures who grow up to be famous knights and finally discover their parentage; one of the most famous is King Arthur.

8. Arnold von Lübeck, *Gesta Gregorii Peccatoris: Untersuchungen und Edition,* ed. J. Schilling, Palaestra 280 (Göttingen: Vandenhoeck and Ruprecht, 1986). An abbreviated version was included as chap. 81 in the influential exemplary anthology, the *Gesta Romanorum*, ed. H. Oesterley (Berlin: Weidmann, 1872), 399–409.

9. See Karin Morvay, *Die Albanuslegende: Deutsche Fassungen und ihre Beziehungen zur lateinischen Überlieferung,* Medium Aevum: Philologische Studien 32 (Munich: W. Fink, 1977). This legend also appears in the *Gesta Romanorum* as chap. 244, though the protagonist is anonymous.

10. This comment is included in a contemporary account of the Cenci scandal translated by Shelley and printed in G.E. Woodberry's edition of Shelley's *The Cenci* (Boston: D.C. Heath and Co., 1909), 133.

11. The story is inserted into the chapter on St. Matthias (Judas' successor among the apostles) by Jacobus de Voragine in the *Legenda Aurea,* ed. J.G. Th. Graesse, 3rd ed. (Dresden, 1990; repr. Osnabrück: O. Zeller, 1969), 184–86. See also Paul F. Baum, "The Medieval Legend of Judas Iscariot," *Proceedings of the Modern Language Association (PMLA)* 31 (1916), 481–563; Dorn, 137f.; Edmonds, 61–67.

12. Of the twelve entries for incest listed in F. Tubach, *Index Exemplorum: A Handbook of Medieval Religious Tales,* FF Communications 204 (Helsinki: Suomalainen Tiedea Katenia, 1969), nos. 2728–39, only one specifically focuses on a man; whether or not the female protagonist initiated the incest, it is her subsequent actions, or refusal to confess, that constitute the main plot in ten of the twelve.

13. An exception in which the son does share responsibility is the poem "Le Dit du Buef," ed. A. Jubinal in *Noveau recueil de contes, dits, fabliaux et autres pièces,* 2 vols. (Paris: E. Pannier, 1839), I:42–72. Here the incestuous mother and son and their daughter are set a penance by the Pope and wander the world sewn into cowhides for seven years; on the night of their reunion all three die, and miracles are associated with the site. But no specific saint's cult is linked to this story.

14. *An Alphabet of Tales,* no. 710, ed. Mary Macleod Banks, Early English Texts Society (EETS) 127, 2 vols. (London: K. Paul, Trench, Trubner, 1905), 475–76.

15. *Dux Moraud,* ed. N. Davis, in *Non-Cycle Plays and Fragments,* EETS S.S. 1 (London: Oxford Univ. Press, 1970), 106–31; five analogous exempla are discussed by W. Heuser in "*Dux Moraud,* Einzelrolle aus einem verlorenen Drama des 14

Jahrhunderts," *Anglia* 30 (1907): 180–208. See also Richard L. Homan, "Two *Exempla*: Analogues to the *Play of the Sacrament* and *Dux Moraud*," *Comparative Drama* 18 (1984): 241–51.

16. *La Manekine*, ed. H. Suchier, in *Oeuvres Poétiques de Philippe de Rémi, Sieur de Beaumanoir*, 2 vols., SATF (Paris: Firmin Didot et cie, 1884), I:3–263; *Emaré*, ed. Edith Rickert, EETS 99 (London: Oxford Univ. Press, 1908, repr. 1958). See also Margaret Schlauch, *Chaucer's Constance and Accused Queens* (New York: Gordian Press, 1927; repr. 1973); Claude Roussel, "Aspects du père incestueux dans la littérature médiévale," in *Mariage, amour et transgressions en moyen âge*, ed. D. Buschinger and A. Crépin (Göppingen: Kummerle, 1984), 47–62; and the chapter on father-daughter relations in my forthcoming study of the incest theme in medieval literature.

17. John Finlayson, "*Sir Gawain* and the Expectations of Romance," *Genre* 12 (1979): 1–24; see also his "Definitions of Medieval Romance," *Chaucer Review* 15 (1981–82): 44–62, 168–81; and Elizabeth Archibald, "Women and Romance," in *Companion to Middle English Romance*, ed. Henk Aertsen and Alasdair A. MacDonald (Amsterdam: Vu Univ. Press, 1990), 153–69, esp. 155–57.

18. For Dympna see *Acta Sanctorum*, Mai. III, ed. J. Bollandus, rev. J. Carnandet (Paris, 1863–1948), 475–87 (15 May); for Oliva see *La Rappresentazione di S. Uliva*, ed. A. d'Ancona (Pisa, 1863), and also Schlauch, *Chaucer's Constance*.

19. Chaucer tells a version of the story without the opening incest episode in his *Man of Law's Tale*, but the unnecessarily elaborate rejection of incest stories in the Prologue draws attention to the fact that incest is often part of Accused Queen stories: see Elizabeth Archibald, "The Flight from Incest: Two Late Classical Precursors of the Constance Theme," *Chaucer Review* 20 (1986): 259–72; and Carolyn Dinshaw, "The Law of Man and Its 'Abhomynacions,'" chap. 3 in *Chaucer's Sexual Politics* (Madison: Univ. of Wisconsin Press, 1989), 88–112.

20. *Yde et Olive*, in *Ausgaben und Abhandlungen aus dem Gebiete der romanischen Philologie* 83, 152 ff.; there is an English version in *The Boke of Duke Huon of Burdeux*, trans. Lord Berners, ed. S.L. Lee, 2 vols., EETS E.S. 40, 41 (London: N. Trubner and Co., 1882–83), II:690 ff. *Lion de Bourges, poème épique du XIVᵉ siècle*, ed. William W. Kibler, Jean-Louis Picherit, and Thelma S. Fenster, 2 vols. (Geneva: Droz, 1980); see also Thelma S. Fenster, "Joie mêlée de Tristouse: The Maiden with the Cut-Off Hand in Epic Adaptation," *Neophilologus* 65 (1981): 345–57.

21. See Büheler, *Königstochter von Frankreich*, ed. J.F.L. Th. Merzdorf (Oldenburg: Shulzer, 1867); and Gutierre Diez de Games, *El Victorial*, II, c. 26, ed. Juan de Mata Cariaz (Madrid: Espasa Calpe, 1940), 177 ff.

22. There are one or two who are propositioned by lecherous stepmothers, as in the Middle English *Generides*, ed. W.A. Wright, EETS 55, 70 (London, 1873; repr. as 1 vol., 1973); but I know no romance in which the hero is harassed by an incestuous mother.

23. *Sir Degaré*, ed. G. Schleich (Heidelberg: Winter, 1929); *Sir Eglamour of Artois*, ed. F. Richardson, EETS 256 (London: Oxford Univ. Press, 1965).

24. Juan de Timoneda, *Patrañuelo*, chap. 5, ed. José Romera Castillo (Madrid: Catedra, D.L., 1978), 117–22. The editor comments that it is impossible to know whether the new ending is Timoneda's invention; no direct source is known.

25. For full discussion and bibliography see Elizabeth Archibald, "Arthur and Mordred: Variations on an Incest Theme," in *Arthurian Literature VIII*, ed. R. Barber (Cambridge: Boydell and Brewer, 1989), 1–27. There are some cryptic allusions to Mordred's incestuous birth in the early thirteenth-century French prose Vulgate Cycle, but the story is first developed coherently in the slightly later *Suite du Merlin*, edited as *Merlin* by G. Paris and J. Ulrich, 2 vols., SATF (Paris: F. Didot, 1886); see I:147–60, I:203–12. Malory seems to have used this version, though he reduces it considerably, for the account in his first tale, *The Tale of King Arthur*; see Malory, *Works*, ed. E. Vinaver, 2nd ed. (Oxford: Oxford Univ. Press, 1971), 27–31, 37.

26. Fanni Bogdanow argues that Arthur's incest is a central theme of the so-called Post-Vulgate *Roman du Graal*, which Malory certainly knew: see *The Romance of the Grail* (Manchester: Manchester Univ. Press, 1966), esp. chap. 6, pp. 138–55.

27. See Helen Adolf, "The Concept of Original Sin as Reflected in Arthurian Romance," in *Studies in Language and Literature in Honour of Margaret Schlauch*, ed. M. Brahmer et al. (New York: Russell and Russell, 1971), 21–29; and Archibald, "Arthur and Mordred," 2–3.

28. See A. Micha, "Deux sources de la *Mort Artu*: II, La naissance incestueuse de Mordred," *Zeitschrift für romanische Philologie* 66 (1950): 371–72; for further bibliography and discussion, see Archibald, "Arthur and Mordred," 3–4.

29. Otto Rank, *The Myth of the Birth of the Hero: A Psychological Interpretation of Myth*, trans. F. Robbins and S.E. Jelliffe (New York: R. Brunner, 1957).

30. Archibald, "Incest in Medieval Literature and Society" (see note 5 above).

31. See note 2 above.

32. Many examples are cited by Duby (note 2 above).

33. See Louis Haas, "Boccaccio, Baptismal Kinship and Spiritual Incest," *Renaissance and Reformation* 25 (1989): 343–56; and Archibald, "Incest in Medieval Literature and Society," 10.

34. John Gower, *Confessio Amantis*, VIII, ll. 148–52 and 164–68, ed. G.C. Macaulay, 2 vols., EETS E.S. 81, 82 (London: K. Paul, Trench, Trubner and Co., 1901; repr. 1957), II:390.

35. There are, however, references to actual or potential incest outside the nuclear family in a number of French narratives of the twelfth and thirteenth centuries: see Archibald, "Incest in Medieval Literature and Society," 8.

36. See, for instance, Pierre J. Payer, "Sex and Confession in the Thirteenth Century," in *Sex in the Middle Ages: A Book of Essays*, ed. Joyce E. Salisbury, Garland Medieval Casebooks 3 (New York: Garland Publishing, 1991), 126–42.

37. This is particularly striking in view of the fact that, in folk song, sibling incest is much the most common form and mother-son is rare; see Paul G. Brewster, "The Incest Theme in Folksong," FF Communications 212 (Helsinki, 1972), 1–35; see 25.

38. See *The Letters of Percy Bysshe Shelley*, ed. F.L. Jones, 2 vols. (Oxford: Oxford Univ. Press, 1964), II:154.

39. Geoffrey de Vigeois, Prologue to the *Chronicon Lemovicense*, ed. Philippe Labbé, *Nova bibliotheca manuscriptorum*, 2 vols. (Paris: J. Henault, 1657), II:279–342 (see 279). The relevant passage is quoted, with a translation, in Archibald, *Apollonius of Tyre*, 224.

THE EMOTIONAL UNIVERSE OF MEDIEVAL ICELANDIC FATHERS AND SONS

Cathy Jorgensen Itnyre

Anyone who reads medieval Icelandic literature quickly becomes accustomed to the many "-sons" appended to personal male names. In the sagas a boy's path in life is determined by his father's status, reputation, and willingness to support his offspring materially. Although we know a great deal about the father-son tie as a factor in transmission of property and keeping track of lineage, little has been done to investigate the feelings that characterized the relationship. Is it possible to learn about the emotional universe of medieval Icelandic fathers and sons? Extensive references to the bond in saga literature suggest that it is. The sagas reflect both the positive and negative features of the paternal-filial tie. Expressions of mutual love, fathers struck with grief at their sons' untimely deaths, paternal advice intended to assist the sons' paths in life—all indicate that the relationship could be a nurturing one. Yet the literature also suggests that, for a variety of reasons, many fathers and sons found little emotional satisfaction in their dealings with each other. Clearly saga authors were interested in the emotional tone of father-son relationships, and it is thus possible to investigate the affective nature of the tie.

Christopher Brooke has noted that "in the history of marriage one cannot afford to ignore any kind of evidence."[1] This observation is particularly relevant to the Icelandic situation: as William Ian Miller writes, "The literary sources are a necessity, for they have the most important characteristic a source must have: they exist."[2] The Icelandic legal code *Grágás* contains inheritance and kinship information, and the legal position of legitimate and illegitimate sons is delineated in the code. But to experience the texture of the tie between fathers and sons, we must turn to the literary evidence. Both the family sagas and the great historical works of the thirteenth century contain a significant amount of information on paternal-filial relationships that are successful or strained. In considering whether it is proper to draw conclusions about actual behavior from literary evidence, it must be stressed that the value of saga evidence has been acknowledged by scholars employing various perspectives, such as Hastrup and Turner from the anthropological view[3] and Miller from the perspective of a legal expert.[4]

In order to investigate paternal-filial relationships in medieval Iceland, I examined a majority of the family sagas as well as the great historical works of thirteenth-century Iceland, *Sturlunga saga* and *Heimskringla*. While noting every reference that dealt with fathers and sons, I was impressed with how often this relationship is featured. To determine the specific nature of the relationship, however, I assigned positive or negative values to a variety of anecdotal evidence. Although saga authors sometimes use explicit phrases like "his father and mother loved him very much,"[5] more often we are left to draw our own observations regarding the emotional tone of the relationship. Based on anecdotal evidence, I identified several elements that helped to define more precisely what it meant to be an Icelandic father or son, at least in the emotional sense. I am aware of the danger of assuming too much (it would be anachronistic to expect medieval saga authors to articulate "feelings"); clearly their purpose was not character delineation in the modern sense. Still, the numerous references to fathers, sons, and their dealings with each other suggest that saga authors considered it a bond well worth mentioning to an audience eager to hear about people like themselves.

Throughout this study, I will examine not only the ties between natural fathers and sons but also what was in some cases the emotional equivalent of this relationship—ties established by fostering, other relatives, and subsequent marriages (stepparenthood). Rearing of children created bonds and obligations that often resulted in mutually affectionate relations; thus, there is good reason to consider foster and stepfathers here, since they performed similar tutelary and economic functions. In this study, I will examine what the Icelandic medieval literary and historical evidence indicates about affectionate and troubled paternal-filial relationships.

Before examining the affective poles of the relationship, however, I want to note that not all father-son bonds were represented by love or hatred. Many, just as today, were characterized by indifference. There is no typical scenario that initiates such a state; it is not caused by an excess of sons, resulting in disinterest in one or more of them. Indeed, having numerous sons enhances a father's status, as we see in *Laxdœla saga*:

> Men say that Hrútr went to the Alþingi one summer accompanied by fourteen of his sons: this is brought up here because it was considered a sign of great splendor and means.[6]

At least in one case, we see a father who had experienced paternal indifference treating one of his sons in the same fashion. As a child, Egill Skalla-Grímsson underwent the silent treatment for a whole winter with his father.[7] Although Egill has several sons whom he loves deeply, as we shall see, one son elicits his antipathy. Most people agree that Þorsteinn Egilsson is a handsome, worthy man, but his father "had no great affection for him, and as far as Þorsteinn was concerned this was mutual."[8] A kind of benign neglect is found in *Haralds saga gráfeldar*, in which Hákon jarl has an illegitimate son, whom all consider to be promising, but "the jarl did not pay much attention to him."[9]

Perhaps the most dramatic example of paternal indifference occurs in *Þorgils saga skarði*. Valgarðr Þorkellsson is at the mercy of Þorgils, who refuses to discuss ransoming Valgarðr with anyone except the latter's father, Þorkell the priest. When Þorkell refuses to pay the amount required to free his son, Valgarðr desperately begs to receive the sacrament of penance from his father. Þorkell's indifference to his son's dangerous situation is emphasized:

> Men thought they heard him ask his father to redeem him, but Þorkell refused. Þorgils now ordered Eyjólfr smiðr to kill him, and Valgarðr was now slain.[10]

Whether Egill's earlier experience of silence from his father caused him to treat Þorsteinn with similar unconcern, or Hákon jarl disregarded his son because of his illegitimate status, or Þorkell's priestly office had something to do with his failure to ransom his son, these examples of paternal indifference stand out in the saga literature because such references are so rare.

Most of the references point to a friendly association between the generations, so I will examine this category of potential relationships first. Today many assume that paternal-filial ties will be imbued with affection; there is some evidence that medieval Icelanders shared this supposition. For example, *Íslendingasaga* relates the death of Bishop Guðmundr Árason, and the author offers the view that episcopal love is paternal in its nature: "they loved him like a brother and asked for his assistance in their services as from a father."[11] The expectation that fathers render assistance to sons is an assumption that underscores the nurturing component of fatherhood. This is reinforced by other references citing friendly cooperation as the usual state of affairs for fathers and sons. Sometimes the ideal is stated negatively, as when Þorgeirr in *Ljósvetninga saga* is warned not to oppose his sons,[12] or when Hallfreðr asks, "Who will be my support if not my father?"[13] Still, these references indicate that the normal condition of father-son relations is positive.

If we want to understand what fathers valued in their sons and vice-versa, we must examine anecdotal evidence in such a way that the underlying attributes of specific cases can be coaxed out. For instance, the time-honored paternal practice of giving advice is a common one in the sagas, but the content of the advice informs us about specific qualities fathers wanted to cherish in their sons. By looking at such factors as advice giving, reactions to paternal and filial deaths, information about economic and living arrangements, and personality and physical traits passed from father to son, a picture emerges of what fathers appreciated in their sons and what sons considered admirable in their fathers.

To put it bluntly, Icelandic fathers wanted sons who were courageous, obedient, sensitive to the family's honor, socially amicable, hard-working, and (preferably) the spitting image of the father. If we examine this wish list one item at a time, it becomes apparent that courage is a high priority for fathers. It is an especially important consideration in *Vatnsdœla saga*. Young Ingimundr has been off pillaging but, when he returns, his father happily welcomes him and entertains him throughout the following winter, "vowing he was overjoyed to have such a son."[14] The more successful Ingimundr is in his viking activities, the prouder Þorsteinn is: "it seemed to Þorsteinn that he was not able to do enough for his son Ingimundr, now that he saw what kind of man he wanted to be."[15] Paternal pride reaches a crescendo in this saga when the aged Þorsteinn finally declares to Ingimundr: "How good now to die, knowing one's son is such a lucky man!"[16] Þorsteinn's fondness for his son is all the more intriguing in light of his formerly troubled relationship with his *own* father, Ketill, who had been a great warrior in his youth. Ketill fears that Þorsteinn is not sufficiently aggressive and ambitious. To inspire his son to try to match his own feats, he harangues Þorsteinn until the son, angry at his father's taunts, ventures out to prove his courage. When they are reunited after Þorsteinn's adventures, "they were the best of friends again."[17]

Þórarinn in *Þorsteins þáttr stangarhǫggs* is another father who fears that his son isn't measuring up to his own heroic past. He tells his son that

> in my younger days I'd never have given way before someone like Bjarni, even though he is a great champion. I'd much rather lose you than have a coward for a son.[18]

In a lengthy lecture to his son, Ketill Raumr in *Vatnsdœla saga* draws several unflattering comparisons between the vigorous, warlike men of Ketill's youth and the lazy, soft specimens of his son's generation.[19]

After courage, medieval Icelandic fathers demand obedience from their sons; it is clear that this is one of the qualities they prize the most—perhaps because it is so difficult to obtain. The evidence that illuminates this virtue is almost always phrased negatively (fathers upbraiding their sons for disobedience), but this only underscores paternal desire to have obedient sons. The tendency to ignore paternal commands starts early: in *Fljótsdæla saga*, Sveinungr chastises his young son for hesitating to comply with his order to bring the sheep to shelter; the boy wants to dress more warmly before he undertakes the task. But Sveinungr tells him: "When I was young . . . we needed neither hood nor mittens!"[20] Skalla-Grímr also encounters disobedience in his son, three-year-old Egill. The little boy—physically precocious—wants to accompany his father to a feast, but Skalla-Grímr denies the request, adding:

> You don't know how to behave yourself when
> there's a crowd doing a lot of drinking.
> You don't seem to know how to behave well
> even when you are sober.[21]

This humorous remark to a three-year-old boy fails to prevent Egill from setting out on his own to the feast at Borg!

Njáll's insistence on obedience from his sons is thwarted several times in *Njáls saga*. His sons are well aware of the deep love he has for his foster son, Hǫskuldr Þráinsson, yet they are responsible for Hǫskuldr's murder nonetheless.[22] When Njáll's enemies prepare to burn his household, he reproaches his sons by referring to their *former* compliance with his wishes:

> Now you are going to override my advice and show me disrespect, my sons—and not for the first time. But when you were younger, you did not do so, and things went better for you then.[23]

In two separate conversations, Njáll expresses his expectation that his sons will obey the terms of any settlement Njáll makes.[24]

In *Prestssaga Guðmundr góða*, we encounter an uncle who takes on the paternal advice-giving role, since Guðmundr is fatherless. His uncle, Þorvarðr Þórgeirsson, attempts to persuade Guðmundr to accept election to the bishopric of Hólar:

You know very well, kinsman, that I am the head of our family, as my father was before me. Your father, and all my other kinsmen, have submitted to my judgement, and I now advise you to do the same.[25]

In this example, Þorvarðr realizes that his family may acquire financial and social benefits from Guðmundr's consecration as bishop, so he is anxious to secure his nephew's acquiescence.

Family honor is a rather nebulous concept, yet medieval Icelanders found it a motivating idea. Richard Bauman observes, "The quest for honor was . . . a quest for reputation, resting on the need to be well talked about."[26] He discusses the hierarchy of values that characterizes the medieval Icelandic notion of honor, with "a jealous guarding of one's status in confrontation with others."[27] Saga literature is replete with allusions to pursuing and maintaining honor; for our purpose of viewing it as a quality that fathers liked to see in their sons, we may turn to a few specific cases. As Bauman suggests, the references involve perceptions of how the family may be viewed by outsiders' eyes: fathers want very much for their sons to maintain the family's prestige, and with words and examples, they advise their sons how to do this. Njáll, for instance, is displeased with his sons for killing his foster son Hǫskuldr, but he nevertheless supports them, "for honor demands that I do not abandon you while I am still alive."[28]

Honor is also the concern of Þorsteinn, Ingólfr's father, in *Hallfreðar saga*. He warns his son to stop meeting with Valgerðr, since Ingólfr does not intend to marry the girl. Þorsteinn believes that Ingólfr's flirtatious behavior demeans the family's honor.[29] *Vatnsdœla saga* casts the father-son confrontation over Valgerðr in a slightly different light, indicating that the concern for "public appearance" might be undergirded with other issues, such as the paternal desire to be obeyed. Þorsteinn says to Ingólfr:

Why are you so set on wronging Óttarr and dishonoring his daughter? You have taken to bad ways, and we will not be in agreement unless you do something about this.[30]

A conversation in *Egils saga* between two old fathers reveals more about paternal insistence that sons maintain the honor of their families. The aged hero of the saga worries with his friend Ǫnundr that their sons' feud will cause people to mock the two old men for their inability to rein in and reconcile their sons. Egill tells Ǫnundr:

I remember the days when neither of us would have considered taking the other to court, or been unable to curb our sons and stop them from making such fools of themselves.[31]

Family honor cannot be upheld if old men are forced to sit by passively while their children bring ridicule on the lineages. Egill and Ǫnundr intervene in their sons' dispute, and the resulting settlement drives a wedge between the two old neighbors—but each is more firmly aligned with his son than previously.[32]

Medieval Icelandic fathers demonstrate an interest in their sons' social behavior, and the desirability of having a well-liked son is linked with the maintenance of family honor. Fathers want their sons to be socially adept, for such behavior affects the family reputation. In *Fóstbrœðra saga*, Bersi spends much of his time looking after his brave yet socially misfit son Þormóðr. We are told that Þormóðr and his close friend Þorgeirr are not well liked because of the disturbances they cause in the neighborhood, yet "they had the help and support of their fathers, as was to be expected, and many men thought that they supported them in their evil ways."[33] Several times Bersi tries to assist his son by avenging his injuries and dispensing advice designed to smooth Þormóðr's social ineptitude. Þormóðr composes a love poem for a woman named Þorbjǫrg, but when he lies to another girl, Þordís, claiming that the poem is intended for *her*, he is in deep trouble with both women. In an attempt to extricate his son from this romantic dilemma, Bersi advises:

> Useless sweethearts you have: from one you get a lasting scar from which you barely recovered, and now from the other one you are threatened with losing your eyes. And now my advice to you is this, that you turn the poem back to what it was in the beginning.[34]

Þormóðr is lucky that his father can assist him in his social dilemmas, because not all saga fathers are aware of what is socially appropriate. In *Bjarnar saga hítdœlakappa*, Björn is invited to stay with his former girlfriend's household for the winter. He seeks his parents' advice on the matter, and his father tells him to accept the invitation, for it will cause Björn to enjoy a deeper friendship with his former love's husband. Björn wisely heeds his mother's advice instead: she recommends that he remain safely at home with his parents.[35] Though Björn's father gives naive advice, we still see his intention to mold his son's conduct into what he considers to be socially advantageous behavior.

Cooperative labor on medieval Icelandic farms was an essential ingredient of a family's economic security. Njáll's sons all remain in close proximity to their father even after they marry, and there are many examples in other sagas of fathers and sons farming together. Fathers naturally want their sons to be hard workers, whether the labor is performed in a jointly owned farm or for wages elsewhere. Hǫskuldr in *Laxdœla saga* asks his illegitimate son Óláfr to accompany him to the Alþingi, but Óláfr declines the invitation because he is too busy working on the farm. Hǫskuldr is proud of his son for demonstrating such an exemplary work ethic.[36]

Hrafnkels saga Freysgoða illustrates the situation of a father with too many mouths to feed and the deleterious consequences this has for the son who is his favorite. To ease the pressure of providing for such a large family, Þorbjǫrn is forced to send his eldest son to find work elsewhere. Still, he reassures Einarr that he has confidence in his ability to make a living and assures him, "It's not for any lack of love that I'm sending you away, I love you more than my other children, but I've been led to this by my poverty and lack of means."[37] Nevertheless, Einarr berates Þorbjǫrn for sending him off to find work so late in the employment season.

Medieval Icelandic fathers often display a preference for sons who look or act like the paternal side of the family. The transmission of physical traits as well as intangible qualities are presented by the saga authors as hereditary results of the father–son relationship. There was an expectation that certain attributes passed naturally from fathers to sons; *Vatnsdœla saga* notes that "men guessed they had as good in Ketill [the father] as in Þorsteinn [the son]."[38]

Good looks, ugly physical features, size, character traits, intelligence, and peculiar qualities are all mentioned as transmissible characteristics in saga literature. Physical resemblance tops the list in terms of frequency. Snorri Sturluson observes that Eindriði inherited his father's stature, although his actual looks are attributed to the maternal side of the family.[39] Lambi Þórbjarnarson in *Laxdœla saga* "resembled his father in appearance as well as temperament."[40] In *Egils saga* there is a noticeable generational pattern of certain traits beginning with Kveld-Úlfr's sons. His oldest son, Þórólfr, is extremely handsome, as are the men of his mother's family, but the younger son, Skalla-Grímr, is "a dark man and ugly, like his father both in looks and disposition."[41] Both Þórólfr and Skalla-Grímr derive their tall physical stature from the paternal side. Skalla-Grímr looks more and more like his father as he ages for, when he reaches his mid-twenties, the saga notes again the striking resemblance: "Skalla-Grímr was like his father not only in stature and strength, but in looks and disposition as well."[42] Finally, Skalla-Grímr continues the paternal tendency toward being "black-haired and ugly."[43] Kveld-Úlfr and Skalla-Grímr have magical, berserker qualities, and Egill displays a greater-than-average proclivity for violence as well: at one point he bites his opponent in the throat and so causes his death.[44] In addition, Skalla-Grímr shares with his son the tendency to grow bald at an early age—indeed, "Skalla-Grímr" means "Bald Grímr."[45]

Besides looks, sagas refer to other traits shared by fathers and sons, and these characteristics sometimes play a role in determining the extent of the pair's emotional affinity for each other. Helgi Njálsson sees into the future like his father, and they enjoy a close relationship;[46] both Glúmr and his son Vigfúss share the unnerving habit of laughing before they kill people.[47] In *Laxdœla saga*, Hǫskuldr feels greater affection for his son Bárðr than for his elder son Þorleikr because the former resembles his father's family in appearance and mental abilities, whereas Þorleikr takes after his mother's side of the family.[48] A similar distribution of family traits in the sons' generation causes Gunnarr in *Njáls saga* to prefer Hǫgni over Grani: "They were men of very different natures; Grani took after his mother, but Hǫgni was a fine person."[49] When his friend Njáll offers to send two of his sons to stay with Gunnarr as protection against an expected attack, Gunnarr declines the offer, but asks Njáll to look after Hǫgni:

> I have only one request—that you look after my son Hǫgni. I do not say anything about Grani, for he does many things that are not to my liking.[50]

Such statements illustrate the paternal tendency to favor offspring who resemble themselves. At one level, a father could be sure that he was indeed the father if the son looked like him; it was one of the few indicators available to "prove" paternity. There has been much discussion in current psychology-of-the-family literature about the tendency of parents to prefer the offspring who most resemble them. The Icelandic examples support this theory of attraction, and it would be interesting to look at medieval literary evidence outside of Scandinavia to see whether the "like attracts like" concept is generally applicable.

Paternal bereavement receives considerable attention from saga writers, and the rich assortment of symptoms accompanying grief can inform us about what roles sons played in their fathers' lives. In saga literature, one finds examples of fathers who survive both the deaths of young sons and grown sons, and the latter tends to produce more extreme reactions of grief. The economic factor, as well as the demographic reality of a high mortality rate among children,[51] must be considered as an explanation for this. Grown sons were needed to support fathers in their old age, and the loss was keenly felt.[52] One exception to my observation that fathers mourn elder sons more than younger ones is Hrútr in *Laxdœla saga*. At the time of his twelve-year-old son Kári's death, Hrútr is eighty years old, and he is plunged into sorrow.[53] But here the disparity between their ages is so extreme, and Hrútr has so many other children (sixteen sons and ten daughters!), that he is hardly a typical example in any case.

On the other hand, when we examine fathers' reactions to the deaths of grown sons, we encounter many symptoms of grief that suggest the depth of the losses. In *Hœnsa–Þóris saga* old Óddr becomes "gravely ill" when he realizes that his grown sons are dead.[54] Hróar, the foster father of Þiðrandi in *Fljótsdœla saga*, "took to his bed in sorrow and died of grief"[55] when Þiðrandi dies. The diminished economic support represented by the loss of grown sons must be considered an important factor in the sagas' portrayal of paternal grief. Also, relatively few fathers attempt vengeance for their sons' deaths compared with sons seeking vengeance for paternal deaths.

Extravagant paternal grief is evident in *Egils saga* (it is a trait that recurs in several generations of this family) when Kveld-Úlfr learns of his son Þórólfr's death:

> It grieved him so deeply that he took to his bed, overcome by sorrow and old age. Skalla-Grímr kept coming and talking to him, and encouraged him to cheer up.[56]

Kveld-Úlfr's sorrow is echoed by his grandson Egill later in the saga; when Egill's favorite son, Bǫðvarr, drowns, Egill is so devastated that he exhibits both physical as well as emotional symptoms. At Bǫðvarr's funeral, Egill's body swells up and bursts apart his tightly fitted clothing. After the funeral, Egill refuses to eat or drink. When his daughter Þorgerðr learns of her father's determination to starve himself, she pretends to join him in this endeavor, and Egill is pleased to have her company:

> You do well, daughter, when you go along with your father; you have shown me a great love. How can I be expected to go on living with such sorrow?[57]

Þorgerðr tricks her grief-stricken father into drinking some milk; since he has inadvertently broken his fast, she says, the only course of action left is to go on with life. She suggests that Egill write a poem to honor his dead son. The resulting elegy is one of the most beautiful in all of medieval Icelandic literature. "Sonnatorek" ("Lament for My Sons") commemorates Bǫðvarr and another son, Gunnarr, who had died earlier. In anguished, stark language, it laments the deep hole left in a family when a young son dies:

> The rough storm has robbed me
> Of my best riches,
> It's cruel to recall
> The loss of that kinsman,
> The safeguard, the shield
> Of the house has sailed
> Out in death's darkness
> To a dearer place.[58]

Many of these images remind us of the economic loss sustained by an aged father when his grown son dies, and the "safeguard . . . of the house" suggests the crucial role sons play in sustaining the lineage—the death of a son threatens the entire family's ability to endure.

Njáll's overwhelming grief at the death of his beloved foster son Hǫskuldr Þráinsson cannot be attributed to economic concerns. After all, his three sons—more than capable of caring for Njáll in his old age—are the very people responsible for Hǫskuldr's death. Here, I think, a relevant consideration is the great lengths Njáll had gone to raise his foster son's status in Icelandic society: he created a chieftaincy for Hǫskuldr so that his foster son could make an advantageous marriage.[59] Hǫskuldr's death is a tremendous blow to Njáll. All of Njáll's work on behalf of his fosterling, including his frequent assertions of love for Hǫskuldr, is undone. Njáll reacts to the news of Hǫskuldr's death as follows:

> This is a terrible thing to hear, for I can truthfully say that it grieves me so deeply that I would rather have lost two of my own sons to have Hǫskuldr still alive.[60]

And the point is reiterated by the saga's author: "This [Hǫskuldr's death] was the only thing that grieved Njáll so much that he could never speak of it unmoved."[61]

In *Sturlunga saga* we encounter paternal bereavement ranging from anger to tears and an inability to resume normal activities. Sæmundr in *Íslendinga saga* is enraged when he hears of his son's drowning, and suggests that Páll was the victim of a plot.[62] Another father, Þorsteinn galti, undertakes a forty-day fast for his son Brandr, who has just been killed.[63]

When Gizurr Þorvaldsson's house is burned in retaliation for Snorri Sturluson's death, he survives by hiding in a vat of whey, but his wife and sons are killed. As the charred remains of his family are brought out of the wreckage, Gizurr tells Páll Kolbeinsson:

> "Páll, kinsman, you may now look upon Ísleifr, my son, and upon Gróa, my wife." And Páll saw that Gizurr turned away, and saw that tears started from his eyes like hailstones.[64]

Gizurr, like Egill Skalla-Grímsson, composes poetry to express his emotional devastation: he admits that his grief will haunt him until he is able to avenge his loved ones' deaths:

> Over and over again I lament my loss,
> My wife burned-in, my lovely lass,
> And three of my sons as well.
> Nor will I grieve the less,
> Nor will I, prey of Göndul,
> Know pleasure again or joy,
> —But live with sorrow alone
> Until my revenge is complete.[65]

Gizurr avenges his losses and goes on to have more children. His grief, like Njáll's for Hǫskuldr, indicates that a father's reputation rests on how well he supports and provides for his sons. It is a cause for grief—and vengeance— when a father's progeny is cut down.

Turning to filial grief in saga literature, I find the reactions of sons to be milder by far than that of fathers. From one point of view, there is always something for sons to gain when fathers die; besides this, the normal expectation is that children outlive the parents. In any case, very few sons display inordinate grief. When such grief *does* occur, it is often that of a fosterling reacting to his foster father's death. For example, in *Hákonar saga Herðibreiðs*, when Ingi Haraldsson learns of the death of his foster father, Grégóríús Dagsson, "it is said that . . . he cried like a baby."[66] Kári, the foster son of Njáll, manifests his grief in sleeplessness after Njáll's death. Though Kári's young son Þórðr died bravely with Njáll, Kári writes a poem that mourns the loss of his foster father and does not even mention Þórðr. Another of Njáll's foster sons, Þorgrímr Asgrimsson, reacts in a spectacular manner when he hears of his foster father's death:

[H]is whole body swelled up and a stream of blood spouted from both ears and would not stop until he fell down unconscious, and then it stopped. Then he stood up and said that he had not behaved like a man.[67]

When we do encounter a case of grief strong enough to move a natural son to tears, it turns out to be that of a six-year-old boy who is actually present at his father's murder.[68]

When Hǫskuldr dies in *Laxdœla saga*, we are told that "[his death] was considered a great loss, especially by his sons,"[69] but no individual reactions are noted. The great outlaw Grettir is hardly moved at all by his father's death: "It is said that Grettir was in no way affected by this news and was just as cheerful as before."[70] Similarly, Þorgeirr in *Fóstbrœðra saga* displays no emotion when he hears of his father's death.[71]

Perhaps because the sagas are more concerned with portraying the active heads of families, there is less evidence that reveals the qualities that sons value in their fathers. Sons generally appreciate the paternal consideration shown to them, they hope for generosity in their fathers, and they prefer their fathers to demonstrate strength and command respect.

While it would be anachronistic to expect saga authors to portray qualities that modern people prize in fathers, such as consideration for sons' feelings, it is nevertheless suggested in several works. In *Óláfs saga helga*, the Swedish king Óláfr Eiríksson demonstrates concern for the well-being of his illegitimate children; his wife "did not behave well towards her stepchildren; therefore, the king sent his son Eymundr to Vinðland to be fostered by his mother's family."[72] *Króka-Refs saga* portrays an uncle, rather than a father, who has extraordinary sensitivity. The hero of this work has a poor relationship with his own parents; their insults and constant nagging have no effect on Refr's lethargic behavior. But when his dynamic and sympathetic uncle Gestr appears, Refr is motivated by Gestr's confidence in him. For example, when Refr admits that he has no practical skills, Gestr responds: "I believe that in some way you are a very skilled man, and I will soon find out what it [i.e., Refr's talent] is!"[73] Inspired by his uncle's faith in him, Refr builds a boat for Gestr, and when the time to test it arrives, Gestr discreetly sails the boat with a very small crew, "since he didn't want everyone to know if the boat were poorly made."[74]

Paternal generosity is often an essential component in sons' successful careers, and it is reasonable to assume that the young men appreciated the benefits they received from material support. Bjǫrn Arngeirsson, who also enjoys an extraordinarily friendly relationship with his foster father,

Skuli Þorsteinsson, receives a good deal of money from both Arngeirr and Skuli so that he can begin a viking career.[75] When Ingimundr of *Vatnsdœla saga* decides to begin his own raiding career, he is confident that his father and foster father will give him the necessary provisions. Before requesting a ship and money from Þorsteinn, Ingimundr thanks his father (Þorsteinn) for having given him such a great foster father.[76] Ásbjǫrn in *Fljótsdœla saga* relinquishes his chieftaincy to his son.[77] Njáll's generosity to his beloved foster son Hǫskuldr is expressed in a similar manner when he obtains a *goðorð (chieftaincy)* for him so that Hǫskuldr can make an advantageous marital match.[78]

Whether fathers contribute property, money, or prestige to ease their sons' paths in life, their generous care for their offspring is one of the factors that determines young men's success. The importance of the paternal role in filial success is stressed by Hrafnkell in his saga: this once powerful man is humiliated by Sámr and Þorgeirr góði, and he is given the choice of obeying Sámr or being put to death:

> Most people would prefer a quick death to such humiliation . . . but I'll do as many others have done and choose life as long as I have the chance. I am doing this mostly for the sake of my sons, for they will have little hope of success if I die now.[79]

Vǫðu-Brands þáttr contains another example of fathers who generously support their sons' careers. Brandr Þorkelsson seeks permission from his father to lodge some Norwegian merchants; although Þorkell expresses some reservations about the risk involved, he admits, "It would seem good to me . . . if there were honor in it for you."[80]

References to filial pride in the sagas suggest that sons prefer strong, independent fathers who are capable of protecting family interests. Sǫlvi in *Egils saga* gives a stirring speech to King Arnviðr, asking that Arnviðr resist the political aggrandizement of Haraldr hárfagri: "My father preferred to die in kingship with honor rather than to grow old as another king's hired man,"[81] he says. Snorri Sturluson repeats this episode in *Haralds saga ins hárfagra*, again stressing Sǫlvi's pride in his father's refusal to submit to the king.[82]

Sons are proud of fathers who can demonstrate composure and aggressive support of family interests. Skarp-Heðinn responds to Flosi's insinuation that the beardless Njáll is feminine:

> It is bad to mock him in his old age, and no brave man has ever done

that before. You may know for sure that he is a real man because he has had sons on his wife. We have left few of our kinsmen unavenged at our door.[83]

Skarp-Heðinn is proud of Njáll's composure when Bergþórshváll is attacked by Flosi and the burners: "My father must be dead now," he observes, "and not a groan or a cough has been heard from him."[84] In *Fljótsdæla saga*, when Ǫlviðr tries to steal some of Ásbjǫrn Hrafnkelsson's horses, people try to deter him by warning that Ásbjǫrn's father does not allow people to steal horses without him exacting vengeance. Fathers who are known to be protective of their family's property and welfare are, then, greatly admired by their sons, for their reputations alone can deter potential aggression.[85]

The many indications that medieval Icelandic fathers and sons shared affection in their dealings with each other are balanced in the saga literature with negative evidence. Thus, we find allusions to hatred, insults, and discontent in both the family sagas and the historical works. It is possible to discern some broad areas of disagreement between the generations. First, I will look at attitudes and activities of Icelandic sons that elicit negative reactions from their fathers. Next, I will point to paternal qualities and actions that sons find disagreeable.

Before dealing with what fathers dislike in their sons, I must caution that it is not always explicitly stated why paternal-filial relations are strained. For example, in *Þorvaldr víðfǫrla*, one learns that Kodrán loves only his elder son, but this preference is not explained. Kodrán displays so little regard for his younger son, in fact, that his mistreatment of him draws the attention of a family friend.[86] Sometimes, paternal dislike has little to do with the *son's* character or behavior: the *father's* condition may be a more relevant factor, as we see in *Eyrbyggja saga*:

> [Þórólfr bægifótr] was getting very old. The older he got, the more violent he became, and there was growing ill feeling between him and his son Arnkell.[87]

Thus, the father's age or state of mind may influence his relationship with his son. Moreover, there is some indication that a child's illegitimate status adversely influences his father's opinion: in *Óláfs saga Tryggvasonar* we encounter a father whose lack of affection for his son is purportedly due to the son's illegitimacy. When Hákon jarl informs Gull-Haraldr of the plot to kill King Haraldr Gráfeldr, he says: "King Haraldr is now very old, and has but one son, and cares little about him, as he is but the son of a concubine."[88]

Hákon's assumption that a father cares less for illegitimate children is perhaps colored by his own experience: later in the saga he demonstrates his preference for his son-in-law Skopti over his own bastard son Eiríkr.[89]

When the sagas indicate reasons for paternal dislike of sons, several sources of discontent emerge. Fathers object when their sons choose associates unwisely; they consider pranks to be signs of disobedience; they expect their sons to answer when addressed; and they object to cowardice, laziness, and lack of foresight in their children. Ásmundr, father of Iceland's greatest outlaw, might serve as the spokesman for fathers who experience filial discord: "He has been difficult for me to deal with!"[90]

Njáll is distressed that his sons have taken up with the disreputable Morðr Valgardsson.[91] Erlingr, father of Magnús in *Heimskringla*'s *Magnús saga Erlingssonar*, also objects to his son's company. When Magnús tries to intercede for a man whom his father considers dangerous, Erlingr warns that Magnús is too easily led by his friends.[92]

Childish pranks are not viewed with amusement by fathers in saga literature. In *Óláfs saga helga*, when Sigurðr Sýr asks his young stepson to saddle his horse, Óláfr instead saddles a goat. Sigurðr takes this as an indication that the future saint will persist in his insubordination:

> It is clear that you will have little regard for my orders, and your mother will think it right that I not order you to do anything against your inclination. It is clear that we are of different dispositions.[93]

Grettir Ásmundarson is another son whose pranks elicit annoyance from his father. Grettir "was not greatly loved by Ásmundr,"[94] and the pranks help us to understand why this was the case. Ordered to watch over the family's geese, Grettir deliberately kills them. When he uses a wool comb on his father's back, the saga author drily observes: "The incident did not improve matters between Ásmundr and Grettir."[95]

When fathers in medieval Icelandic literature issue commands or question their sons, they expect immediate compliance. We have already seen Sveinungr lose patience with his young son because he does not jump to Sveinungr's command.[96] In *Íslendinga saga*, when Sturla Sighvatsson does not respond to Sighvatr's interrogation, tension arises between the father and son.[97] Three-year-old Egill's failure to accede to his father's wish that he remain at home does not result in paternal retaliation, but one suspects this is only because the precocious boy turns out to be the hit of the party. Once his grandfather, Yngvarr, welcomes Egill, he asked why he'd come so late. Egill told him about having had words with Skalla-Grímr, and then Yngvarr gave Egill the seat next to himself and opposite Skalla-Grímr and Þórólfr.[98]

Fathers who suspect their sons of cowardice verbally abuse them, hoping to engender more "manly" behavior; a timid man was not likely to maintain the family's position in a violent and litigious society such as medieval Iceland. The verbal abuse includes insults and insinuations of feminine behavior. Arnkell and Þórólfr are frequently at odds in *Eyrbyggja saga*, and Þórólfr accuses his son of displaying a "cowardly spirit."[99] Þórarinn in *Þorsteins þáttr stangarhǫggs* tells his son, "I'd never have thought I could have a coward for a son,"[100] and Glíru-Halli of *Vápnfirðinga saga* also affirms that he would rather have dead sons than cowardly ones.[101] Guðbrandr in *Óláfs saga helga* accuses his son of cowardly behavior.[102] Þorsteinn Ketilsson reflects on his father's disturbing assessment of his character:

And now, too, came in mind how his father had said he was no better with his weapons than a daughter or other of the women, and that it would be more honorable to the family that there should be a gap in their lineage than such as he.[103]

Ketill accuses his son not only of cowardice but also of laziness—and he gets rather carried away, charging that Þorsteinn's entire generation is guilty of this offense:

Young men are different from when I was a boy . . . [now] young men want to become sticks-in-the-mud and bake themselves by the fire and fill their bellies with mead and beer.[104]

Refr's father also objects to his son's indolence:

[Refr] was a sitter-by-the-fire, and usually had nothing better to do than get in the way of busy people. It seemed a great pity to his parents that their son should be so different from other people.[105]

Just as fathers abhor cowardice in their sons, the reverse is true as well. If we add paternal stinginess, the tendency to hold onto family property too long (from the sons' points of view), and unwelcome paternal advice about their boys' love lives, then we have a fairly complete list of filial complaints. Bárðr accuses his father, Halli, of growing soft with age in *Víga-*

Glúms saga.[106] Commenting on his aging father, Hǫskuldr in *Ljósvetninga saga* says, "It's a shame if my father's courage is failing."[107]

Grettir's father refuses to give him a weapon as the outlaw prepares to comply with the requirements of outlawry by going abroad, and "after that, father and son parted with little affection."[108] Oddr in *Bandamanna saga* responds to his father's lack of generosity by stealing some money so that he can begin a business career.[109] Egill holds a grudge against his son Þorsteinn because Þorsteinn borrows his father's cloak without first asking permission—and the old man retaliates with an ungracious poetic insult:

> No use to Egil,
> His son and heir.
> My child cheated me
> Before death chose me:
> That waterman could have waited
> Until the warriors
> Had built up the burial stones
> Upon my old body.[110]

When fathers do not yield family property to their sons quickly enough, filial impatience can create an unpleasant relationship. In *Íslendinga saga* Órækja Snorrason covets Stafaholt, but Snorri is unwilling to turn it over to him, and to Órækja's chagrin, "it had to be as Snorri commanded."[111] Órækja is not able to obtain Stafaholt until he nearly comes to blows with his father: "Þorleifr and Loftr negotiated between father and son in an attempt to bring them together."[112] An episode in *Egils saga* points to yet another property problem Icelandic sons could face: remarriages of their aging fathers. When old Bjǫrgólfr marries a young woman, his grown son is very annoyed with the prospect of young brothers-heirs, and a long dispute ensues.[113]

When medieval Icelandic fathers try to advise their sons about women, young men are likely to perceive this advice as heavy-handed paternal interference, and this is a source of strife in their dealings with one another. Óláfr allows his father to arrange his marriage with Þorgerðr, daughter of Egill Skalla-Grímsson, but when she hesitates to commit herself because of Óláfr's illegitimacy, the young man angrily blames his father for embarrassing him.[114] In *Egils saga*, Bjǫrn "kidnaps" a willing young woman, but his father Brynjólfr insists that she must be returned to her family. Paternal authority is irksome to the son: "It all had to be done as Brynjólfr wished in his household, whether he liked it or not."[115]

Altogether, saga literature implies that the emotional universe of medieval Icelandic fathers and sons was complex and multifaceted. By looking at how the family and historical sagas portray paternal-filial interactions, one can find evidence that the relationship could be nurturing as well as problematic. To learn about what fathers looked for and strove to produce in their sons, and what attributes sons desired in their fathers, one must often coax such ideals out of texts that present the negative cases. Thus, when we see fathers chastising their sons for cowardice and disobedience, it points to the desirability of the opposite qualities.

It is apparent that Icelandic men admired certain qualities in each other: courage, pride in family, generosity, independence, and an ability to get along in the larger social scene. When a father or son perceives these features in the other, the emotional connection is a positive one; and saga authors draw our attention to it by describing cooperative, affectionate relations. On the other hand, one notices that the characteristics that produce enmity (cowardice, mainly, since it negatively affects the family's ability to get ahead) are also common to both generations. Each generation also seeks to get from the other what it considers essential to its prosperity: fathers demand obedience and are angry when it is not forthcoming; sons above all demand tangible proof (property and advantageous marriages) that they are the heirs, and often their impatience for both is palpable and a source of discontent with the elder generation.

The qualities that are admired and abhorred in the father-son relationship reveal a central underlying principle: the bond between fathers and sons was the main one for preserving the values that created Icelandic society. Jesse Byock writes of the sagas as "a literature of social instruction,"[116] and indeed, we see many elements of the larger society in the paternal-filial link. It's no wonder that the ending "-sons" was ubiquitous.

NOTES

1. Christopher Brooke, *The Medieval Idea of Marriage* (New York: Oxford Univ. Press, 1989), 176.

2. William Ian Miller, "On Beating up on Women and Old Men and Other Enormities: A Social Historical Inquiry into Literary Sources," *Mercer Law Review* 39 (1988): 754. Miller also has written an excellent book that deals with the value of the literary sources for Icelandic historians: *Bloodtaking and Peacemaking: Feud, Law, and Society in Saga Iceland* (Chicago: Univ. of Chicago Press, 1990).

3. Kirsten Hastrup, *Culture and History in Medieval Iceland* (Oxford: Clarendon Press, 1985); Victor W. Turner, "An Anthropological Approach to the Icelandic Saga," in *The Transmission of Culture: Essays to E. Evans-Pritchard*, ed. T.O. Beidelman (London: Tavistock Publications, 1971), pp. 349–74.

4. Miller, *Bloodtaking and Peacemaking: Feud, Law, and Society in Saga Iceland.*

5. *Egils saga Skalla-Grímssonar, Íslenzk Fórnit*, vols. I–xxxv. Reykjavík, 1933ff. Hið íslenzka fornritafélag (hereinafter ÍF), chap. 31, p. 80: "unni honum vel faðir ok móðir."

6. *Laxdœla saga, ÍF* V, chap. 19, pp. 48–49: "Svá segja menn, at Hrútr væri svá á þingi eitt sumar, at fjórtán synir hans væri með honum; því er þessa getit, at þat þótti vera rausn mikil ok afli."

7. *Egill saga Skalla-Grímssonar, ÍF* II, chap. 40, p. 102.

8. Ibid., chap. 79, p. 274: "[Egill] unni honum lítit; Þorsteinn var ok ekki við hann ástúðigr."

9. *Haralds saga gráfeldar*, in *Heimskringla I*, chap. 8, p. 213: "Jarl lét fátt um til hans."

10. *Þorgils saga skarði*, in *Sturlunga saga*, 2 vols., eds. Magnús Finnbogason and Kristján Eldjárn (Reykjavík: Sturlunguútgáfan, 1946) (hereinafter *St.* I or *St* II) chap. 30, p. 158: "Þóttust menn þat heyra, at hann bað föður sinn leysa sik, ok fekkst þat eigi. Fekk Þorgils þá til Eyjólf smið at vega at honum. Eftir þat var Valgarðr drepinn."

11. *Íslendingasaga*, in *St.* I, chap. 19, p. 400: "þeir unnu honum sem bróður sínum ok báðu hann fulltings í bænum sem föður sinn."

12. *Ljósvetninga saga, ÍF* X, chap. 2, p. 8.

13. *Hallfreðar saga, ÍF* VIII, chap. 4, p. 149: "Hverr mun mér þá trúr, ef faðirinn bregzk?"

14. *Vatnsdœla saga, ÍF* VIII, chap. 7, p. 22: "[Þorsteinn] kvazk vel við una at eiga þvílíkan son."

15. Ibid.: "þóttisk Þorsteinn ok aldri fullmikinn geta gǫrt sóma Ingimundar sonar síns, þegar hann sá, hvélíkr maðr hann vildi verða."

16. Ibid., chap. 11, p. 32: "Gott er nú at deyja ok vita son sinn slíkan hamingjumann."

17. Ibid., chap. 4, p. 12: "þá urðu þeir brátt vel sáttir."

18. *Þorsteins þáttr stangarhǫggs, ÍF* XI, p. 75: "því at þar mundi verit hafa minnar ævi, at ekki munda ek bograt hafa fyrir slíkum, sem Bjarni er. Er Bjarni þó inn mesti kappi. Þykki mér, ok betra at missa þín en eiga ragan son."

19. *Vatnsdœla saga, ÍF* VIII, chap. 2, p. 4.

20. *Fljótsdœla saga, ÍF* XI, chap. 19, p. 274: "þá er vér vórum ungir, þurftum vér hvórki hött né vöttu."

21. *Egils saga Skalla-Grímssonar, ÍF* II, chap. 31, p. 81: "Ekki skaltu fara . . . því at þú kannt ekki fyrir þér at vera í fjǫlmenni, þar er drykkjur eru miklar, er þú þykkir ekki góðr viðskiptis, at þú sér ódrukkinn."

22. *Brennu-Njáls saga, ÍF* XII, chap. 111.

23. Ibid., chap. 128, p. 326: "'Nú mun sem optar, at þér munuð bera mik ráðum, sýnir mínir, ok virða mik engis. En þá er þér váruð yngri, þá gerðuð þér ekki svá, ok fór yðr þá betr.'"

24. Ibid., chap. 43, p. 110; chap. 99, p. 254.

25. *Prestssaga Guðmundr góða*, in *St.* I, chap. 25, p. 151: "Veizt þú þat, frændi, at ek hefi verit höfðingi fyrir ætt várri ok minn faðir fyrir mér. Nú hlítti þinn faðir minni forsjá ok svá aðrir frændr mínir, enda ræð ek þér þat."

26. Richard Bauman, "Performance and Honor in 13th-Century Iceland," *Journal of American Folklore* 99 (1986): p. 142.

27. Ibid., p. 143.

28. *Brennu-Njáls saga, ÍF* XII, chap. 118, p. 295: "því at þat er sómi minn at skiljast eigi við yður mál, meðan ek lifi."

29. *Hallfreðar saga, ÍF* VIII, chap. 3, p. 143.

30. *Vatnsdœla saga, ÍF* VIII, chap. 37, p. 99: "'Hví verðr þér þat fyrir, at gera Óttari snepu eða svívirða dóttur hans; hefir þú illt ráð upptekit, ok mun okkr verða at sundrþykki, ef þú gerir eigi at.'"

31. *Egils saga Skalla-Grímssonar, ÍF* II, chap. 81, p. 285: "Man ek þá daga,

at hvárumtveggja okkrum mundi þykkja ólíkligt, at vit myndim sǫkum sœkjask eða stilla eigi sonu okkra, at þeir fari eigi með fíflsku slíkri, sem ek heyri, at hér horfisk til."

32. Ibid., chap. 82.

33. *Fóstbrœðra saga*, ÍF VI, chap. 2, p. 125: "Hǫfðu þeir hald ok traust hjá feðrum sínum, sem ván var at; virðu margir menn sem þeir heldi þá til rangs."

34. Ibid., chap. 11, p. 176: "Óþarfar unnustur áttu, hlauzt af annarri ørkuml þau, er þú verðr aldri heill maðr, en nú er eigi minni ván, at bæði augu springi ór hǫfði þér. En þó er þat nú mitt ráð við þik, at þú snúir aptr kvæðinu á þann hátt, sem þat var ort fyrir ǫndverðu."

35. *Bjarnar saga hítdœlakappa*, ÍF III, chap. 11, p. 138.

36. *Laxdœla saga*, ÍF V, chap. 20, p. 51.

37. *Hrafnkels saga Freysgoða*, ÍF XI, chap. 3, p. 101: "Eigi veldr ástleysi þessari brottkvaðning við þik, því at þú ert mér þarfastr barna minna. Meira veldr því efnaleysi mitt ok fátœkð."

38. *Vatnsdœla saga*, ÍF VIII, chap. 7, p. 18: "ok þóttusk menn hafa iðgjǫld Ketils, þar sem Þorsteinn var."

39. *Haralds saga Sigurðarsonar*, in *Heimskringla III*, ÍF XXVIII, chap. 40, p. 122.

40. *Laxdœla saga*, ÍF V, chap. 22, pp. 61–62: "[hann var] glíkr feðr sínum yfirlits ok svá at skaplyndi."

41. *Egils saga Skalla-Grímssonar*, ÍF II, chap. 1, p. 5: "Grímr var svartr maðr ok ljótr, líkr feðr sínum, bæði yfirlits ok at skaplyndi. "

42. Ibid., chap. 20, p. 50: "Skalla-Grímr var líkr feðr á vǫxt ok at afli, svá ok at yfirlitum ok skaplyndi."

43. Ibid., chap. 31, p. 80: "mjǫk ljótr ok . . . svartr á hár."

44. Ibid., chaps. 1, 40, 65.

45. Ibid., chaps. 20, 56.

46. *Brennu-Njáls saga*, ÍF XII, chap. 85, p. 206.

47. *Víga-Glúms saga*, ÍF IX, chap. 18, p. 62.

48. *Laxdœla saga*, ÍF V, chap. 9, p. 18.

49. *Brennu-Njáls saga*, ÍF XII, chap. 75, p. 182: "Þeir váru menn óskapglíkir: hafði Grani mikit af skapi móður sinnar, en Hǫgni var vel at sér."

50. Ibid., chap. 75, p. 184: "En þess vil ek biðja, at þér sjáið á með Hǫgna, syni mínum. En ek tala ekki um Grana, því at hann gerir mart ekki at mínu skapi."

51. In *Egils saga*, for instance, it is stated that "Skalla-Grímr and Bera had many children but all of the older ones died in infancy." ("Skalla-Grímr ok þau Bera áttu bǫrn mjǫk mǫrg, ok var þat fyrst, at ǫll ǫnduðusk"; chap. 31, p. 80.) There are many indications in the saga literature that their experience was not unusual.

52. For a discussion of the emotional disruption that the death of an adult child could produce (besides the economic uncertainty for elderly parents mentioned above), see Beverly Raphael's *The Anatomy of Bereavement* (New York: Basic Books, 1983).

53. *Laxdœla saga*, ÍF V, chap. 37, p. 106.

54. *Hœnsa-Þóris saga*, ÍF III, chap. 17, p. 46: "tók hann sótt mikla."

55. *Fljótsdœla saga*, ÍF XI, chap. 18, p. 267: "svó at hann leggst í rekkju af harmi ok deyr af helstríði."

56. *Egils saga Skalla-Grímssonar*, ÍF II, chap. 24, p. 60: "varð hann hryggr við þessi tíðendi, svá at hann lagðisk í rekkju af harmi ok elli. Skalla-Grímr kom opt til hans ok talði fyrir honum, bað hann hressa sik."

57. Ibid., chap. 78, pp. 244–45: "Vel gerðir þú, dóttir, er þú vill fylgja feðr þínum; mikla ást hefir þú sýnt við mik. Hver ván er, at ek muna lifa vilja við harm þenna?"

58. The translation of this verse is from *Egil's Saga*, trans. Hermann Pálsson and Paul Edwards, (New York: Penguin Books, 1976), 206. See Carol J. Clover's per-ceptive analysis of the poem "Sonnatorek" in her article "Hildigunnr's Lament" in

Structure and Meaning in Old Norse Literature: New Approaches to Textual Analysis and Literary Criticism, ed. John Lindow, Lars Lönnroth, and Gerd Wolfgang Weber (Odense: Odense Univ. Press, 1986), especially 159–61.

59. Brennu-Njáls saga, ÍF XII, chap. 97.

60. Ibid., chap. 111, p. 281: "'Hormulig tíðendi,' [segir Njáll] . . . 'ok er slíkt illt at vita, því at þat er sannligt at segja, at svá fellr mér nær um trega, at mér þœtti betra at hafa látit tvá sonu mína ok væri Hǫskuldr a lífi.'"

61. Ibid.: "Sjá einn hlutr var svá at Njáli fell svá nær, at hann mátti aldri ókløkkvandi um tala."

62. Íslendinga saga, in St. I, chap. 35, p. 270.

63. Ibid., chap. 141, p. 442. This is in noticeable contrast with Egill Skalla-Grímsson, who undertakes a fast also, but an unlimited one. The Christian significance of a forty-day fast is present in Íslendinga saga; Þorsteinn's fast seems a more formulaic response to grief than Egill's. The latter quite literally loses his appetite for life after his beloved son dies. See Caroline Walker Bynum's fascinating book Holy Feast and Holy Fast: The Religious Significance of Food to Medieval Women (Berkeley: Univ. of California Press, 1987) for a discussion of the general topic of fasting.

64. Íslendinga saga, in St. I, chap. 174, p. 494: "'Páll frændi . . . hér máttu nú sjá Ísleifr, son minn, ok Gróa, konu mína.' Ok fann Páll, at hann leit frá, ok stökk ór andlitinu sem haglkorn væri."

65. Translation of this verse by Julia H. McGrew, in her translation of Sturlunga Saga, vol. I: The Saga of Hvamm-Sturla and The Saga of the Icelanders (New York: Twayne Publishers, 1970), ch. 175, p. 406.

66. Hákonar saga Herðibreiðs, in Heimskringla III, chap. XV, p. 365: "Þat er svá sagt . . . at hann grét sem barn."

67. Ibid., chap. 132, p. 344: "hann þrútnaði allr ok blóðbogi stóð ór hvárritveggju hlustinni, ok varð eigi stǫðvat, ok fell hann í óvit, ok þá stǫðvaðisk. Eptir þat stóð hann upp ok kvað sér lítilmannliga verða."

68. In Gísls þáttr Illugasonar, ÍF III, chap. 5, p. 146, Gísl admits that when he was six years old, his father was killed in his presence; when one of the killers recommended that Gísl and his brother should also be killed, the little boy began to cry.

69. Laxdœla saga, ÍF V, chap. 26, pp. 72–73: "þat þótti mikill skaði, fyrst at upphafi sonum hans."

70. Grettis saga Ásmundarsonar, ÍF VII, chap. 47, p. 148: "Svá segja menn, at Grettir brygði engan veg skapi við þessar fréttir ok var jafnglaðr sem áðr."

71. Fóstbrœðra saga, ÍF VI, chap. 2, p. 127.

72. Óláfs saga helga, in Heimskringla II, ÍF XXVII, chap. 88, p. 130: "[Dróttningin var ríklunduð] ok ekki vel til stjúpbarna sinna. Konungr sendi Emund, son sinn, til Vinðlands, ok fœddisk hann þar upp með móðurfrædum sínum."

73. Króka-Refs saga, in Íslendinga sögur, ed. Guðni Jónsson (Reykjavík: Íslendingasagnaútgáfan, 1953), vol. IV, chap. 6, p. 412: "Ek sé á þér, at þú ert inn mesti íþróttamaðr at nökkurum hlut, en þat mun ek sjá brátt, hvat þat er."

74. Ibid., chap. 8, p. 414: "því at hann vildi ekki, at alþýða sæi, ef ófimligt væri."

75. Bjarnar saga Hítdœlakappa, ÍF III, chap. 2, p. 114.

76. Vatnsdœla saga, ÍF VIII, chap. 7, p. 18.

77. Fljótsdœla saga, ÍF XI, chap. 10, p. 238.

78. Brennu-Njáls saga, ÍF XII, chap. 97.

79. Hrafnkels saga Freysgoða, ÍF XI, ch. 5, p. 121: "Mǫrgum mundi betr þykkja skjótr dauði en slíkar hrakningar, en mér mun fara sem mǫrgum ǫðrum, at lífit mun ek kjósa, ef kostr er. Geri ek þat mest sǫkum sona minna, því at lítil mun vera uppreist þeira, ef ek dey frá."

80. Vǫðu-Brands þáttr, ÍF X, chap. 1, p. 125: "En vel þœtti mér . . . ef þér yrði sœmð at."

81. Egils saga Skalla-Grímssonar, ÍF II, chap. 3, p. 8: "Þat þótti fǫður mínum

vegr, at deyja í konungdómi með sœmð, heldr en gerask undirmaðr annars konungs á gamals aldri."

82. *Haralds saga ins hárfagra*, in *Heimskringla I*, chap. 11, p. 105.

83. *Brennu-Njáls saga*, *ÍF* XII, chap. 123, p. 314: "Illa er slíkt gǫrt at sneiða honum afgǫmlum, er engi hefir áðr til orðit dugandi maðr. Meguð þér þat vita, at hann er karlmaðr, því at hann hefir sonu getit við konu sinni. Hafa fáir várir frændr legit óbœttir hjá garði, svá at vér hafim eigi hefnt."

84. Ibid., chap. 129, p. 331: "Nú mun faðir minn dauðr vera, ok hefir hvárki heyrt til hans styn né hósta."

85. Unfortunately, Ǫlviðr does not listen to this warning, and Ásbjǫrn kills him for stealing the horses. Since Ásbjǫrn's father, Hrafnkell, was famous for killing Einarr for the same offense, the old cliché "Like father, like son" comes to mind!

86. *Þorvaldr víðfǫrla*, in *Íslendinga sögur* VII, chap. 1, p. 440.

87. *Eyrbyggja saga*, *ÍF* IV, chap. 30, p. 81: "Hann tók nú at eldast fast ok gerðisk illr ok æfr við ellina ok mjǫk ójafnaðarfullr; lagðisk ok mjǫk ómjúkt á með þeim Arnkatli feðgum."

88. *Óláfs saga Tryggvasonar*, in *Heimskringla I*, chap. 12, p. 236: "Haraldr konungr er nú gamall mjǫk, en hann á þann einn son, er hann ann lítit ok frillusonr er."

89. Ibid., chap. 20, pp. 248–49. I might add that paternal attitudes about illegitimate children could swing the other way: in *Laxdœla saga*, Hǫskuldr seems to prefer his bastard son Óláfr over his legitimate sons (chap. 13). In *Óláfs saga helga*, the king is overjoyed at the birth of his illegitimate son Magnús (chap. 122).

90. *Grettis saga Ásmundarsonar*, *ÍF* VII, chap. 16, p. 45: "þykkjumikill ok þungr hefir hann mér orðit."

91. *Brennu-Njáls saga*, *ÍF* XII, ch. 108, p. 276.

92. *Magnús saga Erlingssonar*, in *Heimskringla III*, chap. 35, p. 410.

93. *Óláfs saga helga*, in *Heimskringla II*, chap. 2, pp. 3–4: "Auðsætt er, at þú munt vilja af hǫndum ráða kvaðningar mínar. Mun móður þinni þat þykkja sœmiligt, at ek hafa engar kvaðningar við þik, þær er þér sé í móti skapi. Er þat auðsætt, at vit munum ekki vera skaplíkir."

94. *Grettis saga Ásmundarsonar*, *ÍF* VII, chap. 14, p. 36: "Ekki hafði hann ástríki mikit af Ásmundi."

95. Ibid., chap. 14, p. 39: "Ekki batnaði frændsemi þeira Ásmundar við þetta."

96. *Fljótsdæla saga*, *ÍF* XI, chap. 19, p. 274.

97. *Íslendinga saga*, in *St*. I, chap. 128, p. 411.

98. *Egils saga Skalla-Grímssonar*, *ÍF* II, chap. 31, p. 81: "ok spurði, hví hann hefði svá síð komit. Egill sagði, hvat þeir Skalla-Grímr hǫfðu við mælzk. Yngvarr setti Egil hjá sér; sátu þeir gagnvert þeim Skalla-Grími ok Þórólfi."

99. *Eyrbyggja saga*, *ÍF* IV, chap. 33, p. 91.

100. *Þorsteins þáttr stangarhǫggs*, *ÍF* XI, p. 70: "Ekki mundi mik þess vara, at ek munda ragan son eiga."

101. *Vápnfirðinga saga*, *ÍF* XI, chap. 18, p. 63.

102. *Óláfs saga helga*, in *Heimskringla II*, chap. 112, p. 185.

103. *Vatnsdœla saga*, *ÍF* VIII, chap. 3, p. 8: "Þá kom honum ok í hug, at faðir hans segði hann eigi betra til vápns en dóttur eða aðra konu ok meiri sæmð væri frændum, at skarð væri í ætt þeira en þar sem hann var."

104. Ibid., chap. 2, p. 4: "Ǫnnur gerisk nú atferð ungra manna en þá er ek var ungr . . . nú vilja ungir menn gerask heimaelskir ok sitja við bakelda ok kýla vǫmb sína á miði ok mungati."

105. *Króka-Refs saga*, in *Íslendinga sögur* IV, chap. 1, p. 403: "Hann var eldsætinn, ok enga hafði hann aðra iðn fyrir stafni en veltast fyrir fótum mönnum, en þar gengu. Mikit mein þótti þeim hjónum á þessu, at þeira sonr skyldi svá lítt vilja siðu nema annarra manna."

106. *Víga-Glúms saga*, *ÍF* IX, chap. 18, p. 62.

107. *Ljósvetninga saga,* ÍF X, chap. 4, p. 13: "Illt er þat, ef fǫður minn þrýtr drengskapinn."

108. *Grettis saga Ásmundarsonar,* ÍF VII, chap. 17, p. 49: "Síðan skilðu þeir feðgar með litlum kærleikum."

109. *Bandamanna saga,* ÍF VII, chap. 1, p. 295.

110. I am using the Pálsson and Edwards translation of this verse in their *Egil's Saga* (New York: Penguin Books, 1976), p. 219.

111. *Íslendinga saga,* in *St.* I, chap. 90, p. 361: "En þó varð svá at vera sem Snorri vildi."

112. Ibid., chap. 110, p. 388: "Þeir Þorleifr ok Loftr fóru á meðal þeira feðga ok leituðu um samningar."

113. *Egils saga Skalla-Grímssonar,* ÍF II, chap. 7.

114. *Laxdœla saga,* ÍF V, chap. 23, p. 64.

115. *Egils saga Skalla-Grímssonar,* ÍF II, chap. 32, p. 84: "En svá varð at vera allt, sem Brynjólfr kvað á, þar í hans hýbýlum, hvárt er Birni likaði vel eða illa."

116. Jesse Byock, *Medieval Iceland: Society, Sagas, and Power* (Berkeley: Univ. of California Press, 1988), p. 36.

Notes on Family Relationships in Medieval Castilian[1] Narrative

María Luzdivina Cuesta

If someone were to attempt a historical analysis of family relationships in medieval Spain, literature would undoubtedly be a help, but it would never be the main source of information because it expresses a subjective view of reality, frequently conditioned by social preconceptions and prejudices.[2] However, this "defect" can be useful in obtaining an image of the medieval mentality and ideology on this subject. Therefore, by studying family relationships in medieval Castilian literary texts I do not describe historical reality[3] but the view of the family portrayed in these works.

Works of different literary genres reveal different views of family structures. Thus, this brief analysis is limited to narrative texts. I shall include works written in verse (such as epic poems, *romances*,[4] and poems of *mester de clerecía*)[5] and prose texts (such as books of *exempla* and novels). The reader will have the opportunity to see how the treatment of family relationships and the characters changes from one narrative subgenre to another.

Medieval Castilian writers were not very interested in the family. The hero of fictional literature was almost always a man. The most important types of fiction in this period were the epic poems and heroic biographies of mester de clerecía (which unify history and creativity) and novels. The former, relating stories about warriors, dominated literature until the fourteenth century. The latter, which began at that time (before this date there were translations of foreign works, especially Arthurian romances), dominated fictional literature in the fifteenth century, and they combined chivalry and love (romances of chivalry) or analyzed love affairs (sentimental novels).

When the character was a warrior, the family only participated in the plot as a part of his identity, and shared honor and dignity with him. When the hero was a lover, the woman's family was as important as she was. The heroine often had a secondary position.

In the study of the family in the Middle Ages, father and daughter relationships are one of the most interesting subjects. Some of the most famous medieval poems and novels illustrate this type of family relationship *(Poema de Mio Cid, Libro de Apolonio, Cárcel de amor, La Celestina)*,[6] while few medieval Castilian texts speak about relationships between fathers and sons.

In the *Poema de Mio Cid*, the only medieval Spanish epic poem that has been preserved almost in its complete form, the author described the father-daughter relationship and did not refer to Rodrigo Díaz de Vivar's historic son.[7] This work shows scenes in which a complete and united family appear: father, mother, and two daughters. The reader here finds tender scenes in which the characters show affection toward each other: the hero's tears when he must go into exile, his rejoicing when he shows the conquered territories to his family, his blessing of his daughters when they go away with their husbands, his happiness when the family is reunited.

A recurrent theme that is associated with Rodrigo Díaz de Vivar's daughters is their marriages. It is obvious that the author (or authors) could not imagine a more honorable destiny for women than that of marriage. Even at the time of his daughters' childhood, he longs to see the day they wed:

Plega a Dios e a santa María,
que aun con mis manos case estas mis fijas[8]

[May it please God and Saint Mary
for me to live to see my daughters married.]

One of his first conversations with Jimena, his wife, when she rejoins him in exile, is about the wedding of their daughters, doña Elvira and doña Sol (v. 1649).

The second and third parts of the poem center on the daughters' marriages, because the honor that good marriages bring to Elvira and Sol affects the hero's social standing. The unions are arranged by the king.[9] Although El Cid dislikes his future sons-in-law, he does not dare oppose the desire of his monarch. But the king is carrying out a promise made to the *infantes*[10] of Carrión, who desire a union with Cid's family because of his wealth. These are, then, arranged marriages, without love and very much consistent with the customs of the period.[11] Love is not mentioned. But soon the bridegrooms want to dissolve their marriages, arguing that their social status was demeaned by the matches, since El Cid is only an *infanzón*, a nobleman, one who owes his wealth and power to his conquests. Their mistake is their attempt to bring about the dissolution of their marriages by violence and their greedy intention to retain the gifts and dowries their wives had brought to the marriages, for this results in the humiliation of El Cid and his daughters.[12]

The hero maintains a calm appearance throughout in spite of his pain and desire for revenge.[13] Because he loves his daughters very much, he knows that revenge is a poor consolation for them. It is better to offer them compensation for their sufferings: El Cid announces that he is going to find better husbands for them ("que vos vea mejor cassadas d'aquí en adelant"; v. 2893). ["Let us hope I may see you more happily and better wed in the future."] Obviously, El Cid thinks the main responsibility for a father is to provide good marriages for his daughters.[14] The union favored by the king has been unsuccessful and has produced a loss of honor for El Cid and his family: the husbands have treated doña Elvira and doña Sol as if they were peasants. The husbands allege that it was inappropriate for them to have married El Cid's daughters because they did not belong to the high aristocracy and so they were not even good enough to have been their concubines.[15] El Cid must retrieve his honor by arranging more honorable marriages. He achieves this without effort, because the princes of Navarra and Aragón ask if they can marry doña Elvira and doña Sol.

The relationship between El Cid and his daughters is dominated by his desire and responsibility to arrange advantageous marriages for them. The *Poema de Mio Cid* reflects the reality of the period, in which social structure is based on domestic life and family. In this society, the married couple has a dominant position in relation to single men and women, since men and women receive all their rights only when they marry.[16] The daughters return their father's affection in the form of respect and obedience, using the external gestures that a vassal uses in front of his lord:

Amas hermanas, don Elvira y doña Sol
fincaron los inojos antel Çid Campeador.[17]

[The two sisters, doña Elvira and doña Sol,
knelt down before the fighting Cid.]

The *Poema de Mio Cid* shows a good relationship between father and daughters: El Cid loves them as much as his own heart (vv. 2577–78); he feels a closeness with them ("Cuemo la uña de la carne ellos partidos son"; v. 2642). [As nail is torn from flesh, just so painfully do they part.] But sometimes the relationship is a source of conflict, as in some *romances*.

In "Romance de las quejas de noña Urraca," a poem in the *Romancero*, we see women appear in the role of daughters. Doña Urraca[18] claims her share of her father's estate by threatening to prostitute herself:

> a mí, porque soy muger,
> dexáisme desheredada;
> irm'he yo por essas tierras,
> como una muger errada;
> y este mi cuerpo daría
> a quien se me antojara,
> a los moros por dineros
> y a los cristianos de gracia:
> de lo que ganar pudiere,
> haré bien por la vuestra alma.[19]

[Just because I am a woman, you have disinherited me. I shall wander the world as a woman of easy virtue and give my body to whomsoever I fancy: to Moors for money, to Christians at no charge. With whatever I earn in this way I shall pay for masses and give alms for the salvation of your soul.]

This *romance* and the *Cantar del cerco de Zamora*, which is related to it, reflect a tension between two tendencies about the distribution of land during the Middle Ages. On the one hand, there is the Visigothic custom: divide the estate equally among every son and daughter. On the other hand, there was a new custom that spread rapidly over Europe: primogeniture, which gives almost all the territories to the first son and gives money and other minor possessions to the daughters and other sons. Following the new custom, Fernando I's eldest son, Sancho, expected to inherit all the kingdom from his father. But the old king decided to follow the ancient custom, although not completely, because he did not leave kingdoms to his daughters. This was a concession to another new custom about the estate: not to leave lands to women. Doña Urraca rebels against this and claims her right to possess lands and to be a "feudal lord." All her life she defends her claim. Sancho does not accept the terms of his father's will and wages war on his brothers and sisters in order to recover the kingdoms that he considers to be his by right of primogeniture.[20]

The conflict between father and daughter occurs because of his obligation to ensure her future so that she will not be left destitute by his death. Arranging a marriage for the daughter was a solution, since it transferred responsibility from the father to the husband. Without a man's protection, a woman was exposed to a harsh fate if she had no property of her own: this is the root of Doña Urraca's claim and of the allusion to the shameful profession she must take up if her father does not correct his mistaken decision.

In some sentimental novels and romances of chivalry, the main family relationship shown is the one between the father-king and the daughter-princess; the daughter is, in this circumstance, a commercial object in the play for power, a prize to give to another king in exchange for an alliance. Because of this, a princess must marry according to her father's orders.[21] In these instances, fiction is a good reflection of historical reality.[22] If a woman seeks a lover, she risks being sentenced to death as an adulterous woman.[23] In romances of chivalry and in the poems of the *Romancero*, she is able to deceive her father: she maintains a secret love for a time and, afterward, succeeds in imposing her wishes to marry the man she has chosen. This is what happens, for instance, in the "Romance de Gerineldo" and the "Romance del conde Claros de Montalbán." In both cases, the love relationship is sexually consummated and at virtually the same time the lovers are discovered. The king's first impulse is to save his honor by ordering the death of the lover, but then he yields to milder views and overcomes the dishonor by having them marry, to the great joy of all concerned.[24]

The sentimental novel, a genre that achieved its greatest success in the fifteenth century, deals with the same theme in a very different way: the love relationship does not reach a sexual outcome, and the father's reaction is intransigent and intolerant (as in the *Cárcel de amor* by Diego de San Pedro and *Grisel y Mirabella* by Juan de Flores). The father-king is a powerful figure, and he must preserve his honor.

Architrastes in *Libro de Apolonio* (mester de clerecía) allowed his daughter to choose a husband, but Laureola's father in *Cárcel de amor*[25] imprisoned her and is prepared to execute her because of a supposed fault against his honor. Persio libelled her by saying that she was Leriano's mistress. The king did not even consider the possibility of marrying Leriano and Laureola instead of killing his daughter. Preserving his honor was more important than maintaining the father-daughter relationship.

In *La Celestina*, which some critics consider a parody of sentimental literature,[26] there is a real love between father and daughter, but there is also a lack of communication and a mutual lack of understanding: Pleberio imagines his daughter to be a virginal and innocent woman who knows nothing about sex, while she is enjoying the carnal delights with Calisto. This lack of knowledge about his daughter's activities is bound to lead to tragedy. The unhappy outcome of love in the sentimental novel contrasts with the happy ending of the *romances* and works of chivalry, which usually end in a wedding.

Two factors contribute to the prevalence in literary works of the relationship between the king and his daughter: the influence of folklore (the princess always marries the hero, who will become the future king),[27] and the preoccupation with incest, a sin against which the medieval church repeatedly fought by forbidding all kinds of consanguineous unions.[28] The sin of incest is the obsessive subject of *Libro de Apolonio,* a novel in verse written by an author from the literary movement of mester de clerecía who probably based his work on a Latin book.[29] The theme of incest appears from the beginning, when Apolonio, along with other suitors, risks his head in order to marry the princess of Antioquía. King Antioco, the princess's father, had previously forced her to have sexual intercourse with him. In order to prevent the marriage of his daughter, he poses a riddle in which the secret of his sin is hidden. Apolonio solves the riddle, but King Antioco does not accept the solution. Later, Apolonio meets another princess, whose father, Architrastes, is anxious to fulfill his duty to find his daughter a husband. The incest theme culminates when Apolonio encounters his own daughter, Tarsiana, whom he had thought was dead. Tarsiana, not knowing their kinship, is sexually attracted to her father. Fortunately, they recognize each other in the typical *anagnorisis*[30] of the Greek or Byzantine novel, which influences this poem. It is clear that, in the author's mind, the risk of incest between father and daughter is a very real menace.[31] The writer considers it "natural" that the father's and daughter's mutual love develops sexual overtones when the wife and mother has disappeared. In this text, the three kings (Antioco, Architrastes, and Apolonio) have lost their wives before the possibility of incest is posed. The evil Antioco does not overcome the temptation, and even ignores the horror that his daughter feels for his sin.[32] Architrastes, by contrast, is a prudent king and father: he knows that Luciana is at the age of marrying and thinks that his duty is to find a good husband for her. He maintains a distance from his daughter's rooms. She is surprised when Architrastes comes to her chamber: "¿Qué buscastes a tal hora? ¿Quál fue vuestra venida?" (v. 237). [What are you looking for at this late hour? What has brought you here?] Tarsiana does not recognize her father but, noting his sadness, feels the need to make him happy. When she fails, nature impels her to hug him. Their relationship discovered, Apolonio hugs his daughter too, and immediately begins to think about her marriage. He even promises not to shave himself until she marries a good man (vv. 555–558).[33]

The *Romancero* also presents the temptation of incest between father and daughter but avoids the actual sin. In the "Romance de Silvana" and the "Romance de Delgadina" the father—a king in both cases—asks his daughter for sexual intercourse and is ardently refused. In "Silvana" the daughter asks her mother to substitute herself in the father's bed and obtains the king's repentance by this trick.[34] In "Delgadina" the mother notices her husband's desire and kills her daughter. In both cases the main character's mother is alive. Note that this is the reason why incest does not occur: the queen prevents it with good or bad methods.[35]

With regard to the father-daughter relationship in Castilian narrative, we may conclude that there is great interest in analyzing it. However, the texts concentrate on only three aspects of the relationship: marriage of the daughter, preservation of her honor (and the family honor), and incest. The approach differs according to the genre: in epics and poems of the mester de clerecía, the father takes a hand in marrying off his daughter without there being any conflict between them; in the *Romancero* and in the novels of chivalry, the father is deceived by the daughter, who stains his honor, but he forgives the lovers and recovers his honor by allowing them to marry; finally, in the sentimental novels, the father does not find her a husband and, further, does not tolerate her being in love, and so he blocks her happiness. The theme of incest, as a fundamental preoccupation of the Church at this period, appears in poems of the mester de clerecía and in some romances but is absent from the novel.

MOTHER AND SON

The inverse relationship, between mother and son, is not discussed so frequently, but it does appear in Castilian medieval narrative. This lower frequency may be due to the secondary role mothers usually play relative to their male children, since the rearing of sons is the father's responsibility once the son reaches the age of seven.[36] The mother-son relationship is generally described in a stereotypical way. Authors limit themselves to showing two types of women: the good mother, who loves her children, and the bad mother, who is a selfish, evil, and even criminal creature.

In the *Cantar de los siete Infantes de Lara*[37] the mother, doña Sancha, tries to prevent the disaster she perceives to be threatening her brave sons. At a wedding party, knowing that it is possible for fights to break out, she urges her sons to be quiet and isolated. Her brother's wife offends her seriously, but she hides this from her sons in order to prevent trouble between them and her sister-in-law. In spite of her precautions, the infantes of Lara learn of this offense and insult doña Lambra, their new aunt. Lambra incites her husband to vengeance. At the same time, doña Sancha's anxiety concerning her sons is evident. Motherly love is shown by the trouble she takes to protect her sons and to ward off the problems that could affect them. Her care is nevertheless in vain, since her sons are now adults and thus act in accordance with their own ideas.

In the legend *La Condesa traidora*[38] the mother tries to poison her son. The countess of Castile falls in love with a Moorish warrior named Almanzor, enemy of the Castilian people. She then decides to assassinate her husband, the Castilian count Garci-Fernández. To succeed in this, she feeds his horse bran: it becomes fat but also sick and weak. The horse dies of exhaustion in the middle of a battle against Almanzor. Its rider, on foot, is defenseless and is killed. But there is another obstacle preventing the wicked widow from marrying Almanzor: her son, the new count of Castile, carries on the war against the Arabs. Because of this, the countess decides to poison her son, but he, having been warned of the danger, forces his mother to drink the wine she offers him. The legend presents the countess of Castile, Delgadina, of French origin, as an inhuman person.[39] She not only plots to kill her son, but she is partly responsible for her own father's death as well, and also plans the murder of her husband Garci-Fernández's first adulterous wife.[40]

Maternal love is confused with an adulterous relationship in one of the tales of *Conde Lucanor* and in one of the episodes of *Caballero Zifar*. Incest, then, looms not only over the father-daughter relationship but also over the mother-son relationship. However, writers' attitudes toward the latter are decidedly different. Father-daughter incest is more frequent in literature, and what is more important, it sometimes appears not only as just a threat or a suspicion but as a fact (for example, an incestuous relationship between a giant father and daughter produces the monstrous Endriago in *Amadís*).[41] But, in *El Conde Lucanor*, a tale in which the author praises a cautious approach to life, incest is never suspected, even when it is an obvious possibility: a merchant who has been absent from his home for many years returns and finds his wife in bed with another man. He follows the maxim of doing nothing hastily, and thus discovers that this man is his now grown son. The mother sleeps beside the son because he reminds her of her husband, whom she believes to be dead. Neither the narrator nor the main character of this story ever suspect the possibility of incest between mother and son. The blood relationship is, in the author's mind, a real obstacle to incest.[42]

A similar occurrence is found in one of the episodes of the romance of chivalry *Zifar*. A virtuous woman, whose husband and sons went on a journey some years before, comes to a town in search of her spouse. The king of the country is her husband, but she does not recognize him. He orders two soldiers to watch over her during the night. She hears the soldiers talk about their childhood and understands that they are her lost sons (this is a very typical episode in Byzantine or Greek novels). She asks them to come to her room, and they talk all night long. In the morning they are all found sleeping in the same bed, and the woman is accused of adultery. However, when it is discovered that the soldiers are her sons, the woman is set free.[43]

Other cultures have created myths about incest between mother and son (Oedipus, in classical Greek culture; Apollo, in the French *Prose Tristan*), but medieval Castilian culture did not.[44] It is clear that mediaeval Castilian authors felt great respect for the love that mothers and sons ideally have for one another. For this reason, they tried to rid it of any suspicion of sexuality and did not admit the possibility of incest. The relationship between mother and son is one of love and affection, but while the son's dependence on his mother declines as he reaches adulthood (the infantes of Lara do not obey their mother), she never relinquishes her duty to protect the lives of her sons. The role of the mother is always one of protector, whether her sons are adults or children. The heroines condemned to death in the romances "Doña Isabel de Liar" and "El conde Alarcos" suffer more anguish over the future of their offspring, whom they will not be able to feed or care for, than over their own fate; and they even go so far as to request that their own killers hereafter protect their motherless offspring.

The bad mother, when she appears in Castilian literature, is an unnatural and criminal woman. Her lack of affectionate feelings is reflected in her relationship with her son, but not in this alone. A relationship between mother and son that does not imply love and protection on her part seems to the writer impossible to explain without classifying such a mother as a repulsive creature, without morals or heart, capable even of participating in the murder of her own father and husband. This is what happens in the second version of the *Leyenda de la condesa traidora*, which builds on the sparser narrative of the first version by adding parricide and treachery to the list of crimes committed by its protagonist.

FATHER AND SON

The relationship between father and son or mother and daughter is not a favorite subject; it is superficially described, and sometimes, it is problematic. The father-son relationship is absent from the majority of the works, which present their heroes as already adult and bereft of their parents. On those few occasions when a father appears alongside his son, there is no interaction between them.

The epic rarely shows us this type of affectionate relationship, perhaps in order not to diminish the protagonist by praising the knightly prowess of his father. The hero must be of a heroic lineage, but if the author had pushed ahead with detailing this relationship, he risked either having a protagonist with ancestors of doubtful heroism or deprecating the deeds of the son in the eyes of the reader, who would compare him with his father.

The Cid's father does not appear in the *Cantar de Mío Cid*, but is present in the late poem the *Mocedades de Rodrigo*. The public was keen to hear about the early life of the hero, whose deeds as an adult were so well known to all. The father appears merely to keep his impulsive son company; beside the Cid, he looks to be a weak sort of person, and he seems unable to control his son. In the surviving fragment of the lost *Cantar de Roncesvalles*, Charlemagne, who has a fatherly relationship with his nephew Roldán, cries and plucks out his beard in the presence of the latter's dead body. In the *Cantar de Bernardo del Carpío* the relationship between father and son is nonexistent. Bernardo struggles all his life to set his father free from the prison where he has been incarcerated at the king's command, but by the time he succeeds, his father is already dead.

In the *romance* dedicated to the sons of Lara, and in the reconstructed fragment of the lost *Cantar de los siete Infantes de Lara* (or *de Salas*), Lara's sons die when they fall into a trap set by their uncle, who has convinced them to discuss ransoming their father from the Arabs. The father cries heartbreakingly when he sees his sons' heads. In "La venganza de Mudarra," another *romance* from the same series, Gonzalo Gustos' bastard son, who is the infantes' half brother, takes revenge for this by murdering the traiterous uncle. Love for one's father is here manifested in revenge on those who have wronged him.

In the poems of mester de clerecía the father is hardly even a ghost figure: he is mentioned only as the hero's parent. In the case of hagiographies, the father is mentioned only when the author relates how well he has educated his son. In the case of heroic biographies, something similar happens: the author mentions the father's name (and even the grandfather's and great-grandfather's names) and their most worthy deeds, but only in order to set out clearly the hero's lineage. This occurs, for example, in the *Poema de Fernán González*.[45] In the *Libro de Apolonio* there is no information about the main character's father, except that he was the king of Tyre. In both works the heroes' fathers are dead when the story begins. In the Castilian *Libro de Alexandre*[46] Dario's role is limited to ensuring that his son has the best tutors. Aristotle's role is much more important than Dario's, and his relationship with his pupil is stronger. There is no doubt about his influence on

Alexander's opinions and actions. It is Aristotle, not Dario, who advises Alexander on how to treat his troops and what tactics he should use.[47]

In the romance of chivalry there is no strong relationship between father and son either. This is because the author's and the reader's interest is focused on the hero's adventures: battles against monster giants or evil knights, tournaments in which he fights against other knights and beats them, or his love affairs. Since the romance of chivalry is about a hero's early manhood, his parents' role is reduced. This is especially true when the son does not know who his parents are until after he obtains fame and fortune through his own merit.[48] Amadís, Palmerín de Inglaterra, and Palmerín de Olivia, to mention only the main characters of the most famous romances of chivalry, are educated and brought up by a knight, a wild giant, and a farmer, respectively. Esplandián, Amadís' son, is fed and educated by a hermit.[49] Zifar's sons, separated from their parents by the hazards of fortune (always so important in this type of work), are adopted by a bourgeois couple. The *anagnorisis* is always a time for joy and embraces, but the hero soon goes off to look for new adventures. Sometimes the adventurous life puts father and son on different sides in a battle, and they fight without recognizing each other. It is possible that this was the tragic ending of the original *Amadís*: Esplandián unwittingly kills his father and indirectly causes his mother's suicide.[50] In general, the discovery of the family affects the plot of the work in only one way: corroborating the hero's noble origin and justifying the honors that will fall to his lot, while explaining his attractiveness, gallantry, courage, courtesy, and all the other physical and moral qualities typical of a royal lineage.

In the sentimental novel there is no role for the hero's father. Leriano in *Cárcel de amor* has a mother, but no mention is made of his father. The main character of *Arnalte y Lucenda* is an orphan, and his only close relation is his sister. Grimalte in *Grimalte y Gradissa* has no relatives.

Didactic tales show the difficulty of bringing sons up well when they reach adolescence. In Exemplo XXI of *El Conde Lucanor*, the author advises not to argue with a young man and not to punish or reprimand him too much. On the contrary, fathers or tutors must teach them what is right with sweet words and amusing examples, to prevent the young men from hating them. This genre seems to be the only one that takes an interest in this kind of family relationship, and even then, the tales and *exempla* intended to illustrate the theme are few and far between.

Another book of tales, the *Sendebar*, a free translation of a lost Arabic original which, in its turn, derives from Sanskrit culture,[51] shows us a chaste prince who is falsely accused by his stepmother of trying to rape her. The theme is the same as the biblical story of Potiphar's wife and Joseph or the Greek myth of Phaedra and Hippolites: the hero is accused because he refuses to satisfy the sexual desires of a woman. The writer denies the possibility of incest, in which the son becomes the rival of his own father.

We may sum up the presentation of the father-son relationship in Castilian narrative by saying that, for the most part in the epics, the *romances*, the poems of the mester de clerecía, and the sentimental novel, it is practically nonexistent. Either it is of no importance, and the protagonists have long since lost their parents, or it is merely a pretext for vengeance. The novel of chivalry does give the relationship more importance, but even this genre does not develop the theme in depth, since it limits itself to recounting the discovery of the protagonist's real identity and to the son's joyful recognition of his father. Only the didactic tale speaks of the trickier side of the father-son relationship, since it analyzes the difficulties of advising and educating young men or presents fathers and sons as rivals in love.

MOTHER AND DAUGHTER

The mother-daughter relationship, though very common in Peninsular lyric, is hardly noticed in epic. In the *Poema de Mio Cid*, doña Jimena appears briefly bringing up her daughters. There is a tenderness among them, which is expressed in their sad partings and their joyful reunions, but no scenes are related that tell more about the relationship between them. This does not interest the author or authors who center their attention on El Cid.

In the *Romancero*, the amorous rivalry between mother and daughter for the love of a knight is shown in the "Romance del Conde Niño." The mother goes to the extreme of killing the count, thus indirectly bringing about the death of her daughter, who cannot bear her sorrow. In the *Romancero*, as has been noted, cruelty in a mother is not unusual: we need only recall the case of Delgadina.

The mother-daughter relationship does not usually appear in poems of mester de clerecía either. For example, in the *Libro de Apolonio,* the Princess of Antioquía's mother is dead, as is Luciana's mother. Tarsiana, the daughter of Apolonio and Luciana, also grows up without a mother's love, since Tarsiana is believed dead at birth and her supposed corpse is thrown into the sea. One interesting exception is the *Poema de Santa Oria*, in which both mother and daughter have an intense love for each other which overcomes the barrier of death, since Saint Oria appears in a vision to her mother. However, this incident does not demonstrate interest in the mother-daughter relationship on the part of the writer, since the work is based on the saint's biography, written in Latin.

In the *Libro de Buen Amor* doña Endrina's mother makes a very brief appearance in the role of her daughter's guardian. She fails catastrophically, since a procuress, disguised as a peddlar, manages to act as a go-between for the girl and don Melón. This episode, inspired by the *Pamphilus*, ends when don Melón succeeds in consummating a physical relationship with the young woman—a fact that would have caused her dishonor if the kind procuress had not arranged her immediate marriage to the lovesick don Melón.

It would seem that the heroines of the sentimental novel do not have mothers. Nevertheless, there are exceptions. We know of the existence of Laureola's mother (*Cárcel de amor*) because, after her daughter has been condemned to death, another character asks her to seek her husband's pardon for Laureola. When this fails, she visits Laureola in prison, but she does not intervene afterward. The queen is a dull person, completely lacking in initiative.

In *La Celestina*, Melibea's mother, like doña Endrina's mother, plays the role of watching over her daughter's honor and fails. The procuress Celestina manages to talk to Melibea and persuades her to accept the furtive and dishonorable love that Calisto proposes to her. The wedding of the young couple is never planned. It is Melibea's own mother Alisa who imprudently allows the procuress into the house when she arrives at the door peddling thread. Knowing of her ill repute, Alisa nevertheless leaves the procuress alone with the innocent Melibea, who is an easy prey for the experienced Celestina. Alisa never suspects anything, nor is she aware of the changes—obvious to all the other characters—that have occurred in her daughter. Alisa does not even appear in Melibea's suicide scene, but hands the role of chief mourner over to the girl's father.

As with the father-son relationship, the mother-daughter relationship is only superficially described, and on many occasions it is left unmentioned. Either the heroine is an orphan or the mother has virtually no part in the development of the plot. When there is a relationship between mother and daughter, it is fraught with strife: the mother is a rival in her daughter's loves, or she opposes them. Rather than affection, there seems to be mutual fear between mother and daughter: the mother fears her daughter will not preserve her honor as she should, and the daughter fears her mother's watchfulness. The joyful and intimate mother-daughter relationship found in the lyric, where the mother is the confidante to whom the daughter reveals her heartbreaks, is missing from Castilian narrative.

SPOUSES

The relationship between spouses is not a frequent subject in epics. How-

ever, it is present in the *Cantar,* or *Poema de Mio Cid.* Jimena is the proto-
type of the perfect woman, just what moralists would have liked—a good
wife (always supporting her husband, El Cid, and never reproaching him)
and a good mother, since her daughters are perfectly well educated and
well brought up. In this poem, the wife is presented as part of the masculine identity. That is why doña Jimena is always treated with the greatest
respect.

The most outstanding feature of doña Jimena's character is her
strength in adversity. She never complains. She only expresses pain when
separated from her family. She is a deeply religious woman (the first time
we encounter her is when she is praying for her husband when he departs
for Cardeña [v. 239]). She also has theological knowledge, apparent in her
prayer preceding the departure. However, we never see her praying for herself, but only for her husband.

The expression of matrimonial love in this work is social: he embraces
her, she kneels before him or kisses his hand (v. 366 and ff.). There is an underlying submission by the wife to her husband: she treats him just as he would
treat the king. This, however, does not mean that no genuine affection exists.
El Cid shows his love with outward acts: crying over their separation, worrying in an almost obsessive manner about the economic welfare of his wife and
daughters, anxiously waiting for Alvar Fáñez to bring news of them, asking
the king for permission for them to join him (v. 1275), rejoicing at the news
of their liberation (v. 1449), or worrying about their safety and their honor
(vv. 1454–55 and 1466–69). Salinas dedicated an attractive essay to a study
of the relationship between Jimena and Rodrigo (El Cid).[52]

Doña Jimena is respected and looked after by all the characters in the
poem. Even the king makes sure that her journey to Valencia is comfortable
and safe and that she lacks for nothing. Nevertheless, we never see El Cid
consulting his wife on any matter, not even their daughters' weddings. As
Menéndez Pidal[53] points out, the power of marrying off the daughters lies
with both the father and mother, and the passage of *Primera Crónica General* that corresponds to verse 1937b has El Cid consult Jimena. Perhaps the
reference to the fact that El Cid and his nephews should discuss the subject
"en poridad" [in private] means that doña Jimena will be included. In any
case, when in vv. 2187–89 El Cid tells his wife and daughters that the marriage has now been arranged, they do not show surprise but joy, as if it were
expected, and in vv. 2605–6 Jimena shows her support for this wedding:

> Id a Carrión do sodes heredadas
> assí como yo tengo, bien vos he casadas.

[Go to Carrión where you have your property / in my belief I have arranged an excellent marriage for you.]

The impression the poem leaves us with is that doña Jimena is a highly respected woman who is worthy of her spouse, El Cid, the most perfect knight possible. Likewise, she knows how to keep her place at all times, exhibiting neither pride nor humility, bearing misfortunes with steadfastness, and like El Cid, always bearing herself with dignity.

The idea that underlies the poem is that in a marriage, the wife must publicly show maximum respect toward her husband and must honor him as her master. However, in private, it is the husband who should "serve" his wife (El Cid prays to God for the day to arrive when he can serve Jimena and advises the infantes of Carrión: "A mis fijas sirvades, que vuestras mugieres son" (v. 2581). [Serve my daughters, for they are your wives.] The husband should provide for all his wife's needs, watch over her material well-being (money, ladies to serve her), and ensure her personal safety.

In the family, the wife has power in the home, as well as the responsibility for the upbringing of her daughters and her sons up to the age of seven. Castilian law allows the wife to inherit property and to administer it if she is widowed or if she is the sole heiress. This emphasizes that her social role is an important one, albeit vague, since she lives a private life while her spouse has a public life. Outside the house she should remain silent and show respect and subordination to her husband. As we can see, it is a role that appears clearly in the *Poema de Mio Cid*.[54]

The *Romancero* also praises unselfish and faithful women. In the *romance* "La Condesita," or "El Conde Sol," we see how a wife goes in search of her absent husband. He has forgotten her and is going to marry another woman (which is a frequent theme in folklore).[55] In the *romance* "Las señas del esposo," the husband, having been away for several years, checks on the fidelity of his wife by disguising himself and wooing her.[56]

The most frequent theme of the *Romanceros* is a husband's revenge for his wife's infidelity ("Romance de Bernal Francés," "La Blanca Niña"). Attempts by the wife to murder her husband for financial gain is an additional theme often found in both epic and legends and in the *Romancero* ("Romance de Landarico"). The legend *La Condesa traidora* is a perfect example of both themes.

Naturally, given the misogynistic milieu of the Middle Ages, the adulterous wife rarely triumphs. If she does, the discovery of her crime and subsequent punishment soon follow. The *romances* are not blind to reality, however, and in many cases they offer an excuse for a wife's infidelity (the husband is unfaithful, abandons her, ignores her sexually, or mistreats her), but even if this is clearly seen as the husband's fault, adultery is never forgiven in the wife (for example, the *romance* "La bella malmaridada").

Male adultery, with the consequent rivalry between the lawful wife and the mistress, arises in various poems in the *Romancero*. On certain occasions, it is the wife who dies at the request of the mistress ("De cómo hizo matar don Pedro el Cruel a doña Blanca de Borbón"). The mistress who is a victim of the wife is also very common ("Doña Isabel de Liar").[57] In cases of male adultery we see the mother suffer great pain when she is torn from her children. One writer makes special reference to a young baby whom the mother can no longer breast-feed ("El conde Alarcos"). The need to abandon their children weighs more heavily on the protagonists' minds than the pain of a husband's unfaithfulness or being separated from a lover.

The mester de clerecía briefly shows some married couples. In the *Poema de Fernán González* the hero's wife risks her life twice to free him from prison.[58] She also helps her husband, when he is in chains, to kill an evil priest who attempts to rape her. The relationship between the spouses is, in this case, one of mutual aid, but passionate, sexual love is not ruled out either. In the *Libro de Apolonio* there is praise for the marital love of Apolonio and Luciana and for their fidelity even when they believe each other dead. In this case, too, married love is not devoid of desire, as is demonstrated by Luciana's illness, which is caused by the love she feels for Apolonio, which keeps her sick in bed until she marries him.[59]

The romance of chivalry and the sentimental novel do not address the sexual aspect of couples, since these genres concentrate on the process of falling in love, which occurs prior to marriage, or else they deal with permanent separation due to the death of one of the protagonists—a theme characteristic of the sentimental novel. The heroes usually maintain fidelity in their love relationships. For example, the knight Zifar does not consummate his second marriage, since he is not sure of his first wife's death.

The tale, because of its exemplary and didactic character, is more realistic and establishes a model that the spouses should follow in their relationship.[60] The *Libro del conde Lucanor* shows this aspect clearly. In this work by Juan Manuel, the role of the woman fits that associated with contemporary morality. Women are portrayed only in the role of wife. The tales suggest that there are two kinds of wives: good wives, ever obedient to their husbands, and bad wives, disobedient and whimsical.

Intelligence is associated with the obedient wife. Although there are various tales that could exemplify these attributes of the female gender, the most obvious is Exemplo XXVII, "lo que sucedió con sus mujeres a un emperador y a Alvar Fáñez Minaya," which deals with two cases. In the first case, the emperor rids himself of a disobedient and stubborn wife by asking her lovingly not to touch a poisonous ointment. In the second case, Alvar Fáñez and his wife love each other very much and they live in perfect harmony, but one day a nephew of the husband reproaches him for letting himself be dominated by his wife. Alvar Fáñez, after showing him several proofs of his wife's perfection, replies:

[V]os digo verdat: que del día que comigo casó, que nunca un día le bi fazer nin dezir cosa en que yo pudiesse entender que quería nin tomava plazer, sinon en aquello que yo quis; nin le vi tomar enojo de ninguna cosa que yo fiziesse. Et siempre tiene verdaderamente en su talante que qualquier cosa que yo faga, que aquello es lo mejor; et lo que ella a de fazer de suyo o le yo acomiendo que faga, sábelo muy bien fazer, et sienpre lo faze guardando toda mi onra et mi pro et queriendo que entiendan las gentes que yo so el señor, et que la mi voluntad et la mi onra se cumpla; et non quiere para sí otra pro, nin otra fama de todo el fecho, sinon que sepan que es mi pro, et tome yo plazer en ello. Et tengo que si un moro de allende el mar esto fiziesse, quel devía yo mucho amar et presçiar yo et fazer yo mucho por su consejo, et demás seyendo ella tal et yo seer casado con ella.[61]

[I tell you truthfully, since the day when she married me I have never once seen her do or say anything because of her own desires or wishes, but rather to please me; nor have I ever seen her angry at anything I have done. Moreover, she always truly believes that whatever I do is best. What she must do for herself or because I ask her to do it, she does extremely well, taking care of my honor and property. She always wants people to realize I am the lord and wishes my will to be obeyed. For herself she desires no advantage or praise for what she does other than for all to know that it benefits me and that I am pleased with it. I think that even if a Moorish infidel from overseas did this for me, I should appreciate and cherish him and follow his advice. How much more so, then, with this woman who is so honorable and my own wife.]

However, the conclusion is that the affection the spouses have for each other should not go beyond reasonable bounds:

... ca si el omne, por aver grand amor a su muger, quiere estar con ella tanto porque dexe de yr a los lugares o a los fechos en que puede fazer su pro et su onra, faze muy grand yerro; nin si por le fazer plazer nin complir su talante desa nada de lo que pertenesçe a su estado, nin a su onra, faze muy desaguisado; mas guardando estas cosas, todo buen talante et toda fiança que el marido pueda mostrar a su muger, todo le es fazedero et todo lo deve fazer et le paresçe muy bien que lo faga. Et otrosí, deve mucho guardar que por lo que a él mucho non cumple, nin le faze gran mengua, que non le faga enojo nin pesar et señaladamente en ninguna guisa cosa que puede aver pecado.[62]

[... for if a man, through his great love for his wife, desires to be with her so much that he ceases to visit those places and perform those actions that bring him profit and honor, great indeed is his error. Likewise if to please her or to fulfill her wishes he fails to do what befits his rank and honor, then he is mistaken to act thus. Excepting only this, however, whatever goodwill and trust that the husband can show his wife he should demonstrate toward her, and it is right and proper that he should do so. Further, he should avoid angering her or causing her sadness over any trivial thing that brings him no great profit or serious loss, all the more so if this could give rise to sin.]

This final sentence is a clear allusion to male infidelity, which should be avoided by the husband. The texts suggest that, within the marriage, the feeling of affection that exists between the spouses is defined as *dilectio* on the part of the husband and *reverentia* on the part of the wife, but not as love, a passionate feeling that remains outside this grave and sacred institution.[63]

The various genres approach the marriage relationship from different points of view. The epic values the family and sees marriage as the fundamental support for it. The relationship between husband and wife is one of mutual assistance and is based on reciprocal respect. Both partners have their functions and obligations toward the other spouse. Didactic tales propose the same sort of relationship, although they insist heavily on one feature that the epics barely consider: the wife's obedience to her husband. For their part, the poems of mester de clerecía allow passion within the marriage context. The *Romancero* seems obsessed with the negative consequences of infidelity within marriage. When the man is involved, misfortunes ensue. If it is the woman, then punishment of the adulteress is not long delayed. The sentimental novel and works of chivalry are not interested in the marriage bond except as the reason for the engagement preceding it, which, in the case of the latter genre, does not exclude sexual intercourse. The adultery of the *roman courtois* is altered in the novel of chivalry into love outside marriage (sometimes legitimized by a secret wedding)[64] between unmarried lovers who owe no fidelity to any third party. The husband-wife-lover triangle becomes a different triangle, more acceptable to the morals of the age and consonant with the pro-marriage attitude of Castilian literature[65] than the father-daughter-beloved triangle. A public wedding takes place at the end of the book. The novel of chivalry thus defends the idea of marriage for love. The sentimental novel, on the other hand, sees the love relationship as a virtually unavoidable failure as a result of social morality, and has no place for marriage or sexual intercourse. Its heroes remain unmarried, or die of grief when rejected by the women they love.

BROTHERS AND SISTERS

The fraternal relationship is hardly developed at all, although it does exist between some famous brothers and sisters in the *cantares*, or epic poems. In the *Poema de Mio Cid*, two pairs of sisters and brothers are opponents and meet in confrontation at the end of the poem: on one side, the daughters of El Cid, and on the other, their husbands, the *infantes* of Carrión. In both cases the brothers and sisters show a common identity. Normally one of them speaks for both. When the *infantes* of Carrión converse, their voices seem complementary, as if they are speaking as a duo. In the same way, in the reconstructed fragment of *Los siete Infantes de Lara* (or *de Salas*) all the brothers act as one and have the same character. They are the multiplication of one character.

The brother-sister relationship is not always a peaceful one. This is shown by the fratricidal wars that are the theme of the *Cantar de Sancho II o Cerco de Zamora*. Sancho fights against his brother and sisters with the goal of gathering back into his own hands all of the territories that his father had divided among his children. He is besieging his sister doña Urraca, the lady of Zamora, when he is murdered, a crime that the *Cantar* blames on doña Urraca. In several *romances* ("Jura de Santa Gadea de Burgos") and in the epic *Las mocedades de Rodrigo,* King Alfonso is forced to swear that he has had no part in the treachery that led to his brother's death.

Fratricidal brothers are not absent from the *Romancero*. The "Romance del maestre de Santiago" tells how King Peter the Cruel has had his brother executed at the instigation of his mistress doña María de Padilla. Fraternal love also interested the anonymous authors of the *Romancero*. One family scene is encountered in the *romance* "Don Bueso y la hermana cautiva." The hero meets an attractive captive of the Moors and hopes to have a relationship with her, but he finds out eventually that she is his sister. When he introduces her to their parents, they all rejoice.

The idea of brother-sister incest also shows up in the *Romancero* in "Amnón y Tamar."[66] A re-creation of the classical myth of Procne, Philomel, and Tereo is found in the *romance* "Blancaflor y Filomena," in which Blancaflor avenges the rape and mutilation of her sister by offering her guilty husband the flesh of their son. She then kills the husband, and receives no punishment.

In the sentimental novel *Arnalte y Lucenda*, the hero's sister gives him advice on his unfortunate love affairs and tries unsuccessfully to help him. Whatever the result, the story shows the intimacy established between brother and sister, since she acts as a confidante to the lovesick Arnalte and even adopts the role of matchmaker for her friend Lucenda.

As we have already noted, the heroes of the sentimental novel usually have no close relations. The heroines, likewise, have no brothers or sisters. The reason for this must be found in the fact that this type of novel is based on psychological introspection and analysis of the world of feelings, so that any character not having a clearly defined role is superfluous. The universe of the novel is reduced to the smallest compass, and is generally composed of the lover, his beloved, her father, a confidant of the couple, and an enemy of the lover. Thus, if a sister is present, she takes on one of these functions.

In the novel of chivalry, it is not unusual for the hero to have a brother. In the first home-grown novel of chivalry, *El caballero Zifar*, Garfín and Roboán, the children of Zifar, exemplify fraternal love. However, Roboán prefers to leave the kingdom so as not to dwell in the shadow of his brother. This gives rise to a series of adventures that form the final part of the book. Roboán becomes the absolute protagonist and attains a heroic stature denied to his brother. In the most important Castilian novel of chivalry, Amadís is brought up unaware of who his parents and siblings are. When at last he finds out, the ensuing meetings are effusive. The affection among them seems to rest on the importance of common "blood."

As can be seen, examples of sibling relationships are few and far between, and the relationship is not developed. There are, of course, some exceptions (for example, Arnalte and his sister, or the famous brothers of the epics). In general, though, medieval Castilian authors do not seem to have the slightest interest in the sibling bond unless it touches on the well-known incest theme, or unless it is used to celebrate the great love and rejoicing that results when siblings unaware of each others' existence are reunited.

CONCLUSION

It is important to point out that the observations made here are by no means conclusive. This is only an initial approach to the subject and is based on a small corpus of the most representative works in medieval Castilian literature in a narrative style. Family scenes are rare, and even rarer are the works that show complex relationships within a complete family. Authors normally select certain components of the family structure and analyze their relationships, and they pay little or no attention to the role played by the rest of the family group. The favorite characters are the father and the daughter, with the mother and the son in second place. In both relationships the theme of incest is raised, probably because the medieval Church was obsessed by this sin. The relationship between father and daughter is usually centered on the girl's marriage. The relationship between mother and son presents maternal and filial love as desirable and inevitable, except when the mother has a criminal personality. The other family relationships arouse little interest in authors and remain practically undeveloped in the literature. When they do appear, it is normally in a stereotypical form: the perfect mother who loves and protects her sons or watches over her daughter's honor; the heroic father who ensures that the protagonist will be brave; exemplary husbands or unfaithful wives; brothers who have a strong affection for each other even though they barely know one another.

Medieval Castilian writers rarely focus on the description of situations or scenes of everyday family life; rather, they focus on the relationships that are established between the characters and their families. In many cases, the relationships described are based on power and repression. This is especially the case in the father-daughter relationship when there is the possibility of a forced marriage, which causes a conflict between love and the family honor. It is also the case in the mother-daughter relationship, characterized by the mother's all-powerful hold over the girl (we have seen that she may have her daughter's life in her hands, kill the girl's lover, or, more usually, prevent their love).

Among the genres, there are noteworthy differences in the treatment of certain family relationships. The positive attitude toward marriage for love in the novel of chivalry and the *Romancero* versus the negative view of this taken by the sentimental novel is particularly striking, as is the fundamental absence of the mother-daughter relationship in the novel as compared to the lyric. In all probability, the explanation for these differences is to be sought in the sociology of the audience at which each genre was aimed. For instance, a favorable attitude toward marriage must have been present in court circles of the fifteenth century, as is demonstrated by the lyrics of Jorge Manrique.[67] Nevertheless, this was seen as an ideal, possible in the fantastic and magical world of works of chivalry but not in the sentimental novel. The latter prefers to show us the conflict between the ideal and current morality, demonstrating the disastrous consequences that ensue from this.

The study of family relationships in medieval Castilian narrative reveals that the interests of both medieval authors and their public were narrowly focused on certain themes such as marriage, incest, adultery, and the conflict between love and honor. Each of these themes was given special treatment in specific genres. Marriage interested virtually all genres; incest was a preferred topic in poems of the mester de clerecía, didactic tales, and the Romancero; the Romancero also frequently touches on adultery; sentimental novels and works of chivalry concentrate on the conflict of love and honor. Those family relationships not suitable for developing one of these themes were relegated to a superficial treatment or totally ignored.

NOTES

1. I prefer to use the adjective "Castilian" because of the ambiguity of "Spanish." "Spanish" and "Castilian," when they are used as nouns, refer to the same language but, as adjectives, refer to different geographic regions: Castile is a region of Spain. It is therefore possible to say that Catalan is a Spanish language but not that it is a Castilian language. This article is on works written in Spanish (or Castilian) but not in other Spanish languages.

2. See Jacques Heers, *El clan familiar en la Edad Media* (Barcelona: Labor, 1978 [original ed. *Le Clan familial au Moyen Age*, Paris, PUF]), p. 7: "es de todos conocido que las obras literarias . . . ofrecen una imagen muy deformada de la sociedad; suelen presentar tipos elaborados a veces con elementos muy dispares; sobre todo, reflejan el estado de ánimo o las intenciones de sus autores y los convencionalismos vigentes en tal o cual espectáculo. . . . Además, los tipos literarios así presentados suelen evolucionar muy lentamente; lo frecuente es que permanezcan fijos y se perpetúen durante varios siglos en una forma estereotipada y convencional, de acuerdo con unos esquemas invariables que se asemejan muy poco a la realidad."

3. There are many books on this subject. A general work about family history is *Historia de la familia* by A. Burguière, C. Klapisch-Zuber, M. Segalen, and F. Zonabend (with prefaces by C. Lévi-Strauss and G. Duby) (Madrid: Alianza, 1988 [1st ed. Paris: A. Colin Editeur, 1966]), especially vol. I: *Mundos lejanos, mundos antiguos*, "Tiempos medievales," 281–461. About sex in the Middle Ages, see the excellent annotated bibliography collected by Joyce E. Salisbury, *Medieval Sexuality: A Research Guide* (New York: Garland, 1990).

4. *Romances* (roughly equivalent to ballads) are poems defined by their metric form, with a narrative, epic, or lyric nature. The *Romancero* is all the *romances* known. The *romances* written in the Middle Ages go under the name of *Romancero viejo*. Because of their subject matter, most of them are related to the epic cycles or chronicles and medieval novels. They are anonymous and are supposedly traditional and popular in origin. Two good didactic anthologies of *Romancero viejo* are *Romancero*, ed. Michelle Débax (Madrid: Alhambra, 1982), and *Romancero viejo (Antología)*, ed. M.C. García de Enterría (Madrid: Castalia, 1989).

5. The *mester de clerecía* is a literary movement that blossomed in the thirteenth and fourteenth centuries and is characterized by its use of the same strophic form (the *cuaderna vía*), by its use of sources (especially Latin and French) freely translated, by the didactic nature of their stories (frequently hagiographies), and by the cultural knowledge that the authors show, which is why they were denominated *clérigos*.

6. See M.R. Lida, *La originalidad artística de La Celestina* (Buenos Aires: EUDEBA, 1962), for a discussion of the literary genre of *La Celestina*.

7. There is a large bibliography on the relationship between the *Cantar o Poema de Mio Cid* and history. This relationship has greatly interested the critics because it affects one of the most debated theoretical questions concerning epic: some critics state that *cantares de gesta* (epic poems) were created by people who participated in the heroic events and wrote the news a short while after these events occurred; others claim that a learned author, centuries after these events, wrote about them in order to increase the fame of a family or a monastery, making use of chronicles or legends. See, for example, Jules Horrent, *Historia y poesía en torno al "Cantar del Cid"* (Barcelona: Ariel, 1973).

8. *Poema de Mio Cid*, ed. Ian Michael (Madrid: Castalia, 1987), vv. 282–282b.

9. On the role of matchmaker adopted by the father and lord in the poem, see Georges Martin, "Famille et feodalité dans le *Poema de mio Cid*," in *Le Texte familial (Textes hispaniques)*, ed. G. Martin (Université de Toulouse-Le Mirail, 1984), 30–31.

10. "Infante" is a title of nobility ranking above count (earl) or marquess. All sons (other than the firstborn crown prince) of the kings of Spain are entitled infantes. The title may also be bestowed by royal decree on descendants of the royal house and line. Even today, the daughters of the king of Spain bear the title "Infanta" and not Princess.

11. According to medieval moralists, marriages for love had awful consequences. See "Las mujeres en el orden feudal (siglos XI y XII)," in *Historia de las mujeres en Occidente, vol. II: Edad Media*, ed. G. Duby and M. Perrot (Madrid: Taurus, 1992), 247– 99.

12. Before the ninth century, Roman, Hebrew, Germanic, and Celtic custom allowed marriages to be dissolved. This was especially easy when the husband initiated the process and he belonged to the elite. In the presence of witnesses, the couple expressed their wish and divided their possessions following customary rules. See the chapter "Mujeres de los castillos y señoríos" in B.S. Anderson and J.P. Zinsser, *Historia de las mujeres: una historia propria*, vol. I (Barcelona: Crítica, 1991 [original ed. *A History of Their Own: Women in Europe from Prehistory to the Present*, vol. I, New York: Harper & Row Publishers, 1988]), especially 364–65. Although the date of *Poema de Mio Cid* is uncertain (between the beginning of the twelfth century and the beginning of the thirteenth century), the historic Cid and his daughters lived in the eleventh century. The wedding with heirs of Carrión is a fiction without parallel in historic reality, but the texts reflect the situation of divorce in Castile in this period. Colin Smith, "On the Distinctiveness of the *Poema de Mio Cid*," in *Mio Cid Studies*, ed. A.D. Deyermond (Londres: Tamesis, 1977), 161–94, and David Hook, "On Certain Correspondences between the *Poema de Mio Cid* and Contemporary Legal Instruments," *Iberorromania*, n.s., XI (1980): 31–53, have studied the legal and administrative attitudes in the *Poema*. When the marriage is dissolved, the dowry and wedding gifts must be returned. See also M.N. Pavlovic and R.M. Walker, "Money, Marriage, and the Law in the *Poema de Mio Cid*," *Medium Aevum* LI (1982): 197–212.

13. M. Eugenia Lacarra, *El Poema de Mio Cid: realidad histórica e ideología* (Madrid: Porrúa Turanzas, 1980), 96–102, explains that the essential objective of the author is to make evident the opposition between revenge and public justice. Because of this Lacarra imagines the episode of "the outrage of Corpes" (the heirs of Carrión leave their wives in the forest, after beating them and thinking that they cannot sur-

vive and will be food for wild beasts). According to the general structure of epic poems, El Cid must take revenge, but Rodrigo Díaz de Vivar waits patiently for the king's judgment at court.

14. G. Martin states that "le texte fait du héros un être pour l'alliance. Sur l'héritage des filles les maris seront souverains. Leur sang, leur lignage, leurs biens sont destinés à se fondre dans d'autres, seuls perpétués par un nom. Aussi triomphale, aussi gratifiante soit-elle pour lui-même, l'aventure du Cid est vouée à cette aliénation. C'est pourquoi le mariage est le fond de la quête cidienne: la réussite, l'heureux prolongement de celle-ci dépendent de la valeur d'un serment, seul contrat de garantie." G. Martin, "Famille et feodalité dans le *Poema de mio Cid*," in *Le Texte familial (Textes hispaniques)* (Université de Toulouse-Le Mirail, 1984), 31.

15. *Historia de la vida privada*, vol. 2: *De la Europa feudal al Renacimiento*, ed. Ph. Ariés and G. Duby (Madrid: Taurus, 1988 [original ed. *Histoire de la vie privée*, Paris: Editions du Seuil, 1985]), 128: "En busca de prestigio, los linajes tratan de encontrar para el primogénito una esposa de rango superior o igual al suyo." The infantes married for economic motives and they remember too late their high nobility. The poet ridicules the infantes' ambition. He chose as a hero a man who has won honor and riches by his own value (vv. 3107–08: "Quando lo vieron entrar al que en buen ora naçió, / levantós en pie el buen rey don Alfons"; v. 3116: "[the king:] maguer que algunos pesa, mejor sodes que nos"). This is why some critics think that the *Poema de Mio Cid* is an ideological battle between the hereditary court nobility and the low aristocracy composed of warriors, in which the author is partial to the latter. See Diego Catalán, "*El Mio Cid*: nueva lectura de su intencionalidad política," in *Symbola Ludovico Mitxelena septuagenario oblata*, vol. II (Vitoria: Universidad del País Vasco, 1985), 807–19.

16. See H. Dillard, *Daughters of the Reconquest: Women in Castilian Town Society, 1100–1300* (Cambridge: Cambridge Univ. Press, 1984), 21–26.

17. Vv. 2592–93. The daughters kneel down in front of their father. This is a sign of respect also used in the ceremony of knighthood. See R. Lull, *Libro de la orden de caballería*, ed. L.A. de Cuenca (Madrid: Alianza, 1986). A further sign of respect is the kissing of hands (*besamanos*), a rite showing a vassal's homage to his lord. G. Martin has shown that of the fifty-three occasions on which this ceremony appears in the poem, thirty-three cases are of homage paid to the king and twenty-nine are to the Cid. More than half of the latter occur within the family context. He infers from this fact that there is a parallel between family relationships and the feudal system. See G. Martin, "Famille et feodalité dans le *Poema de mio Cid*," 27–30.

18. She is a historical person, King Fernando I's daughter. She inspired many legends and *romances* because of her authoritarian and brave temperament. A lost *cantar de gesta* (epic poem) the *Cantar del cerco de Zamora* or *Cantar de Sancho II* (some fragments are preserved), narrated her opposition in war to her brother King Sancho. The legend presents her falling in love with El Cid (See S.G. Armistead, "The enamored doña Urraca in Chronicles and Balladry," *Romance Philology* IX [1957–58]: 26–29), and maybe—it is unproven—she ordered a knight from Zamora named Vellido Dolfos to assassinate her brother Sancho to prevent him from conquering Zamora, the town that was her estate (see "Cantar de Sancho II," in *Epica medieval española*, ed. C. Alvar and M. Alvar [Madrid: Cátedra, 1991], 271–308).

19. *Romancero*, ed. M. Débax, 201.

20. B.S. Anderson and J.P. Zinsser summarize women's situations on estates during the Middle Ages in *Historia de las mujeres: una historia propia*, 322–28, 341–48.

21. For example, Lisurate, Oriana's father, wants her to marry the emperor of Rome in *Amadís*, unaware that she has secretly married the hero. This act leads to a war between the army of Amadís and those of the emperor of Rome and king Lisuarte. The problem caused by the king's failure to understand his daughter's feelings takes up the better part of books III and IV of *Amadís* (Garci Rodríguez de

Montalvo, *Amadís de Guala*, ed. J.M. Cacho Blecua [Madrid: Cátedra, 1991], chaps. 72–112).

22. As late as this century women have not been free to select a husband, but men have not had much more freedom in this respect. See Jean-Louis Flandrin, *La moral sexual en Occidente* (Barcelona: Ediciones Juan Garnica, 1984), 99.

23. This topic arose in Arthurian literature. This cruel custom originally appears in the *Tristan en prose*, ed. R.L. Curtis (Cambridge: D.S. Brewer, 1986), t. I, páras. 209–10, 119–20. Apparently, it was transmitted from this to *Amadís*, and from the latter to the chivalric and sentimental novel. See G.S. Williams, "The *Amadis* Question," *Revue Hispanique* XXI (1909): 62, 115, 118, 130.

24. M. Débax points out an evolution in the "Romance de Gerineldo." The happy ending, frequent in the earlier versions of the poem, does not occur in some of the later variants, found principally in Andalusia but gradually spreading out as time goes by. In these variants, Gerineldo rejects the proposed marriage on the grounds that he will never marry a woman with whom he has already had sexual relations. M. Débax believes that the change in the romance is a direct consequence of the moral views prevailing in the areas where this version has been kept. See M. Débax, "Histoires de famille dans le *Romancero* traditionnel. Les Amours de l'infante et du page dans le Romance de Gerineldo," in *Le Texte familial (Textes hispaniques)*, ed. G. Martin (Université de Toulouse-Le Mirail, 1984), 35–58.

25. See *Novela sentimental española*, ed. C. Hernández Alonso (Barcelona: Plaza y Janés, 1987). This edition has the advantage of offering, in the same volume, other sentimental novels, among them *Arnalte y Lucenda*.

26. See M. Eugenia Lacarra, *Cómo leer la Celestina* (Madrid: Júcar, 1990).

27. V. Propp, *Las raíces históricas del cuento* (Madrid: Fundamentos, 1984), 499–506, considers this characteristic of folklore tales to be derived from prehistoric customs in which the old king had to die in order to be replaced by a young king. The youth had to demonstrate his power by killing his predecessor. This situation, incomprehensible in later periods, was reflected in the tales as a transmission of power by means of the new king's marriage to the old king's daughter. In the tales, instead of killing the old king, the hero must prove to be worthy of marrying the princess (and obtaining the throne) by performing some tasks. Roman mythology (remember the high priest of the wood of Nemi) and some primitive rituals of succession suggest the same fact. Many Indo-European people preferred the matrilineal estate to the more uncertain patrilineal estate, in which paternity is essentially unprovable. See J.G. Frazer, *La rama dorada: mágia y religión* (México-Madrid–Buenos Aires: Fondo de Cultura Económica, 1991 [original ed. 1890]). In the matrilineal estate, the estate is transmitted from king to his sister's son. But sister or daughter, there is a woman whose conquest means the throne. Jean Markale has suggested that in primitive Arthurian romances Guinevere represents the sovereignty. See J. Markale, "The Thème de la reine infidèle," in *Le Roi Arthur et la société celtique* (Paris: Payot, 1976), 257–69.

28. Many studies have been written about the importance and repercussions of this obsession in the Middle Ages. Some historians think that this is one of the keys to understanding the evolution of family and noble clans. Jack Goody, in *The Development of the Family and Marriage in Europe* (New York: Cambridge Univ. Press, 1983), 32–47, suggests that the policy of the Church on marriage, adultery, and divorce produces more families without heirs and more opportunities for the Church to increase its property. Because of that, or for fear of abnormal children born of consanguineous unions, the Church forbade marriages between relations as far as the seventh degree. This was very damaging for noble and royal interests. The Lateran Council of 1215 modified incest definitions from the seventh to the fourth degree of relationship. The significance of incest in literature has also been studied. A good book about this theme is Paloma Gracia, *Las señales del destino heroico* (Barcelona: Montesinos, 1991). On the theme of incestuous opportunities (distribution of beds inside families' homes), see Burguière et al., *Historia de la vida privada*: vol. 2: *De la Europa feudal al Renacimiento*, 91.

29. For discussion of the sources of the Castilian *Libro de Apolonio*, see Carmen Monedero's introduction to her edition of this poem (Madrid: Castalia, 1987), 15–25. E. Klebs demonstrated an immediate dependence on a Latin source, from which French and Provençal versions are also derived: the *Historia Apollonii Regis Tyri*.

30. A character is unaware of his real identity because he has been separated from his parents as a young child. At a given point in the plot, the family meets by chance, and clues that have been accumulating as the tale progressed reveal to the hero and his family the true nature of their relationship. This procedure is much used also in the comedies of Plautus and Terence.

31. See C.C. Phipps, "El incesto, las adivinanzas y la música: diseños de la geminación en el *Libro de Apolonio*," *El Crotalón (Anuario de Filología)* 1 (1984): 807–18.

32. Strophes 7–8 of *Libro de Apolonio*, ed. C. Monedero (Madrid: Castalia, 1987).

33. The obsession with marrying the daughter off may be motivated by the desire to settle her future securely and ensure her rights to the estate. Fathers were reluctant to leave their heritage to a single daughter because she might be an easy prey for neighboring lords. Because of that, they try to marry her at an early age. Historians note that, in France, beginning in the fourteenth century, some feudal lords who had only a daughter asked their sons-in-law to adopt their names and emblems in order to prevent the extinction of their lineages (Anderson and Zinsser, *Historia de las mujeres*, vol. I, 346–47).

34. This is a variant of two folklore motifs recorded by S. Thompson in *Motif-Index of Folk-Literature: A Classification of Narrative Elements in Folktales, Ballads, Myths, Fables, Medieval Romance . . .* (Bloomington, Ind., and London: Indiana Univ. Press, 1955): "Chaste woman refers lover to his wife" (motif K1231.1) and "Chaste woman sends man's own wife as substitute" (motif K1223.2.4).

35. See Manuel Gutiérrez Esteve, "Sobre el sentido de cuatro romances de incesto," in *Homenaje a Julio Caro Baroja*, eds. A. Carreira, J.A. Cid, M. Gutiérrez Esteve, and R. Rubio (Madrid: Centro de Investigaciones Sociológicas, 1978), 551–79.

36. This is illustrated in the *Libro de Alexandre*, vv. 16a, 38c. See M. Eugenia Lacarra, "Notes on Feminist Analysis of Medieval Spanish Literature and History," *La Corónica* 17:1 (1988–89): 17. The same topic is covered by G. Duby, "Por una historia de las mujeres en Francia y en España. Conclusiones de un coloquio," in *El amor en la Edad Media y otros ensayos* (Madrid: Alianza, 1990), 104–10, especially 105.

37. In *Epica medieval española*, ed. C. Alvar and M. Alvar, 175–270.

38. In *Epica medieval española*, ed. C. Alvar and M. Alvar, 319–29.

39. On misogyny in the Middle Ages see, for example, J. Ornstein, "Misogyny and Pro-Feminism in Early Castilian Literature," *MLQ* 3 (1942): 221–34.

40. See C. Acutis, *La leggenda della Contessa traditrice* (Torino: Rosa, 1985), 11–33; and D.G. Pattison, "La condesa traidora," in *From Legend to Chronicle: the Treatment of Epic Material in Alphonsine Historiography* (Oxford: Society for Study of Mediaeval Language and Literature, 1983), 57–69. It is necessary to note that the first adulterous-wife story appears only in the most modern version of this legend.

41. *Amadís*, book III, chap. 73.

42. Exemplo XXXVI: "De lo que conteçió a un mercadero quando falló su muger et su fijo durmiendo en uno," in Don Juan Manuel, *El conde Lucanor*, ed. J.M. Blecua (Madrid: Castalia, 1982), 202–5.

43. *Libro del caballero Zifar*, ed. Cristina González (Madrid: Cátedra, 1983), 207–13.

44. See Albert Mordell, "The Oedipus Complex and the Brother and Sister Complex," in *The Erotic Motive in Literature* (Oxford: Plantin Publishers, 1990), 36–46.

45. *Poema de Fernán González*, ed. A. Zamora Vicente (Madrid: Espasa-Calpe, 1970).

46. *Libro de Alexandre*, ed. J. Cañas Murillo (Madrid: Editora Nacional, 1983), vv. 48a–85d.

47. This advice is similar to what Fernán González puts into practice in the *Poema de Fernán González*. A. Zamora Vicente suggests a connection between both texts in his introduction to his edition of this work, xv–xvi.

48. According to Cristina González (introduction to her edition of *El caballero Zifar*, 52), this fact has social implications. P. Gracia considers it an important part in heroic biography (*Las señales del destino heroico*, 192–95).

49. See *Amadís, Las sergas de Esplandián* (ed. Pascual de Gallangos, *Libros de caballerías*, vol. I [Madrid: Rivadeneyra, 1857], 403–561), *Palmerín de Inglaterra* (*Libros de caballerías*, part 2 [Madrid: Bailly-Baillière, 1908], 1–374), *Palmerín de Olivia* (Giuseppe Di Stefano, *Studi sul Palmerin de Olivia*, t. I: *El libro del famoso e muy esforçado cavallero Palmerín de Olivia* [Pisa: Instituto de Letteratura Spagnola e Ispano-Americana dell'Università di Pisa, 1966]).

50. See M.R. Lida, "El desenlace del *Amadís* primitivo," *Romance Philology* VI (1952–53): 283–89.

51. *Sendebar*, ed. M. Jesús Lacarra (Madrid: Cátedra, 1989).

52. Pedro Salinas, "La vuelta del esposo (Ensayo sobre estructura y sensibilidad en el *Cantar de Mio Cid*)," in *Ensayos completos*, vol. III (Madrid: Taurus, 1983 [1st ed. *Bulletin of Spanish Studies* XXIV (1947)]), 27–37.

53. R. Menéndez Pidal, ed., *Poema de Mio Cid* (Madrid: Espasa-Calpe, 1971), 210, note v. 1937b. He develops an opinion of E. de Hinojosa, *Estudios sobre la historia del derecho español* (Madrid, 1903), 103.

54. See M.E. Lacarra, "Notes on Feminist Analysis of Medieval Spanish Literature and History," *La Corónica* 17: 1 (1988–89), 17.

55. See W.J. Enwistle, "El Conde Sol o la Boda estorbada," *Revista de Filología Española* XXXIII (1949): 251–64.

56. See S. Thompson, ed., *Motif-Index of Folk-Literature*, motif K1813: "Disguised husband visits his wife."

57. In the *Baladro del Sabio Merlín* the same tale is told, based on a historical occurrence that greatly impressed contemporaries: the death of doña Inés de Castro, ordered by the king of Portugal with the aim of permitting a new marriage for the prince. In the romance the king's role is transferred to the new wife. See M.R. Lida, *Estudios de Literatura Española y Comparada* (Buenos Aires: Eudeba, 1966), 147.

58. A. Deyermond has emphasized the importance that sex and women have in the Castilian epic, which is thus sharply differentiated from the French epic. One of the most significant examples comes from this poem. Fernán González falls into a trap when he goes to negotiate his marriage to his enemy's daughter, doña Sancha de Navarra. She falls in love with him and sets him free when she receives his pledge to become her husband. They flee together, facing a range of dangers, and he e 'en has to carry her on his shoulders for a spell. Some time after his marriage, the count is taken prisoner by the king of León. Doña Sancha gets permission to see him and to have him released from his chains by explaining to the king that she wants to have sexual intercourse with her husband. Once they are alone, they exchange clothes and Fernán González escapes from the prison by pretending to be his own wife. The various sexual symbols that appear in the poem have been commented upon by A. Deyermond, "La sexualidad en la épica medieval española," *Nueva Revista de Filología Hispánica* XXXVI (1988): 767–86, especially 775–76.

59. "Tanto fue en ella el amor ençendiendo / fasta que cayó en el lecho muy desflaquida" (*Libro de Apolonio*, vv. 197c–d). [Love grew so strong in her that she fell ill.]

60. On the theme of the adulterous wife in tales, see M. Jesús Lacarra, "Algunos datos para la historia de la misoginia en la Edad Media," in *Studia in Honorem profesor M. de Riquer*, vol. I (Barcelona: Quaderns Crema, 1986), 339–61, and especially 340–43.

61. *El conde Lucanor*, 174.

62. *El conde Lucanor*, 175.

63. See M. Eugenia Lacarra, "Notes on Feminist Analysis of Medieval Spanish Literature and History," 17.

64. See J. Ruiz de Conde, *El amor y el matrimonio secreto en los libros de caballerías* (Madrid: Aguilar, 1948).

65. On the pro-marriage attitude of medieval Castilian literature, see the opinions of Jesús Menéndez Peláez in *Nueva visión del amor cortés* (Oviedo: Universidad de Oviedo, 1980) and in the introduction to his edition of *Juan Ruiz, Arcipreste de Hita, Libro de Buen Amor* (León: Everest, 1985), 7–73.

66. See M. Alvar, "El romance de Amnón y Tamar," in *El Romancero: Tradicionalidad y pervivencia* (Barcelona: Planeta, 1970), 163–245.

67. Manrique dedicated several of his love poems to his wife, both before and after he married her. See Jorge Manrique, *Obras*, ed. A. Serrano de Haro (Madrid: Alhambra, 1986). This attitude in favor of marriage may also be noted in other fifteenth-century court poets, for example, Pedro Manuel de Urrea, Fernán Pérez de Guzmán, and Gómez Manrique.

THREE-GENERATION FAMILIES

SEARCHING FOR GRANDPA AND GRANDMA IN LATE MEDIEVAL ENGLAND

Joel T. Rosenthal

Were I to open this article by making a general comment on the human condition, or were I to offer a reflection on the personal or the lyrical, I could
turn without trouble to the poetry of Ricardian England for a pithy quotation: either Chaucer or Langland or the Gawain poet would serve us well.[1]
Or if I were attempting to link poetic musing to an aphorism on the condition of the body politic, the public weal, and the link between fortune's and
each man or woman's own fate, the lesser but still adequate expressions of
any one of a number of fifteenth-century writers would serve to make the
point.[2] But since I am concerned with talking about three-generation families, with grandparents who knew their grandchildren, and vice-versa, I am
forced to turn to Lydia Maria Child ("Over the river and through the wood/
To grand-father's house we go") to catch the appropriate tone of nostalgia
and sentimentality. The thin thread of human relationships is not easily
picked out in weak light.

Admittedly, if I wanted to begin on a bleaker note on this theme, I
could do much worse than to begin with Peter Laslett's warning about such
matters: "You could not with any confidence expect to see your grandchildren in the world we have lost."[3] And if I wanted to suggest an existential
framing of the discourse about family continuity, there is always
Shakespeare's bald if perceptive exchange as offered in *Two Gentlemen of
Verona:*

> Who begot thee?
> Marry, the son of my Grand-father.[4]

This essay—in which I report on some efforts to investigate the three-
generation family in late medieval England, as defined in terms of people
from (at least) the first and third generations who are alive at the same time—

has two motives or goals, two reasons for being of professional interest. The first, as is often the case, is methodological. The search for records and information about the overlapping of lives between the first and the third generations, let alone for any material on interaction (I hesitate to say affection and personal bonding), poses a test for our ability to coax the laconic sources we have from this world into some part in our conversation.[5] Can we get these terse and often disinterested records to talk about an aspect of private life that has engaged social scientists, looking at the function and structure of both modern industrial (and postindustrial) society and of the world that has existed (at least until very recently) alongside but beyond the boundaries of the Western industrial state?[6]

One of the games social historians play with or upon the people of the past is to make the latter answer questions (for the sake of the curiosity of the former) that had not been particularly prominent in the original cultural or social agenda. I will pick out and expand upon some material on grandparents and grandchildren that was commonplace to, and even made explicit on occasion by the late medieval observer had he or she but cared to pay it much heed and to do some simple analysis; I will try to put very few of our words into their mouths. In this quick study I will concentrate on three different kinds of material and sources, sufficient in quantity and/ or quality for the grounding of some suggestions about survival, family continuity, and relations between the generation that was about to leave the scene and that other, one down the line, now waiting to be called into place.

Other than the methodological challenge of coaxing reluctant sources, we have a concern for the inherent substantive value of our findings in terms of late medieval society, social structure, and patterns of family interaction. By means of an analysis of intergenerational links, we are delving into the tangled world of personal and social networks, into the kind of historical data that might help us define self and other. When we chart and analyze the overlap of the generations, we are looking for a way of gauging the depth and richness of the contemporary fabric of private and family life and experience.

Our scholarship on late medieval English society—whether at the level of biography, prosopography, or county and regional studies—regularly seeks to explicate the lives of the men and women whom we track through the complex amalgam or mosaic of the extant sources. We talk much of such motivating forces and policies (for individuals and their families, over time) as the arranging of felicitous and upwardly mobile marriages, of the role of heiress-daughters and marriage settlements, and of the need and demand for the children who would serve as basic pawns in the game, the raw material for the next round at the bargaining table or in the bedchamber. We recognize, as a common mind-set of upper-class culture and socialization (and probably for others farther down the social hierarchy as well, had we their records), a deep and persistent interest in and knowledge of family background and genealogy, an ability to identify and remember a wide circle of relationships, a fierce pride over coats of arms and heraldic devices, and a long memory of family burial sites and of favorite religious houses. And it was all—or so we are wont to say—for the sake of the family enterprise; patriarchy and the patrimony became—for the fortunate families who bred male children, who won their lawsuits, and who survived—as one.[7] I suggest here that an additional ingredient in this recipe for worldly pride and success was the preservation of life and descent (continuity and procreation) into the next-plus-one generation. When the children's children were on the scene, then (and perhaps only then, could we but know the full story) was patriarchy fully valorized.

How reliable a guide is Peter Laslett, with his gloomy prognosis about sitting on the lap of grandpa and grandma? He offered his somber reflection in 1965, at the very beginning of the scholarly movement or revolution that we then presumed to call "the new social history," when just posing the questions sufficed to get our engines going. In essence, and with the benefit of three decades of hindsight and of much research from many willing and able hands, I think we can say today that he probably overstated the negative case, perhaps even by some considerable degree, at least as far as his generalization can be applied to those who survived infancy and childhood and who lived to become parents. Whether we want to say the glass of the three-generation family is 80–90 percent empty or 10–20 percent full, the odds on grandparent-grandchild overlap seem to have been a bit better than his early bookmaking would have indicated.

In this inquiry we deal with a tale whose full explication is irretrievably embedded in sources that largely focus on eldest sons (and sometimes on those sons' sons); ignored, to a great extent, are younger brothers and sisters, along with grandmothers and most other women. In many instances, once the son-and-heir was on the scene and survived to outlive his father, not even the son's own children were of great interest for the records on which we must rely; the narrow concern of such written materials and the contemporary value placed upon and surrounding the oldest son, almost to the exclusion of all others, seems to coincide to a striking degree. As we say to our students, "It is no accident" that we know some things and not others about people in the past, even about their births and their deaths (not to speak of their copulations). As rich a source for family history as the

Paston Letters mostly gives us documents that concentrate on the instrumental occasions of family life (courtship and marriage, the coercion of recalcitrant daughters, etc.) rather than shed much light on the processes of domestic life and the give-and-take of those lesser boys and girls farther down or beside the main line. I doubt if the Pastons' lives, especially those of the peripheral children whose existence is often mysterious and whose births tend to go unnoted, were as dominated by the patriarchy of John and the matriarchy of Margaret as the letters would lead us to believe.[8] But where, with any precision and confidence, can we go from here? It is easy to be skeptical about the gap between the agenda as set (long after the fact) by the extant sources with a legal slant, and life as it was lived within the family, uneventful day by uneventful day, unrecorded milestone by unrecorded milestone. Beyond the boundaries of recorded records, it is not so easy to be enlightening.

For the parliamentary peerage, at least, the tolerable genealogical material that is at hand indicates that about forty-eight aristocratic families, between 1399 and 1485, had at least one three-generation link, as against thirty-seven who did not.[9] This tally is less precise than it sounds, though the reasons for this have little to do with three-generation survival. The mere naming and counting of peerage families is a male-defined business, governed by primogeniture and peerage law. The tally ignores the affective symmetry of cognatic and agnatic kinship links that may have loomed large in many lives, even those of eldest sons and male heirs.[10] The number of families that I report here as having had at least one three-generation link, like the data we will look at below in Inquisitions Post Mortem, indicates the reality of one slim thread; it invariably is insensitive to the presence of younger children and surviving grandmothers (as opposed to surviving grandfathers). Nevertheless, if we take these findings as representing the minimalist answer about grandparents and grandchildren, the enumerated tip of a large and silent iceberg, we are glimpsing a brighter picture about three-generation families than the first forecast indicated. Some families, like the Percys and the Cliffords, accommodated both an inordinate number of deaths by violence *and* the frequent overlap of grandparents and grandchildren.[11] Other high-born families moved through the century with less drama and more longevity, and stretched out their peers' lives so the simultaneity or coevality of the males of the first and third generation was less dramatic and more in keeping with the natural order, at least as the natural order was reified for those who survived.[12]

Genealogical information is apt to be relatively accurate, where we have it at all, and in many respects it represents a floor, not a ceiling, for the kind of data we are after. It offers virtually no guide to interaction or social relations, but it is a reasonable *sine qua non* with which to begin. If we move on to what we can learn from the Inquisitions Post Mortem (IPMs), we are travelling in the same direction: from the minimalist toward the fuller-if-unrecorded. The purpose of an IPM proceeding was to determine the identity and age of the next heir to real property held in chief from the lord king, and the proceeding was held fairly soon after the death of the previous land-holder. Thus the inquisitions offer a vast database from which we can extract pertinent information about age and identity or relationship, and if we are cautious about believing what they tell us, we can add a good deal more substance to our patchwork quilt of family reconstruction.

From the mass of inquisitions, ranging from the late fourteenth to the early sixteenth centuries, I have picked out a number of published collections and subjected them to some simple-minded statistical analysis.[13] The largest group of heirs named, in each separate collection of IPMs and in the whole group in aggregate, consists of children of the body of the deceased landholder: mostly sons, a few daughters. Of this large group—some 79 percent of all the heirs named, or 1,519 heirs for 1,913 males (the now-deceased women who held property being omitted here, for brevity's sake)—the age brackets of the new heirs upon coming into the property are as follows: 22 percent named as being aged 10 and below, 29 percent between 11 and 20, 25 percent in their twenties (i.e., between 21 and 29), 17 percent in their thirties, and 7 percent named as being 40 and above.

It was inherent in the working and recording of the administrative proceeding that created the IPM that if there was a son of the deceased landholder, the inquisitorial or investigative procedure ground to a logical halt (regardless of the son's age) when he was named and identified. Thus, in the majority of the Inquisitions, we are left with no inkling as to whether the son named as the heir had any younger brothers (let alone sisters, be they older or younger) or whether, when his own age made it not unlikely, he already had children of his own. We are stretching neither late medieval probability nor late twentieth-century credulity to suggest that some significant proportion of those men (and, occasionally, women) identified as heirs and named as already being in their thirties (or beyond) were fathers (or mothers). And if we can take this step, we can argue that the odds in favor of parenthood were not all that bad for some of the son-heirs still in their twenties, and that they were a great deal better for those in their forties or more.

This is speculative, to be sure, but hardly very far out on the thin ice of wish fulfillment; if pre-modern demography moved only on certainties, it would rarely move at all. If men in post-plague England were marrying by their middle or late twenties, as we generally accept, then they were likely to be moving from bachelorhood to fatherhood—in many if not in most instances—by the time they had entered their fourth decade. And for women of propertied families, marriage came by, if not before, the mid-twenties, in most instances, and once wed, we trust that they sought to move as quickly as possible toward and into motherhood. Thus a whole wave of grandchildren—unreported and covered over by the limited curiosity of the king's writ that spurred the creation of the Inquisition Post Mortem—must have been on the scene when grandpa (and grandma) finally shuffled off. A whole reserve army of procreation was thereby slighted from the written memory of historical consciousness.

In about one instance in every twenty or so IPMs, the deceased landholder's eldest son had predeceased him but had had the decency to leave a son of his own before departing. In such cases, the grandson is explicitly named in the IPMs as the next heir to the old man and to his land. Thus we have, from the goodly body of Inquisitions that we have utilized and aggregated, some 107 instances of succession under which the property (and the patriarchal torch) went directly from grandfather to grandson. To make the material even more intriguing, we can see that the ages of the grandchildren often indicated something well beyond mere infancy, beyond a mere fact of survival that might suffice to keep the family's male-bonded linkage alive in such an exiguous fashion. The ages of the third-generation heirs were spread across the board: 18 percent of them were named as being 10 or below; 31 percent were between 11 and 20; and 51 percent were at least of legal age. Discounting the insoluble dilemmas of exaggeration and inaccuracy in the IPMs, we seem to have a profile of (recently deceased) grandparents that argues for some impressive survival, in terms of incidence, and also for some considerable years of three-generational overlap.

Though the data from the Inquisitions are hardly incontrovertible, the argument in favor of using them seems persuasive in view of the largish amount of material and the on-the-spot identification of the grandchildren. But once again, we can turn to the "but." One obvious "but," and one that leads us to our next body of sources, is that data from IPMs, except for demographic usage and what we might fill-in regarding any families of note or those whose subsequent (or prior) history can be tracked, are two-dimensional at best. As we like to say today, it is tolerably reliable for quantitative matters but woefully thin if we wish to turn to qualitative issues.

There is a third body of sources we can tap in this exercise, perhaps coming to our rescue at this point. These are the largish number of last wills and testaments that have been preserved from the late fourteenth and fifteenth centuries. Here, as with the IPMs, the contemporary voice governs our access to the facts of the matter, except that now the controlling or authorial voice is that of the testator (at least as he dictated), and the direction and tone of the voice are probably pretty much as he or she chose. If grandchildren are not exactly thick on the ground in the wills, at least it is not because their appearance was precluded by some legal rationale shaping the very creation of the form and purpose of the primary source on which we rely. If they do not appear very often, it is either because they really did not exist when the will was made, which was usually less than a year before the death of the testator, or because the putative grandmother or grandfather chose—for whatever reason (and we will turn to this shortly)—to ignore their existence.

In quantitative terms, wills are by no means a rich source on which to base an argument about the frequency or strength of the three-generation family as a player in the game called variations in the structures of family and alternative tracks of personal/private life. If we turn to some of the published collections of wills from "the long" fifteenth-century, we find that only a small proportion talk about benefactions that moved along the lines we have been charting. In the wills from the Hustings Court of the City of London between 1399 and 1509, there are only 16 wills (of 561, a mere 3 percent of the group) that make an explicit and unambiguous reference to a grandparental bequest to a grandchild.[14] If we move a bit up the social and economic ladder and look at the wills in Archbishop Chichele's Register, we can see if people of more affluence and higher social visibility were different in this regard.[15] The answer seems to be yes, but is not accompanied by any deafening chorus of farewell shouts between grandparents and grandchildren: 13 percent of the wills in Chichele's Register refer to a three-generation bequest.

Given the low percentages that we encounter in these two collections of printed wills, there seems little point in reporting in with numbers or percentages from other counties and other collections: York, Somerset, Richmondshire, Nottinghamshire, and so forth. The demographic information in the IPMs argues for a higher incidence of three-generation links than is reflected in any way, shape, or form in this large aggregation of soft data. The rather disappointing returns from the wills, at least in quantitative terms, just has to be accepted as a fact of life or—more accurately and with better professional expression—death, and of late medieval modes of family linkage and articulation. Between what the law, custom, and the Church dictated to shape and channel individual options regarding the transmission of property and the distribution of personal wealth, there was usually little inclination to write a will that embraced more than a certain fraction of potential family beneficiaries. Arguing from negative evidence, it seems likely that bequests from parents to children often covered over or subsumed (to the point of totally ignoring and excluding) those children's children. Though there are a fair number of exceptions in which we find both generosity and some sign of a bond, we have to accept that for the overwhelming bulk of the instances, the genuine glimpse into the world of the three-generation family offered by the wills is, almost always, through an exceedingly narrow window.

Furthermore, when grandchildren are mentioned in a will, they rarely seem to have been cut in for anything particularly impressive. The small sums of money and the wide distribution of personal, religious, and household items that dominate the list of bequests in most wills of any substance tend to be their wonted portion. The granddaughter's haul of "a caldron, a pot, and a littell ponset" may have gone toward setting up her own household when the time came, but it was hardly a princess's trousseau.[16] We spot what may be more personal concern in the bequest of £20 left for young John Rochfort, "son of Johanna, my doughter, late the wyff of Henry Rochfort." This sounds like a case of a widowed daughter-mother and young grandchildren.[17] It is both poignant and unusual.

Our quick exploration nears its logical end. As so often with topics in social history, how we choose to wrap up the case—either for the defense or for the prosecution—depends a good deal on what we had hoped to find, whether new lines of inquiry have been suggested or stumbled across, how inclined we are to be generous gatekeepers when assessing behavior, and what we can deduce about motivation and identity. If we started with Laslett's cautionary hypothesis as our guiding light, then clearly the returns have been moderately impressive, coming in distinctly, if not strongly, on the positive side. At a bare minimum, you had a one-in-ten chance of knowing your grandparents personally, as well as chronologically and structurally, if you survived the ravages of infant mortality and if they avoided the hazards on their side of the slope. After all, everyone starts with four grandparents, and if any of these lasted much past 20 or 25 they were even-money to get at least pretty close to age 50 by the end, and perhaps a fair stretch beyond that.[18]

But if we start with a Laslett-plus picture of the demography, we have to be struck by the fact of how many more three-generation links there may well have been than we are able to track down, let alone to pick apart for a more nuanced analysis and explication. The law did not very often have any need to determine the presence and identity of grandchildren, and when it did, a son's son was almost always sufficient; only rarely do we move, in the IPMs, to such rich material as a distribution of the property between a group of daughters' children (both sons and daughters). Nor, we are sorry to say, did grandparents need them or feel any need to trumpet their existence, either when making wills or when recording many other types of transactions that have come down. If a grandchild stood to be the heir at law, he or she would be taken care of regardless. When the grandchildren were on a family track that stood outside the law's main concern, they were likely to serve their years in the family's history without much explicit support or recognition—sometimes even of their identity itself, let alone of their coming and going.

Were we to turn more of our attention to women of property, the tale would be a little bit richer. In the IPMs of women (now widows, and therefore with older children or with a longer survival span during which their own children might have died), we find a few more grandchildren as heirs, and the grandchildren we do encounter are older than they had been for the late husbands. In this pool of third-generation heirs, the grandchildren are divided almost evenly among those who were named as being under age 10, those who were between 11 and 20, and those identified as being 21 and more. But the material is richer in its potential for speculation about the quality of life and relationships than it is in statistical terms. In other ways, the wills of widows are much in line with those of the men; only a few refer to grandchildren, and when they do so, they rarely transmit much beyond those pleasant tokens of affection we find all over the world of testamentary disposition. And since the death of the widow-cum-grandmother was likely to represent the final breakup of the household of the oldest generation, the restraint covering both affection and enrichment, as she made her final disposition, is worth noting if only for its high quotient of disappointment.

What we seem to be searching for, by now, is some indication of a rich two-way exchange between the alternate generations. Such a complex and colorful fabric is easier to postulate than to uncover. We are told by anthropologists that, in many cultures, the aged grandparents provide a significant buffer against the pressures that parents feel they are expected to put upon their children. In addition, since older people can be gently cycled out of the most demanding roles in the labor force, they are willing and able to assume less demanding domestic chores—bringing them into contact with the very young—and to become the transmitters of lore, myth-history, and family memory to the generation yet to come, along with offering a lot of discount-price baby-sitting.[19] To look at the bonding of alternative generations is often a useful tool in social analysis. However, it is not a tool that gets picked up very often when we try to hammer away at late medieval English social structure and patterns of family life.

Hints of such a role, recast into the idiom of late medieval life, may be found, though they are hard to confirm or to build up beyond mere suggestion. In the dowager households that we know (such as those of Cecilly of York or the Stafford dowagers), we easily picture the granddaughters and perhaps the great nieces and even very young great nephews who were a regular part of the menage; primary education, manners, religious instruction, and the practical training for whatever station in life they would be called to fulfill were taught as part of a routine that covered bed, board, and service.[20] But against this lurch toward sentimentality, we can set the table of a Londoner who left a minimal bequest to a servant girl and a trifle more to the servant's brother, now identified as the testator's grandson.[21]

There are a few brighter patches. John of Gaunt remembered his son Henry Bolingbroke's young son, the future Henry V, with "un hanap d'or," with the same for John, future duke of Bedford. But nothing here for the infants, Thomas and Humphrey.[22] Nor did many of the high and mighty, even when we know of the existence of grandchildren, bend even this far. And when they did, we have no reason to expect to find signs of any custom that dictated that if one member of the next generation were being remembered, then all members of that cohort had to be. Such sensitivity about other (and presumably lesser) siblings, let alone for first cousins by the testator's other children, remained for a more egalitarian or more introspective world. Margaret Paston's will *might* bespeak a desire for a reconciliation with an estranged daughter, expressed in part by bequests to the daughter's children: perhaps posthumous reconciliation was better than no reconciliation at all.[23] An odd northern will worries about "Alice Watton, my daughter, xl s., to help hir and hir childir."[24] But for the most part, if we see wills as instances of instrumentality and social control as much as of benefaction and spiritual solace, the grandchildren were just more cannon fodder in the armory of family dynamics, and rarely used ones at that.

If we look at Laslett almost thirty years on, we are fairly confident that he understated the case for survival, if not for interaction. If we accept the bulk of the seemingly precise information the records give—and much of the thrust of demography today is to be trusting in this regard—we are more sanguine about age and longevity, about survival and procreation, and about replacement rates than we once were. But if we are looking for a new day as marked by signs of visible affection, of sentimentality and nostalgia and personal satisfaction, we are barking up the wrong tree. How much of this is due to the nature of the extant sources and to the motives and conventions that shaped them, how much is due to the hazards and pitfalls of demography and the life course, and how much is due to the fact that these people were socialized to be curt and formal in their written intercourse is for us to play with. But at least, in statistical or actuarial terms, there was a reasonable chance that you might survive birth and the first year and live to go over the river and through the woods and come to grandma's and grandpa's place. There was also some chance they would still be alive when you got there. On the other hand, once you got there, they would probably indicate that—as a grandson or a granddaughter—you were much better seen than heard, and not even that all too often.

NOTES

1. A shorter version of this article was read at the meeting of the Medieval Academy of America, April 1993 (Tucson), and I wish to thank Constance Bouchard, who asked me to offer the paper and who arranged the panel, and Cathy Itnyre, who persuaded me to revise it for publication. They are not responsible for errors and insensitive comments. The material I use here is part of a longer study I am completing on old age in late medieval England.

2. The autobiographical laments in Hoccleve's works commend themselves in this context: H.S. Bennett, *Six Medieval Men and Women* (Cambridge: Cambridge Univ. Press, 1955), 69–99; and A. Compton Reeves, "Thomas Hoccleve, Bureaucrat," *Mediaevalia et Humanistica* n.s. 5 (1974): 201–14.

3. Peter Laslett, *The World We Have Lost* (2nd ed., New York: Scribner's, 1971), 103. Though I think these voices are too pessimistic (as I argue below), they probably represent the common scholarly view. For more in this vein, see Jean Fourastie, "From the Traditional to the 'Tertiary' Life Cycle," in William Petersen, ed., *Readings in Population* (New York: Macmillan, 1972), 29–38, and Jennifer C. Ward, "Wealth and Family in Early Sixteenth-Century Colchester," *Essex Archaeology and History* 21 (199), 110–17, on the general absence of references to three-generation families among even a privileged database.

4. According to the *Harvard Concordance to Shakespeare*, compiled by Marvin Spevack (Cambridge: Belknap, 1973), in the canon there are nineteen uses of "grandam," nine of "grandame," one of "grandchild," thirteen of "grandfather," four of "grandmother," and twenty-four of "grandsire" (plus two occasions where it is used in the plural). As with so much else in this essay, we are free to decide whether these data indicate many uses or not many uses of terminology depicting three-generation family links.

5. When I read an earlier version of this essay at the Medieval Academy, Don Queller urged me not to be so reluctant to say that people in past times, as their culture shaped their expression, "loved" each other. His stricture against falling back upon the equivocal "affect" and "affective relationship" is a good one, and I thank him for his advice and support, not for the first time.

6. Relations between the first and third generation are of interest to contemporary observers, and they were a significant topic in the post–World War II heyday of urban sociology. Grandparent-grandchild links figure prominently (as shown in the indexes) of such agenda-setting studies as Michael Young and Peter Willmott, *Family and Kinship in East London* (Harmondsworth: Penguin Books, 1962); Peter Townsend, *The Family Life of Old People: An Inquiry in East London* (Harmondsworth: Penguin, 1963); Raymond Firth, Jane Hubert, and Anthony Forge, *Family and Their Rela-*

tives: Kinship in a Middle-Class Sector of London (London: Routledge, 1969). The focus in these studies is on such issues as the frequency of visits, how freely the grand-children just drop in, the role of grandparents (mostly the grandmother) as a surro-gate parent while the parents are at work or following their own inclinations, and where afternoon tea is provided.

7. I have spelled out a good many of these issues in detail in my *Patriarchy of Privilege in Fifteenth-Century England* (Philadelphia: Univ. of Pennsylvania Press, 1991). But they are also the bread and butter of many of the local and community studies of recent years: Nigel Saul, *Knights and Esquires: The Gloucestershire Gentry in the Fourteenth Century* (Oxford: Clarendon Press, 1981), and his *Scenes from Pro-vincial Life: Knightly Families in Sussex, 1280–1460* (Oxford: Clarendon Press, 1986); Simon J. Payling, *Political Society in Lancastrian England: The Greater Gentry of Nottinghamshire* (Oxford: Clarendon Press, 1991).

8. For the rich if less than satisfying tale of Paston family life, we can still be-gin with H.S. Bennett, *The Pastons and Their England* (Cambridge: Cambridge Univ. Press, 1932). More recent works that look at these issues include Colin F. Richmond, *The Paston Family in the Fifteenth Century: The First Phase* (Cambridge: Cambridge Univ. Press, 1990); Ann S. Haskell, "The Paston Women in Marriage in Fifteenth-Cen-tury England," *Viator* 4 (1973): 459–71; Philippa Moaddern, "Honour among the Pastons: Gender and Integrity in Fifteenth-Century English Provincial Life," *Journal of Medieval History* 14 (1988): 357–71.

9. The information on peerage families is basically as extracted from Vicary Gibbs et al., *The Complete Peerage*, 12 vols. in 13 (London: St. Catherine Press, 1910–59).

10. A fair number of fifteenth-century peers inherited their peerage from their wives, i.e., they were their fathers-in-law's heir *to* or *in* the House of Lords. In such cases, the wife was a mere transmitter, of course, but certainly the threads of patriar-chy must have been seen to have become frayed. Such peerages include claims to such lofty titles as the earldoms of Warwick and of Salisbury. For a general survey, see J. Enoch Powell and Keith Wallis, *The House of Lords in the Middle Ages* (London, 1968), in the index under "marriage portion . . . as cause for summons or dignity."

11. Between the death of Henry, Lord Percy in 1368 and that of the IV Earl in 1489, five of the six males in the patriarchal line died by violence. And yet three of the Percy grandfathers lasted long enough to see the eldest son's eldest son born (at the very least). Actually, the years of three-generation overlap were more than a mere token; the years of overlap between the new boy and the old man were four (for Hotspur, x. 1403), fifteen for his son (x. 1455), and six for the IV Earl. The Cliffords had four consecutive peers die by violence, but here too one of them (Lord, 1388–x. 1422) overlapped with his grandfather for a year or two.

12. The Scropes of Bolton are a striking case of a direct patriarchal line that lasted through the century: seven direct father-son links in the long chain of succes-sion. And yet they are at the other pole of three-generation overlap, with only Rich-ard (1327–1403) living long enough to see a grandson (Richard, III Lord Scrope, 1394–1420) on the scene.

13. The printed IPMs that have been analyzed are *Calendar of Inquisitions Post Mortem, XVII (15–23 Richard II)* (London: Mackie, 1988); *Calendar of Inqui-sitions Post Mortem, XVIII (1–6 Henry IV)*, ed. J.L. Kirby (London: Mackie, 1987); *Calendar of Inquisitions Post Mortem, Henry VII*, vol. 1 (London: Mackie, 1898), for 1–12 Henry VII; *Calendar of Inquisitions Post Mortem, Henry VII*, vol. 2 (Lon-don: Mackie, 1915), for 13–20 Henry VII. The data from these four volumes have been tallied and aggregated in this presentation. The validity of the material contained in an IPM has often been questioned; both the formulaic nature of the responses and the pseudo-precision of the responses seem suspect. The case against them is well stated by R.H. Hunnisett, "The Reliability of Inquisitions as Historical Evidence," in *The Study of Medieval Records: Essays in Honour of Kathleen Major*, ed. D.A. Bullough

and Robin L. Storey (Oxford: Clarendon Press, 1971), 206–37. The value of the IPMs, despite their faults, has been defended: Josiah Cox Russell, *British Medieval Population* (Albuquerque: Univ. of New Mexico Press, 1948), 92–117; more recently, and with sophisticated statistical reasoning, L.R. Poos, *A Rural Society after the Black Death: Essex, 1350–1525* (Cambridge: Cambridge Univ., 1991).

14. As edited, and probably calendared rather severely, by Reginald R. Sharpe, *Calendar of Wills in the Court of Hustings, London, A.D. 1258–1688*, 2 vols. (London: J.C. Francis, 1889–90).

15. E.F. Jacob, ed., *The Register of Henry Chichele, Archbishop of Canterbury, 1414–1443* vol. II (Oxford: Clarendon Press, 1938).

16. James Raine, Jr., ed., *Testamenta Eboracensia, IV*, Surtees Society 53 (1869), 198.

17. *Testamenta Eboracensia III*, Surtees Society 45 (1865), 185.

18. Russell, *British Medieval Population*, 175–91, for life tables and a general discussion of longevity.

19. I have looked, in a perfunctory fashion, at some aspects of retirement in "Retirement and the Life Cycle in Fifteenth Century England," in *Aging and the Aged in Medieval Europe*, ed. Michael M. Sheehan (Toronto: Pontifical Institute of Mediaeval Studies, 1990), 173–88. The ties between elderly serfs who turn over their holdings in return for care and maintenance are examined by Elaine Clark, "Some Aspects of Social Security in Medieval England," *Journal of Family History* 7 (1982): 307–20, and "The Quest for Security in Medieval England," in *Aging and the Aged*, 189–200. Since investigations like those of Professor Clark have to look either at normative contracts, made when the turnover is instituted, or at the anomalies of litigation and breakdown, it is virtually impossible to re-create what bonds an aged grandparent, sharing a household with a child's children, forged with the alternate generation. Oral history for the fifteenth century is still beyond our reach.

20. For Cecilly's household, see Society of Antiquaries, *A Collection of Ordinances for the Royal Household* (London: John Nichols, 1790); for her life as revealed by the ordinances, see C.A.J. Armstrong, "The Piety of Cicely, Duchess of York: A Study in Late Medieval Culture," in *For Hilaire Belloc: Essays in Honour of his 72nd Birthday*, ed. Douglas Woodruff (London: Sheed and Ward, 1942), 73–94. For the dowagers of the Stafford family and their households, see Carole Rawcliffe, *The Staffords, Earls of Stafford and Dukes of Buckingham* (Cambridge: Cambridge Univ. Press, 1978).

21. Sharpe, *Calendar of Wills in the Court of Hustings*, 558–59.

22. John Nichols, *A Collection of Wills* (London: J. Nichols, 1730: repr., New York: Kraus Reprint, 1969), 145–73.

23. James Gairdner, *The Paston Letters, 1422–1509*, 3 vols. (London: AMS Press, 1985), III:281ff.

24. *Testamenta Eboracensia IV*, 109.

CONTRIBUTORS

Elizabeth Archibald is associate professor of English at the University of Victoria, British Columbia. She took her Ph.D. in medieval studies at Yale. She has published articles on a range of medieval topics, including Chaucer, the "Scottish Chaucerians," macaronics, the Arthurian legend, women and romance, and medieval incest stories, as well as a book on the treatment of the *Historia Apollonii Regis Tyri* in the Middle Ages and Renaissance (Boydell and Brewer, 1991). She is now working on a study of the incest theme in medieval literature and society.

Albrecht Classen received his doctorate from the University of Virginia and currently holds the rank of full professor with tenure at the University of Arizona. He has published extensively on medieval German literature, feminism, comparative literature, and epistolary. He has written several monographs and anthologies, has written numerous articles, and is currently preparing a new monograph on communication theory in the German Middle Ages. Dr. Classen is the editor of *Tristania*, co-editor of *Mediaevistik*, and member of the advisory board of *Fifteenth-Century Studies*.

María Luzdivina Cuesta is a professor of Hispanic philology at the University of León (Spain). She specializes in medieval Spanish narrative. Her publications include studies on Arthurian Spanish literature, and especially on the subject of Tristán (*Aventuras amorosas y caballerescas en las novelas de Tristán*, 1991). Currently she is working on a book about literary kings in medieval Spanish fiction.

Carolyn Edwards received her degree in history from the University of California at Santa Barbara. The winner of a Javits Fellowship, she completed her doctoral course work at the University of Notre Dame and is currently completing her dissertation research on monastic houses in thirteenth-century Regensburg as a Fulbright scholar in Munich.

Philip Gavitt received his Ph.D. in history from the University of Michigan. He has taught at the University of Tennessee, Knoxville, and is currently associate professor of history and director of the Center for Medieval and Renaissance Studies at Saint Louis University. He is the author of *Charity and Children in Renaissance Florence* (Ann Arbor: University of Michigan Press, 1990). He is currently working on a book-length study of the relationship between gender, inheritance, abandonment, and convents in sixteenth-century Italy, and also plans to write an intellectual biography of the sixteenth-century Florentine humanist scholar and antiquarian Vincenzo Borghini.

Louis Haas did his graduate work at the University of Illinois and is assistant professor of medieval and early modern history at Duquesne University. He has published articles on godparenthood in late medieval England and Florence, and is writing a book about birth and infancy in late medieval and Renaissance Florence.

Aline G. Hornaday is a visiting scholar of the history department at University of California, San Diego. She has served as Professor Stanley Chodorow's assistant for his edition of *Regesta Decretalium (1140–1200)* and, with Dr. Ann Elwood, co-founded the *Journal of Unconventional History*. Dr. Hornaday has published several papers, most recently "Les saints du 'Cycle du Maubeuge' et la conscience aristocratique dans le Hainaut médiéval," *Revue du Nord* (1991). Currently she is researching the involvement of monasteries in the riverine trade patterns of early medieval Europe.

Cathy Jorgensen Itnyre teaches history and philosophy at Copper Mountain College in Joshua Tree, California. She was educated at the Catholic University of America and Rutgers University, and was a Fulbright scholar at the University of Iceland. Currently she is working on a book about family relationships in medieval Iceland.

Kimberly Keller received her undergraduate education at Michigan State University and is at present enrolled in the doctoral program at Indiana University. She is completing her dissertation on the Chaucer apocrypha.

Timothy S. Miller is currently an associate professor in the department of history at Salisbury State University, Salisbury, Maryland. His first book, *The Birth of the Hospital in the Byzantine Empire*, examined the sophisticated medical hospitals that the East Roman government and church maintained in Constantinople and in other towns of the eastern Mediterranean. From hospitals he moved to the care of orphans. He is now writing a monograph on the Orphanotropheion (orphanage) of Constantinople and on other ecclesiastical institutions for the care of homeless children in the Byzantine Empire.

Joel T. Rosenthal has his degrees from the University of Chicago, and he teaches in the history department of the State University of New York at Stony Brook. He has worked on Anglo-Saxon England but in recent years has mostly concentrated his research on the social structure of late medi-eval England, with special attention to family history and the role of women.

Fiona Harris Stoertz received her undergraduate education at the University of Calgary, and is currently in the doctoral program at the University of California at Santa Barbara. Her dissertation, "Youth in Medieval Culture," will examine changing definitions and activities of youths and adolescents, with particular emphasis on the transformations of the twelfth-century Renaissance. She teaches history at the University of Trent in Peterborough, Ontario.

INDEX

stepmothers, 171 n. 22, 208
stillborns, 107, 108
Stricker (the), 47
Sturla Sighvatsson, 188
subfumigation, 105, 112
Sudden Infant Death Syndrome (SIDS), xiii,
    138, 140–41, 142, 143, 145, 146,
    147, 150–51 n. 20
suicide, 161, 207, 209
Sulpicius Severus, 8
Syria/Syrian, 127, 129

Terence, 9, 222 n. 30
Theodore Prodromos, 131
Theodore Stoudites, 125, 126, 132
Theodosian Code, 23
Theodosius, 124
Theophanu, 4 (fig. 1), 12, 13, 15
Theutberga, 30, 32
Thietmar of Merseburg, 11
Thomas of Canterbury, St., 108, 110, 112
Thomas of Cantilupe, St., 109
Timokletos, 131
Turkish, 130
Tuscany/Tuscans, 87, 137, 138, 148, 149
Twelve Tables (XII Tables), 123, 134 n. 11

uncle(s), 24, 123, 126, 177, 185, 206
unguents, 106
universities, 105
unnatural presentation, 108

vengeance/revenge, 179, 182, 184, 187, 204,
    206, 208, 220 n. 13
virginity, 9, 82 n. 8
Visigothic, 200
Volksbuch, 53, 54, 57

von Aue, Hartmann, 42, 43, 46, 61 n. 23,
    159, 160
von der Vogelweide, Walther, 50
von Eschenbach, Wolfram, 41, 42, 50, 57,
    61 n. 22
von Montfort, Hugo, 50, 53, 57, 58
von Nassau-Saarbrücken, Elisabeth, 57
von Ringoltingen, Thüring, 53, 54, 55, 57–58
von Strassburg, Gottfried, 45, 46, 57
von Tepl, Johannes, 50, 51, 52, 53, 57, 58, 59
von Trimberg, Hugo, 46, 47
von Wolkenstein, Oswald, 47, 49, 50, 53,
    57, 58, 59, 64 n. 72

Waldrada, 30, 31, 32
Warbeck, Veit, 57
weaning, 141, 146, 148, 149, 153 n. 56
wergeld, 22
Wernher the Gartenaere, 46, 47
wetnurses, 91, 95, 96, 97, 129, 137, 139,
    140, 141, 142, 143, 144, 145, 146,
    147, 148, 149 n. 3
widows/widowhood, 12, 13, 14, 16, 26, 70,
    82 n. 8, 123, 124, 127, 165, 232,
    233
Widukind, 8, 14
Wilfred, St., 110
William (Archbishop of Mainz), 4 (fig. 1), 9,
    10
William of Norwich, 107
wills, 124, 230, 231, 232, 234
witches, 90, 117 n. 32
Wittenwiler, Heinrich, 52, 53
women, 13, 16, 17, 52, 68, 104, 105, 134 n.
    10, 157, 163

Zotikos, 129